Sherds of History

UNIVERSITY PRESS OF FLORIDA

Florida A&M University, Tallahassee
Florida Atlantic University, Boca Raton
Florida Gulf Coast University, Ft. Myers
Florida International University, Miami
Florida State University, Tallahassee
New College of Florida, Sarasota
University of Central Florida, Orlando
University of Florida, Gainesville
University of North Florida, Jacksonville
University of South Florida, Tampa
University of West Florida, Pensacola

Sherds of
HISTORY

Domestic Life in Colonial Guadeloupe

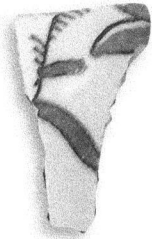

Myriam Arcangeli

University Press of Florida

Gainesville/Tallahassee/Tampa/Boca Raton

Pensacola/Orlando/Miami/Jacksonville/Ft. Myers/Sarasota

Published in the United States of America

First cloth printing, 2015
First paperback printing, 2024

29 28 27 26 25 24   6 5 4 3 2 1

A record of the cataloging-in-publication data is available from the Library
of Congress.
ISBN 978-0-8130-6042-2 (cloth) | ISBN 978-0-8130-8058-1 (pbk.)

The University Press of Florida is the scholarly publishing agency for the State
University System of Florida, comprising Florida A&M University, Florida Atlantic
University, Florida Gulf Coast University, Florida International University, Florida
State University, New College of Florida, University of Central Florida, University
of Florida, University of North Florida, University of South Florida, and University
of West Florida.

University Press of Florida
2046 NE Waldo Road
Suite 2100
Gainesville, FL 32609
http://upress.ufl.edu

To Greg, for the volcano and all

To Mary, a great teacher

Contents

List of Illustrations   ix

Acknowledgments   xi

1. A Ceramic Culture   1

2. From Kakukera to Guadeloupe   17

3. Just Add Water: Domestic Water Reserves and Water-Storage Ceramics   36

4. A Canari in the Kitchen: Creole Cooks, Foods, and Cuisine   64

5. The Creole Art of the Table   99

6. For Healthy Bodies and Clean Houses   145

7. Conclusion   175

Notes   183

Bibliography   187

Index   205

Illustrations

Tables

1.1. Probate inventories selected for analysis 10

2.1. Occupations recorded in the inventory sample 28

Figures

1.1. Typical forms in Guadeloupe's ceramic culture 2

1.2. Reconstruction of Basse-Terre, ca. 1780 9

1.3. Map of Guadeloupe showing the areas from which probate inventories were sampled 11

3.1. Biot water jar and local drip jars 44

3.2. Possible local coarse earthenware water jars 46

3.3. Faience and faience fine sherds from probable wall fountains 51

3.4. Locally made coarse earthenware pitchers 54

3.5. Traditional stone water filter from Peru 58

4.1. Stoneware cannes (storage pots) and Vallauris canaris (cooking pots) 79

4.2. Locally made coarse earthenware cookware 81

4.3. French coarse earthenware saucepans 85

4.4. French coarse earthenware bowls 86

5.1. Faience brune tureens 103

5.2. Faience salad bowl 104

5.3. Faience tableware with refined floral patterns 118

5.4. Faience tableware in floral patterns with daffodils and carnations 119

5.5. Common eighteenth-century faience tableware pattern with flowers, buds, tendrils, and serrated leaves 120

5.6. Common eighteenth-century faience tableware pattern with flower arrangement 121

5.7. Common rim patterns on colonial faiences 122

5.8. Faience pitchers in the Lambrequin style 123

5.9. Porcelain tableware 124

5.10. Pearlware bowls and saucers 125

5.11. Faience fine tableware with transfer-printed decorations 126

5.12. Faience fine tableware with hand-painted and stenciled decorations 127

5.13. Blue transfer-printed plate with colonial pattern 128

5.14. Average-quality faience floral pattern from Rouen 130

5.15. Re-creation of an eighteenth-century table setting 131

5.16. *Une famille métisse*, Le Masurier, 1775 139

6.1. Coarse earthenware, faience, and faience fine chamber pots 147

6.2. Delftware barber's bowl, coarse earthenware *albarelle,* and faience fine pill box 152

6.3. Faience fine soap dishes 154

6.4. Incised marks on local coarse earthenware ceramics 172

Acknowledgments

For their guidance and support, my sincere gratitude to Kirsteen Anderson, Gregory Arcangeli, Mary Beaudry, Andrea Berlin, Sonia Dickey, Mark Hauser, Kenneth Kelly, Karen Metheny, Nevil Parker, and Gregory Waselkov. All errors are mine.

CHAPTER ONE

A Ceramic Culture

If pots could talk, their most interesting stories would be about ceramic cultures. In the mind of an archaeologist, this statement might conjure up an antiquated notion that dates from the culture-historical era of her discipline. People without written records appear to us as cultural entities mainly through the ceramics they left behind. For instance, the Pit-Comb and Linear cultures of Neolithic Europe are both named after the type of decorations they applied to their ceramic wares. Other societies, labeled as pre-ceramic or non-ceramic, are characterized by their lack of pottery. The phrase *ceramic culture* can be freed from this narrow traditional definition and reformulated to designate a different kind of approach. Since culture history theory led to the first methods for dealing with ceramic objects (such as seriation), it is only fitting that a term it popularized be reapplied to modern ceramic studies.

In order to understand a ceramic culture, it is best to observe local potters or local ceramic industries to determine, for instance, what kind of vessels people made themselves and which objects they acquired through trade. Yet this type of approach is not restricted to the craft of pottery. It also goes beyond evaluating consumers' choices or knowledge about ceramic objects, although how and why people acquired those objects does matter. The principal aim of this concept is to assess the relationship between ceramics and users. If possible, this point should be considered in any archaeological analysis, since what people did with their vessels is important. For instance, during the early modern period in France, coarse earthenware potters everywhere made cooking pots for their local market. Yet each region had its own culinary tradition, principal ingredients, and preferred cooking methods, so that the range of dishes prepared in a single type of vessel was wide. It is these recipes, more than the characteristics of the pots themselves, that embodied regional cultural variations. In addition, from the late Middle Ages to the end of the nineteenth century, people's tastes and food repertoires changed greatly. They discovered new ingredients, in particular those coming from the New World, abandoned exotic spices for local ones, and invented new cooking techniques—for instance, skilled cooks started making broths and mousses. Yet despite these important changes, the shape and technology of common ceramic cooking pots remained quite stable.

Ceramics are helpful for characterizing early civilizations, but their usefulness does not diminish in historical times. Until the advent of plastics and other modern materials, ceramics were quite ubiquitous in daily life. They came in a great variety of sizes and shapes, and could be made, for example, waterproof, portable, decorative, or fashionable. At the same time, ceramic objects needed to be replaced on a regular basis because they aged, broke, went out of fashion, or lost their utility. In Guadeloupe, for instance, ceramic items were used to store, transport, and purify water; prepare and cook foods; host formal dinners or serve beverages at social gatherings; clean houses; and take care of bodily needs, including treating illnesses (figure 1.1).

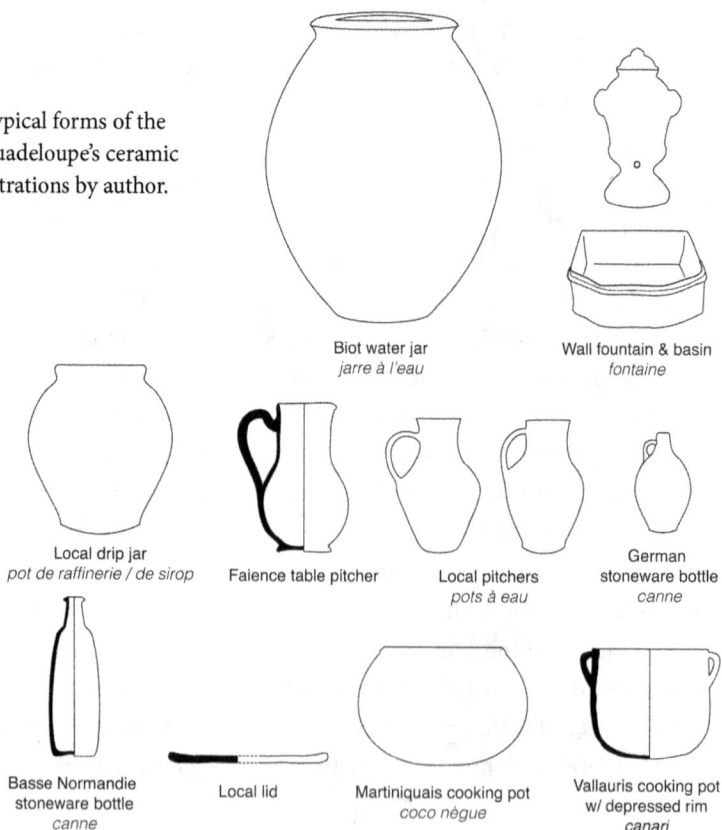

Figure 1.1. Typical forms of the objects in Guadeloupe's ceramic culture. Illustrations by author.

Biot water jar
jarre à l'eau

Wall fountain & basin
fontaine

Local drip jar
pot de raffinerie / de sirop

Faience table pitcher

Local pitchers
pots à eau

German
stoneware bottle
canne

Basse Normandie
stoneware bottle
canne

Local lid

Martiniquais cooking pot
coco nègue

Vallauris cooking pot
w/ depressed rim
canari

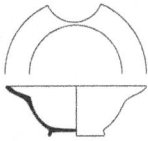

Barber's bowl
plat à barbe

Footbath
bain de jambes

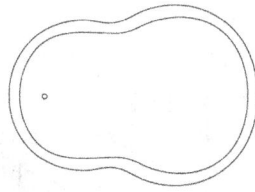

Bidet

Chamber pots
pots de chambre

Soap dish

Albarelle

Drug pot
pillulier

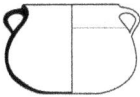

Vallauris teardrop
cooking pot
canari

Vallauris straight-sided
cooking pot
canari

Vallauris saucepan
casserole

Saintonge bowl
terrine

Huveaune bowl
terrine

Local bowl
terrine

Local flanged bowl
terrine

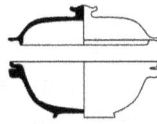

tureen
soupière

Albisola plate
assiette

Round dish
plat rond

Faience plate
assiette

Salad bowl
saladier

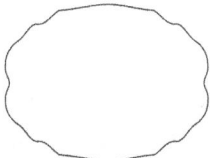

Sauceboat
saucière

Mustard pot
moutardier

Saltcellar
salière

Oil & vinegar set
huilier

Oblong dish
plat ovale

Bowl
bol

Bottle cooler
seau

Cup
tasse

écuelle

Teapot
théière

Coffeepot
cafetière

This study of colonial-era ceramics on the island of Guadeloupe, in the Lesser Antilles, takes an archaeological look at materiality and applies an archaeological method for analyzing material culture (Hicks and Beaudry 2010). It reflects on people as users of artifacts. Because ceramics are so common, they have long served a variety of purposes in archaeology, including defining cultures and geographical ensembles or dating sites. More recently, studies such as Tamara Bray's (2003) reevaluation of imperial Inca culinary pottery have demonstrated the extraordinary potential of also embracing ceramics for what they fundamentally were—that is, material, concrete, and useful everyday objects. By determining what people did with their cookware and serving vessels, Bray shed new light on the relationship between food, politics, and gender in the Inca state and explored the significance of its commensal practices.

Analyzing a ceramic culture in this way requires a focus on ceramic users ahead of ceramic makers, sellers, buyers, or consumers, especially when these groups consist of different individuals. In colonial Guadeloupe, the masters did most of the choosing and buying, but enslaved servants did a lot of the using and handling. The ties between ceramics and their users can reflect very diverse experiences within the context of a single society (Cochran and Beaudry 2006: 194). Some concepts deriving from behavioral archaeology can further illustrate this point. *Cadenas* (chains) are theoretical constructs representing the chain of interactions that arise between artifacts and people during the life histories of things (Walker and Schiffer 2006). They map the relationships between a given object, other objects that come in contact with it, and people. As networks linking all of the activities that take place around a material culture object from conception to discard, cadenas can vary greatly in size and complexity. In effect, this concept has led behavioral archaeologists to focus mostly on technology, or how objects were conceived and made, as well as artifact acquisition processes. Nevertheless, it fully acknowledges the role of users in such chains of cultural interactions. In Guadeloupe's case, the creation and acquisition of vessels may matter, but what happened after the ceramics were made, shipped, and bought turned out to be the most valuable and original point of entry into Creole colonial society and culture.

This study shows that the cadenas of ceramics in Guadeloupe tended to be long and heterogeneous. They usually involved masters and slaves and included non-ceramic objects as well as several types of vessels. As William Walker and Michael Schiffer (2006) note, social power, or the ability to influence the relationships between people and artifacts, manifests itself and is negotiated through these chains of activities. It is important to distinguish, as these authors do, between two forms of social power: structural power, which allows a group such as Guadeloupean heads of households to directly affect how others interact with artifacts—essentially by buying or ordering the ceramics for use in their houses—and "actual" social power, which stems from the ensemble of practices that surreptitiously shape normative people-artifact interactions. In Guadeloupe the ways in which slaves repeatedly handled ceramics affected both Creole society and culture. As Walker and Schiffer make clear, subordinates are especially able to exercise this kind of agency in domestic activities. Guadeloupe's ceramic culture suggests that enslaved servants influenced some local ceramic choices based on practical criteria that their masters might not necessarily have been aware of. It is possible to go even further and claim that enslaved female domestics, who had no recognized form of structural power, determined a great deal of their masters' health and well-being and also helped shape the overall Creole culture. This, in essence, gave structurally powerless slaves a form of unspoken but nonetheless undeniable "actual" effect on their environment, and perhaps helped them regain a modicum of control over their lives (see chapter 4).

Methodologically, studying a ceramic culture requires embracing whole assemblages as they exist in the archaeological record. It demands taking into account the complete range of objects retrieved from a particular context, including all materials, from coarse earthenware to refined ware and from locally made to imported vessels (Cochran and Beaudry 2006: 193). It thus utilizes the extensive typological work and research done on ceramics excavated at French colonial sites (in particular, Avery 2007; Bernier 2002; Brassard and Leclerc 2001; Décarie 1999; Genêt 1980; Lapointe and Lueger 1997; Moussette 1996; Waselkov and Walthall 2002), an array of ceramic studies from France (Abel and Amouric 1995; Amouric et al. 2006; Costes 2010; Forest et al. 1996; Guilhot and Richard 1995; Guillemé Brulon 1998a, 1998b; Maire 2008; Petrucci 1991, 1999; Rosen 1995), and both early and recent enquiries about local French Caribbean potteries (Beuze 1990; De Roo Lemos 1979; Gabriel 2004; Gibson 2007; Kelly et al. 2008; Vérin 1967; Victor 1941).

My objective is to conduct a detailed, data-driven, contextual analysis of ceramics in order to understand their roles. In Guadeloupe, ceramics were essential to domestic Creole life. Initially, the French word *créole* designated any island-born person, either free or enslaved (Garraway 2005).

In time however, créole took on a racial connotation and referred specifically to white colony-born individuals. Modern French Caribbean literature returned to the word's original meaning, using it to designate people with strong local roots and a culture that is Caribbean but neither African nor European. My work embraces both the original and postcolonial meanings: *Creole* essentially describes locally born men and women but also any individuals who lived in Guadeloupe and took full part in the local culture.

Ceramics help us consider aspects of the daily life of Guadeloupeans who do not appear in conventional histories because they were hidden, unacknowledged, or dismissed as unimportant. The topics I research—water management, cooking, formal dining, and health and hygiene—do not exhaust the list of possible themes. Yet they cover a wide enough scope to offer an understanding of important aspects of Guadeloupe's culture and to illustrate the potential of this kind of approach. This study is based on two major data sets: archaeological collections from four sites in the capital of Basse-Terre and probate inventories originating from Basse-Terre and the surrounding countryside, which required separate critical review (Beaudry 1988; Wilkie 2006). It also teases information in a very holistic way from an array of relevant sources, including personal papers, diaries, travel accounts, historical political statements such as that of Victor Schoelcher (1842), modern cookbooks, and historical paintings (Beaudry 2006; Beaudry and Symonds 2011; Wilkie 2009: 340).

A similar inclusive method applies to the analysis of ceramics: in order to understand what ceramics did for Guadeloupeans, I believe it is best to examine as many of their relevant attributes as possible, whether functional, technological, aesthetic, or chronological. Finally, my broad comparative approach also draws on previous scholarship in archaeology, history, ethnography, and cultural studies (see Beaudry 2006; Beaudry and Symonds 2011). Comparative data come from places situated throughout and beyond the French Atlantic world: at its center are places like the port of Bordeaux, which was involved in the French Triangle trade; more remotely under Atlantic influence are Paris or Toulouse; and located outside of its geographical boundaries but sharing social or cultural similarities are places like Ile Bourbon in the Indian Ocean or India under British rule.

Sources of Data

Guadeloupe, located in the eastern Caribbean and earlier a French colony, nowadays is considered a part of France, but distinct from continental

France, which is called the *metropole*. Like any other French region, Guadeloupe has a governmental service—the Service régional de l'archéologie, or SRA—that administers all of its archaeology. SRA employees oversee both research programs and cultural resource management (CRM) in archaeology. When they do not lead projects themselves, they contract local professionals or members of INRAP (Institut de recherches archéologiques préventives), a nationwide organization that undertakes most of the compliance archaeology in France. The archaeological collections that can aid us in understanding Guadeloupe's ceramic culture come from colonial sites excavated in Basse-Terre for CRM prior to scheduled construction or renovation.

The nature of these sites departs from the common fare in Caribbean archaeology. First, they are located in an urban area, which sets them apart from the abundant terrestrial archaeology done on rural plantations (Armstrong and Hauser 2009). In Guadeloupe as well, one of the first research programs in colonial archaeology centered on the excavation by Kenneth Kelly (2011) at the slave village of La Mahaudière, a sugar plantation in Grande-Terre. Plantations played an important role in Caribbean history, but the concentration of archaeology on plantation sites tends to overshadow the contribution of Caribbean cities to both local societies and the wider Atlantic world (Pérotin-Dumon 2000). Second, many studies of ceramics in the Caribbean have focused on local potteries and locally made ceramics (e.g., Hauser 2008; Haviser 1999; Kelly et al. 2008; Loftfield 2001). Yet imported vessels that were manufactured overseas represent the largest portion of the ceramics excavated at many Caribbean colonial sites, including at slave housing and slave villages (Armstrong and Hauser 2009: 596; Wilkie 1999: 265). Therefore, it is important to take these objects into account as well.

Working with collections excavated for CRM reasons, rather than for research, has specific challenges. In Guadeloupe, even though all compliance archaeology follows the same general guidelines, each team adapted its methods to the nature of the site, the field conditions, and their resources. This led them to conduct a large open excavation at one site and the equivalent of a Phase 2 survey at another. They also all used a mechanical excavator to remove the top layers, a practice that is common in French CRM archaeology. The sherds found in the mechanically excavated dirt pile were assigned a discrete provenience. Since the depth of the mechanical stripping did not neatly fit the stratigraphies, this meant that ceramics from very different contexts were mixed together. Finally, each team could decide whether or not to screen the colonial layers, which determined whether they retrieved the smaller sherds and how much cross-mending was possible in the post-excavation phase.

Unfortunately, none of the field reports had a detailed artifact or artifact bag catalogue, and the provenance recorded on some bags did not fit with any information from the site reports. Nonetheless, it is often possible to adapt research designs to existing collections, especially when doing so helps revive data that were never used in the first place. This is a thrifty, "green" kind of archaeology that contributes to the preservation of archaeological resources and extends the relevance of archaeological archives. One needs simply to critically review the fieldwork, as one would any other source, and recognize its limits. As it turns out, the study of a ceramic culture is a program that can be applied to many types of assemblages.

The four colonial sites selected for this study yielded good-sized ceramic assemblages and close to 2,000 sherds. They include the fortified mansion of Charles Houël, the founder of Basse-Terre and one of Guadeloupe's most influential leaders; the cemetery for the first colonial hospital (Palais de Justice); the former cemetery of the Cathedral of Basse-Terre (Cathédrale); and the yard of a house at 28 Rue Amédée Fengarol occupied by a series of middling Creole families (figure 1.2).

In comparison to the archaeological record, the probate inventory record starts late, in 1774. In June 1776, French authorities required that copies of notarial records from the colonies be sent to the metropole, with the exception of probate inventories. As a result, the original inventories archived in Guadeloupe are the only extant copies. Only a small portion of the local archives has been microfilmed so far, so in most cases, the original inventory must be consulted in situ. Compounding the problem, several documents have suffered considerable damage due to the humid climate, frequent fires or hurricane-related floods, insect and rodent infestations, and acid in the paper.

Inventories were selected for analysis based on availability, state of preservation, and focus on those notaries who recorded the most information about ceramics. Sources from the 1770s and 1780s proved to be the most useful, but the sample stretches into the 1830s (see table 1.1). It also includes households not only in the city of Basse-Terre but also in the surrounding countryside (figure 1.3). The selected sample consisted of 145 inventories containing 1,287 entries about ceramics and describing more than 20,000 objects. These entries touched upon a series of attributes of ceramics: material,

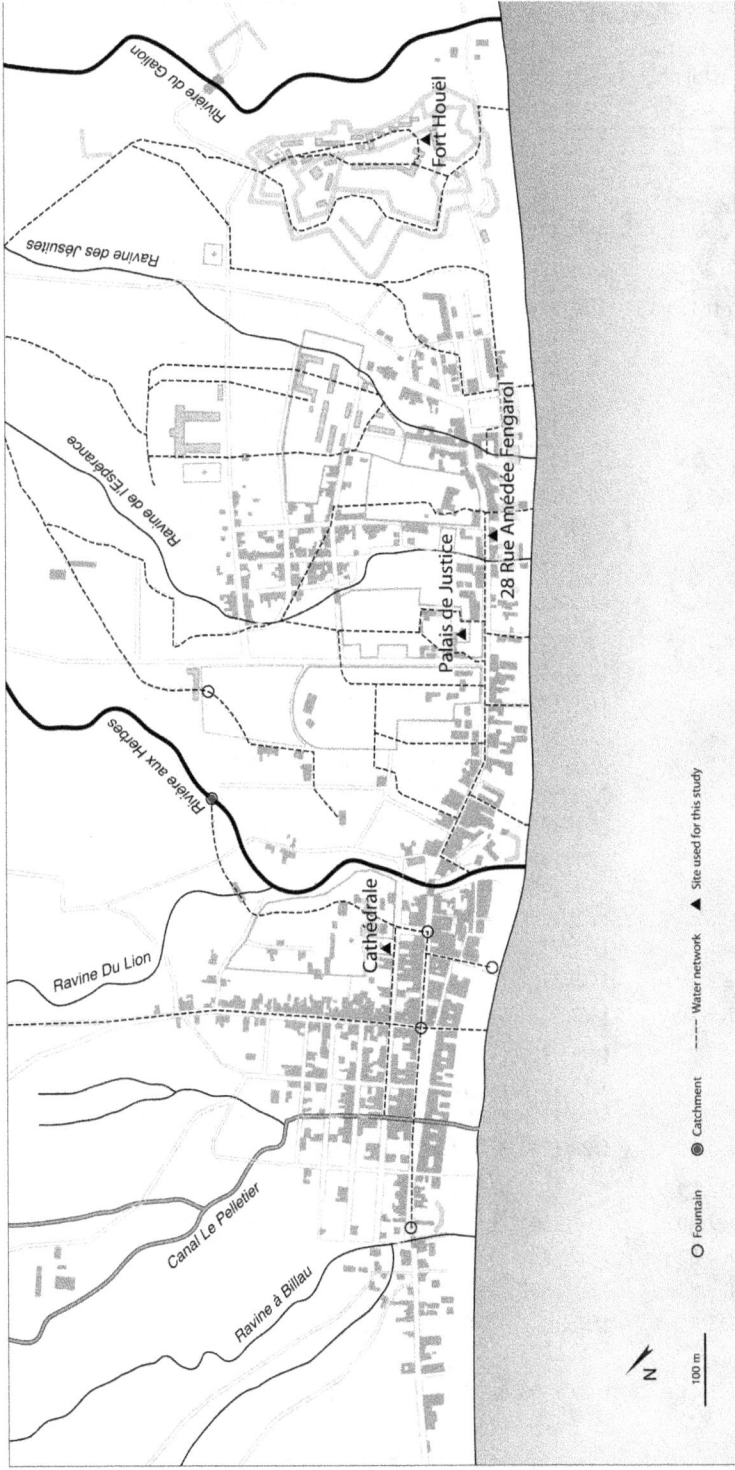

Figure 1.2. Reconstruction of Basse-Terre, ca. 1780, showing the locations of the four archaeological sites analyzed in this study. Illustration by author adapted from Desmoulins 2006, 63.

Table 1.1. Probate inventories selected for analysis

Notary officer	Archive ID number	Date (month/day/year)
Barbier	2E 3/75	3/9/1789
Chuche	2E 3/74	1/2/1778, 2/12/1778, 3/2/1778, 3/26/1778, 4/3/1778, 4/21/1778, 5/26/1778, 8/18/1778
	2E 3/75	1/26/1780, 2/3/1780, 4/12/1780, 5/18/1780, 6/27/1780
Debort	2MI 153-155	9/8/1775, 10/23/1775, 3/21/1776, 5/20/1777, 2/24/1778, 2/27/1778, 7/7/1778, 8/15/1778
Dupuch	2E 2/22	11/10/1789
Fontaine	2 E 3/5	7/27/1778, 8/20/1778, 11/23/1778, 1/8/1779, 6/11/1779, 7/1/1779, 7/28/1779
Jaille	2E 3/6	10/23/1786, 11/18/1786, 8/7/1788, 8/27/1788, 1/15/1789, 1/30/1789, 2/5/1789
	2E 3/7	3/6/1790, 12/14/1790, 6/14/1793
Joly	2E 3/179	11/22/1823
Mimerel	2E 2/195	10/19/1774, 12/20/1774, 3/22/1775, 8/19/1775, 12/7/1775, 12/20/1775
	2E 2/196	1/23/1776, 4/1/1776, 4/18/1776, 6/27/1776, 9/9/1776, 1/29/1777, 3/26/1777, 4/5/1777, 5/13/1777, 5/16/1777, 7/3/1777, 9/23/1777
	2E 2/197	2/4/1778, 2/11/1778, 2/28/1778, 3/5/1778, 3/12/1778, 4/13/1778, 7/24/1778, 8/18/1778, 8/26/1778, 1/7/1779, 3/10/1779, 7/30/1779, 8/26/1779, 9/27/1779, 10/5/1779, 10/19/1779
	2E 2/198	2/4/1780, 2/18/1780, 3/6/1780, 3/11/1780, 4/17/1780, 6/27/1780, 7/24/1780, 8/5/1780, 8/25/1780, 9/21/1780, 11/14/1780, 12/8/1780, 2/20/1781, 2/24/1781, 7/21/1781, 11/26/1781, 12/19/1781
	2E 2/199	1/29/1782, 2/14/1782, 4/16/1782, 5/14/1782
	2E 2/200	10/2/1783, 3/27/1784
Mollenthiel	2E 3/79	10/31/1777, 1/9/1778, 2/14/1778, 3/5/1778, 4/25/1778, 8/18/1778, 9/7/1778, 9/9/1778, 9/29/1778, 10/9/1778, 11/4/1778, 3/16/1779, 10/22/1779, 11/10/1779, 12/6/1779, 12/13/1779
	2E 3/80	1/27/1780, 3/16/1780
Nesty	2E 2/79	1/20/1829, 1/26/1829, 3/31/1829, 5/6/1829, 5/25/1829, 8/4/1830
	2E 2/80	2/9/1830, 2/12/1830, 2/13/1830, 2/23/1830, 4/3/1830
	2E 2/82	9/16/1831
	2E 2/84	1/21/1833, 2/3/1833, 2/11/1833, 3/21/1833, 3/25/1833
	2E 2/85	4/10/1833, 4/24/1833, 4/29/1833, 5/9/1833, 6/10/1833, 6/20/1833, 6/28/1833
Roydot	2E 3/11	1/30/1806, 4/12/1806, 6/7/1806, 7/12/1806, 8/2/1806

Source: Archives Départementales de la Guadeloupe (ADG), Notariat, Basse-Terre.

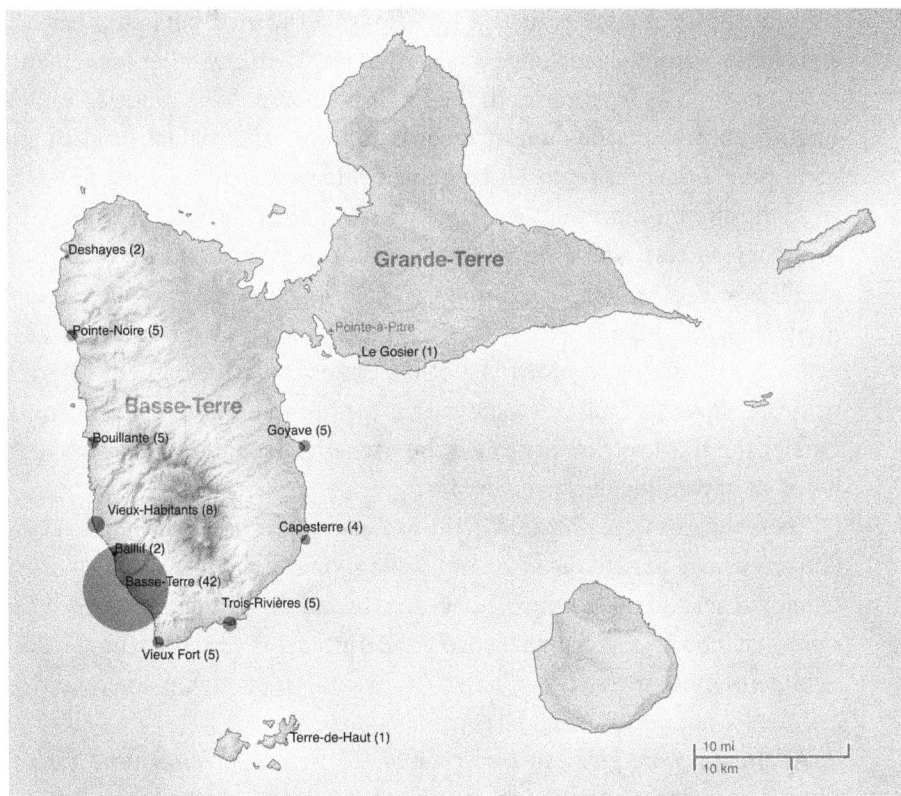

Figure 1.3. Map of Guadeloupe showing the areas from which probate inventories were sampled. Illustration by author adapted from a photo courtesy of Sémhur (available at http://commons. wikimedia.org/wiki/File:Guadeloupe_Places_of_interest_map-fr.svg).

provenance, quality, color, decoration, the existence of sets, object type, function, shape, size, capacity, condition, and patina. These data, combined with those from the archaeological collections, helped write the story of Guadeloupe's ceramic culture.

Under French law inventories were made after major life events: when children lost a parent, a spouse was widowed, a couple separated, or two people remarried. By law an inventory had to be filed within three months of a death (Pardailhé-Galabrun 1988: 32). Based on available information, it seems 70 percent of Guadeloupean inventories were completed within that time frame—and on average, slightly earlier than in Paris: 27 days in Guadeloupe versus 30 to 45 days in Paris. The inventory would not necessarily represent all an individual's possessions, because in the four weeks between the triggering life event and inventory filing families would have had time to sell some possessions or rearrange a house as they wished, but in this respect, an inventory from Guadeloupe was no different than any other French one.

Just as probate inventories in the English colonies were modeled on the English source, Guadeloupean records followed the format used in the metropole. French inventories contained three sections. The first summarized the circumstances of the triggering event: the date, who instigated the inventory process, where the inventory would take place, and who was present. The second section listed all of the material possessions of the relevant individuals, with the inventory often conducted room by room. Then, there would be a description of the rest of the estate; in Guadeloupe this started with the slaves (chattel) then moved on to the land, buildings, and crops. Finally, the third section presented the parties' personal papers as well as a list of all of pending debts and credits.

These records were prepared in the presence of the notary or his clerk, the persons who requested the inventory, three appraisers, and several witnesses. Often the head of the inventoried household and the appraisers pursued the same livelihood—merchants tended to be involved in inventorying the possessions of other merchants, planters in inventories of other planters, and so on—so the appraisers could be considered experts.

Appraisals were given in *livre coloniale,* a fictive currency used for accounting, analogous to the *livre tournois* used in the metropole. Much like the English system of pound-shilling-pence, 1 livre equaled 20 sols, and each sol equaled 12 deniers. Originally, the *livre coloniale* was worth 133 percent of the French *livre tournois,* but the relative value increased over time and fluctuated across the colonies, so it is difficult to make direct price comparisons between the colonies and mainland France (Buffon 1979). Given the dire monetary situation of the French colonial islands, the livre coloniale represented an essential economic tool. There was no central bank until the mid-nineteenth century, and each island had to import all of the currency it used (Buffon 1979). As a result, a hodgepodge of French, foreign, and counterfeit money circulated, and people often settled on a price in livre coloniale then paid that value in coffee, sugar, or foodstuffs. The livre disappeared in 1826, when France decided to replace it with the franc, which had been used in the metropole since 1795.

For Guadeloupe, Nicole Vanony-Frisch (1985: 41–47) compared slave prices in probate inventories and sale records between 1770 and 1789 to evaluate the accuracy of inventory appraisals. She found only a slight overall discrepancy: the median inventory value for slaves was 14 percent higher than the median market price. She concluded that the conflicting interests of family members, witnesses, and appraisers ensured that inventory appraisals remained close to current market rates.

Fortunately, during the inventory process in Guadeloupe, ceramics were almost always appraised in situ, instead of being moved elsewhere or bundled. In addition, notaries often inventoried a house room by room and recorded details about the location of each inventoried item within that identified room. Inventories of poorer households generally lacked such rich contextual data: the smaller the living space, the more people had to keep their possessions haphazardly clustered together, and the less notaries felt they needed to give spatial details. The material context recorded in the inventories is important because the function of ceramic objects can often be inferred based on their location within the house and their relationship to other objects. For example, a faience pitcher kept in a bedroom next to a basin was likely used for daily washing.[1] The same item located in a dining room china cabinet might be solely for display.

Organization of the Book

Chapter 2 summarizes the history of Guadeloupe and provides the socio-historical context necessary to understand how its inhabitants used their ceramics. More details about the sites in Basse-Terre and their assemblages follow. Then a demographic analysis of the inventory sample illustrates how these documents offer a broad survey of Guadeloupe's Creole society. Although all-white households predominate, there are records for a number of households of freed mixed-race individuals—called *gens de couleur* in French—as well as interracial couples. The sample also encompasses a broad cross-section of Guadeloupe's residents, from poor widowers to wealthy planters. To further elucidate the identity of ceramic users, I also classify the 145 households into three main wealth categories. These data show that, because of its relative commercial isolation from the metropole and the fact that a majority of its population was island-born, Guadeloupe is a good place to study the ceramic culture of a typically French Creole society.

In chapter 3 I analyze the uses of ceramics, in particular the vessels that served to collect, transport, store, and purify water. Although they might appear inconsequential to modern readers, such tasks were crucial in premodern times and constituted a central function of ceramics. Before tap water was delivered to homes, keeping reserves of water at home and managing them well were critical to domestic survival and to people's health and well-being. This theme is also fairly new for ceramic studies in archaeology, as well as for the archaeology of water in general. The latter tends to dwell on systems put in place to control and deliver water to an entire population, rather than on water management within the domestic sphere (Arcangeli 2014).

This part of the analysis concentrates on Basse-Terre because it is an ideal location. The city had enough freshwater rivers to enable its residents easily to build a simple distribution system that delivered running water to individual households. Yet the ceramic evidence shows that even in this excellent setting, most households kept water reserves. This domestic storage was not only prudent and practical, but also helped improve water quality. Seemingly, female servants were in charge of managing these reserves, and the types of ceramics they employed for doing so, such as recycled sugar drip jars, reflected that reality.

Chapter 4 reveals that enslaved female servants performed further essential work that was not acknowledged in historical sources, namely, cooking for their masters. Probate inventories and other sources document that Creole kitchens, which were often detached from the main house, were workspaces for slaves. They were not only isolated and minimally furnished, but also contained no objects of value, except for some common metal cookware. French historical sources often mention the existence of enslaved professional chefs, who were almost exclusively men. Yet the very small number of male chefs compared to the total number of households in need of a cook implies that female servants were in charge of preparing food in most cases.

The cookware these women used included coarse earthenware cooking pots, saucepans, and bowls; sherds from these vessels were found at the four sites. The use-wear of these objects was particularly intense, showing that this equipment was not only sparse but could also be used for a lengthy time. Yet reviews of the foods listed in the inventories, the kinds of foods grown in Guadeloupe during the colonial period according to historical sources, and modern French Caribbean cookbooks suggests that slave women were able to concoct an array of balanced and varied dishes.

Chapter 5 discusses the fundamental importance of hospitality and commensality in Creole society, which led to the creation of *salles* and *galeries*, spaces inside Creole homes entirely devoted to hosting guests. Glassware, silverware, and tableware were often stored near or inside these areas, which were more directly under the control of the masters.

Guadeloupean tableware included many vessels adapted to serving Creole foods, such as tureens and bowls, plus beverage services for coffee and tea. Evidence suggests that Creole homes were at least as well equipped with tableware as their French metropole counterparts, which underscores the importance of the ceramic material culture in Guadeloupe. This situation was all the more remarkable given that none of this tableware was made locally, so everything had to be imported. The majority was of French origin: assemblages were dominated by French faiences in the eighteenth and early nineteenth centuries, and by a variety of French refined ceramics (called *faiences fines*) afterwards. Yet the trading connections between Guadeloupe and the metropole were often tenuous, and Guadeloupeans did not hesitate to import complementary foreign vessels when it suited their needs. The fact that so much of their tableware was of French origin was clearly not dictated entirely by circumstances or ceramic availability. Aesthetics might have been an added motivation for this choice: most of the faiences Guadeloupeans owned had simple decorative patterns that facilitated putting together mismatched but visually coordinated services. Given that historical sources are unequivocal in relating the importance of formal dining and commensal hospitality in Creole society, it is plausible that French faiences and faiences fines were preferred because they helped heighten the function and meaningfulness of such events. Beverage services, in contrast, seem to relate more directly to such commensal practices among Creole women.

Chapter 6 rounds out this story by considering Creole health and hygiene. Based on the ceramic evidence, it is plausible that, compared to people in France, Creole Guadeloupeans had more extensive and modern hygienic practices. Local households used comparable or greater numbers of chamber pots, bidets, and barber's bowls, and Creole society seemed to have a less complicated and fearful relationship with water. Bathing outdoors, for instance, seemed more common in the colonies.

The greater cleanliness of Creole bodies is also supported by local beliefs about health. While their masters largely followed Western colonial medical practices, local enslaved healers developed water- and herbal-based therapies that have survived in modern Antillean folk medicine. Because these beliefs extended to maintaining the cleanliness of foods and homes, they concern not only specialized therapeutic ceramics, such as footbaths or drug pots, but also some common utilitarian objects most often handled by servants. Incidentally, such beliefs may explain the markings that servants engraved into some of these vessels.

The conclusion briefly revisits these findings, and summarizes what Guadeloupe's ceramic culture shows about the nature and distribution of social power throughout its slave-based society.

CHAPTER TWO

From Kakukera to Guadeloupe

It was Christopher Columbus who named Guadeloupe when he visited the island during his second trip to the Caribbean in November 1493. Columbus stopped there to replenish his water reserves, and as it turns out freshwater is an important topic in the island's ceramic culture and a fundamental source of the island's allure. The Arawak people who preceded Columbus had already recognized this and called Guadeloupe "Kakukera" (island of beautiful waters), probably in reference to the picturesque waterfalls, cascades, basins, rivers, and hot springs found throughout its lush tropical forest.

Guadeloupe proper consists of two islands separated by a narrow saltwater channel, which gives it a butterfly shape. The mountainous western wing, called Basse-Terre, is covered with tropical forest and is home to La Grande Soufrière, the highest volcano of the Lesser Antilles. Some of the beaches in Basse-Terre—especially near the colonial capital, also named Basse-Terre—are made of black volcanic sands. Meanwhile, the eastern wing of Guadeloupe, Grande-Terre, is a relatively flat limestone plateau with a more arid climate. The limestone has produced some idyllic landscapes of white sand beaches and excellent terrain for sugarcane fields.

In its entirety, Guadeloupe is actually a small archipelago: in addition to these two main islands are a number of outlying ones, the largest of which are La Désirade, Marie-Galante, and Îles des Saintes. The last is composed of several islets, two of which are inhabited: Terre-de-Bas and Terre-de-Haut. This cluster is close to Basse-Terre, the geographical focus for this study, and is also relevant because it housed a major local pottery during the colonial period.

About 120 miles to the south is the island of Martinique, which became a French colony at the same time as Guadeloupe and is likewise now a department of modern France. Guadeloupe and Martinique share a common Creole culture but followed different trajectories during the colonial period. Pierre Belain d'Esnambuc, a French colonist established in nearby Saint-Christophe—known today as St. Kitts—initiated colonization plans for the two islands in 1633. With the support of King Louis XIII, d'Esnambuc went to Martinique in 1635, while two other expeditioners, Charles Liénard de l'Olive and Jean du Plessis d'Ossonville, debarked in Guadeloupe with 500 men. The first few years of their settlement there were miserable and characterized by conflict with the local Caribs. Not long thereafter, in the 1640s, France became embroiled in wars, financial problems, and a cycle of cold, wet weather that contributed to a serious food crisis. These problems diverted France's attention from the colonization of the Caribbean and ushered in an era of private proprietors (Boucher 2008). Charles Houël, who had been appointed governor of Guadeloupe in 1643, bought the island and became its sole rightful owner for about 15 years.

Houël was instrumental to Guadeloupe's development in several ways. First, he gave the sugar economy a boost. Louis XIII had already legalized the use of African slaves for plantation work in 1638. Yet the first colonists in Guadeloupe were mostly small farmers who grew subsistence crops and tobacco with the help of some French indentured servants called *engagés*. In the 1650s, however, Houël welcomed Dutch and Jewish refugees who had been driven out of Brazil by the Portuguese. They brought better techniques for making sugar as well as valuable relationships with Dutch merchants, which allowed Houël to begin buying slaves on credit. The new technologies and enslaved workforce spurred the development of sugar plantations. The historian Philip Boucher (2008) estimated that by 1660, African slaves already made up one-third to one-half of the Guadeloupean population.

It was also Houël who chose to make Basse-Terre the capital. Basse-Terre was a tiny port on the southern end of Guadeloupe's western coast, where a community of Jacobins (Dominicans) had established a plantation (Pérotin-Dumon 2000). In order to take control of this area, Houël expelled the Dominicans and replaced them with Carmelites and Jesuits. He then built himself a fortified masonry mansion that towered above the town, west of the river called Rivière du Galion.

During that time, Guadeloupe and Martinique were in essence part of the Dutch commercial empire. Dutch ships helped the colonists to market their products without paying any colonial taxes as well as to acquire staples and cheaper manufactured goods. Guadeloupe benefited the most from this alliance, and sugar production took off faster there than in Martinique.

The situation changed dramatically in the 1660s, when Louis XIV assumed personal control of France and consolidated his power. With his finance minister Jean-Baptiste Colbert, he sought to reestablish control over the former colonies in the West Indies. They implemented a series of political, economic, and social reforms; appointed new colonial governors; and established mercantilist policies called the *exclusif*, which required that the colonies trade exclusively with France. By the 1680s the colonies had been extracted from the Dutch empire, and French merchants received state support to supply them.

Both sugar output and the slave population continued to rise in the French West Indies in the 1670s and 1680s. Louis XIV's religious intolerance also led to the expulsion of Jewish planters in 1683, and to restrictions on the rights of Huguenots and Dutch Protestants. The economic side effect of these measures was that they helped increase the control of French traders and merchants over the colonial market.

France was not alone in coveting a piece of the Dutch trading empire. In England, Cromwell and Charles II enacted mercantilist laws to drive Dutch merchants out of their colonies as well (Pluchon 1982). In trying to regain control over their islands, European nations brought war to the Caribbean. The era of maritime conflict lasted until the signing of the Treaty of Utrecht in 1713. In particular, Basse-Terre was attacked and briefly occupied by the English governor of the Leeward Islands, Christopher Codrington, in both 1691 and 1703, while a well-known chronicler of the colonial French West Indies, Jean-Baptiste Labat (1722), was actively involved in its defense.

In 1685, Louis XIV also passed the first draft of the Code Noir regulating the conditions of slavery. The intent of this document was to uphold public order and curtail the overexploitation of slaves, but in effect it codified many existing customs and reinforced the rights of masters (Boucher 2008). Historians acknowledge that it is very hard to assess the conditions of slavery in the pre-plantation phase, as well as to estimate the size of the slave population. The French slave trade was very small before the 1700s, and most slaves still had to be acquired from Dutch traders. By Philip Boucher's estimation, there were 33,000 enslaved workers in the French Caribbean by 1700, about 6,500 of them in Guadeloupe, which was far fewer than in the English colonies.

The free mixed-race French population was still small but growing, because the code technically required masters to manumit their mixed-race children when they came of age and to marry the child's mother. Permanent maroon communities of fugitive slaves were also already established in both Guadeloupe and Martinique.

Unlike in the proprietor era, Martinique prospered in the late 1600s as it assumed a prime administrative role. Its main port, Saint-Pierre, was transformed into the "Paris of the Islands." Meanwhile, in the Greater Antilles, the French colony of Saint-Domingue started its rise. The soil was richer and less depleted on that island than in the Lesser Antilles, and the cultivable area was vast—26,000 km², more than double the size of Jamaica, the largest English island (Pluchon 1982). Saint-Domingue would become the most important sugar island of the Caribbean and would remain so until at least the 1780s. Its slave population increased in consequence, reaching circa 47,000 in 1720. By comparison, Guadeloupe likely had only about 17,000 slaves.

Unlike Martinique and Saint-Domingue, Guadeloupe was progressively bypassed in the legal French transatlantic trade, and its merchant class came to rely on local contraband smuggled in by raft (Pérotin-Dumon 2000). The most thriving trade took place with the Dutch colonies of Curaçao and St. Eustatius: in 1745, for example, among the ships that visited Guadeloupe one was from France and 168 were from St. Eustatius (Pluchon 1982).

The British occupation of Guadeloupe in 1759–63, during the Seven Years' War, intensified this trend and gave Guadeloupe's economy a sudden and remarkable boost. Under British rule, the island was temporarily relieved from its dependence on Martinique as well as the restrictive policies of the exclusif. Its planters were finally able to import the workforce they desperately needed, and a staggering 18,000 additional slaves arrived on the island in short order. This in turn favored the development of sugar plantations in Grande-Terre and the founding of Pointe-à-Pitre, a new port that was more centrally situated than Basse-Terre and would become the largest city on Grande-Terre. Guadeloupean merchants took full advantage of the British occupation to legally expand their foreign trade.

The departure of the English cut off the supply of slaves but not the trading activity. Direct connections with North America actually intensified: in 1788, Basse-Terre was visited by 309 American ships versus 48 English and 42 French ones (Pluchon 1982). Seventy percent of Guadeloupean syrup and tafia went to North America. In return, the island imported foodstuffs, in particular salt cod, from ports in New England, Virginia, and North Carolina (Pérotin-Dumon 2000).

The end of the Ancien Régime represented the height of Guadeloupe's economic prosperity. In the 1780s and early 1790s, French-based traders began opening offices for the first time in both Basse-Terre and Pointe-à-Pitre.[1] Over time, the two ports became quite specialized: Pointe-à-Pitre focused on the bulk importation of staples and foreign commerce, while Basse-Terre handled the export of high-quality sugar in exchange for luxury items, weapons, and slaves. This focus would later hurt Basse-Terre. During the revolutionary era, the French transatlantic trade broke down and was replaced by contraband trade conducted out of Pointe-à-Pitre.

The onset of the French Revolution in 1789 brought a period of unrest to the colonies, during which each island charted its own course. Slave revolts intensified in Saint-Domingue after 1791, ultimately leading to the creation of independent Haiti in 1804. Meanwhile, in Guadeloupe, insurgent slaves allied themselves politically with the French Republicans and radicalized the conflict with white royalist planters (Dubois 2004). They also claimed that as defenders of the Republic they deserved full citizenship, and won their struggle when slavery was temporarily abolished in Saint-Domingue, Guadeloupe, and French Guyana in 1794 (Dubois 2004). Martinique, in contrast, welcomed British occupation from 1794 to 1802, in order to shield its planter class from abolition.

When the British attacked Guadeloupe in 1794, France sent troops under Victor Hugues to take it back. With the help of newly enlisted black soldiers, Hugues conquered the island in a little more than six months and became its new leader. Hugues's autocratic regime lasted until 1798. Many white planters left the islands, and Hugues tried without success to force their former slaves, now called *cultivateurs*, to return to work on the plantations. To make up for the lack of sugar production, he also authorized privateering, which brought short-term wealth but would lead to conflict with the United States when privateers started preying on the American merchant fleet (Pérotin-Dumon 2000; Pluchon 1982). When Napoleon Bonaparte rose to power in 1799, he decided to revive colonial agriculture by reverting to the policies of the Ancien Régime. In Guadeloupe, slavery was reinstated and the former colonial order reestablished.

France also lost its economic grip on the international sugar trade, and both Guadeloupe and Martinique were left with the metropole as their sole outlet, while metropole farmers started large-scale production of sugar beets to compete with cane sugar. In response to these new conditions, Caribbean planters greatly increased the surface area of their plantations and focused on making cheap, raw sugar that was sent to France for processing (Butel 2002).

On the social front, free gens de couleur kept fighting for reforms, exacerbating racial tensions (Pluchon 1982). A wave of poisonings in Martinique in the 1820s terrified the local planter class. In France, the July Revolution of 1830 led to the creation of a more liberal constitutional monarchy. Free gens de couleur in the colonies obtained civic equality and were finally allowed to participate in local elections. Through manumissions the number of slaves diminished, falling in Guadeloupe from 97,339 in 1831 to 87,732 by 1845 (Butel 2002). French public opinion was tilting against slavery, and famous abolitionists such as Victor Schoelcher called for its immediate end. On April 27, 1848, the Second Republic proclaimed its unequivocal abolition.

Planters, bankers, and traders pooled their resources to modernize the colonial sugar economy. Guadeloupe's first industrial sugar plant opened in 1844. In the second half of the century, industrial plants like these monopolized sugar production and forced the sale or demise of many plantations. Later in the 1880s, as competition from cheap beet sugar increased, these industrial plants also embraced rum distillation. In need of workers, sugarcane plants encouraged the immigration of laborers from India, China, and Africa. Politically, the middle class de couleur was prominent in the 1870s and 1880s. Later black socialist leaders such as Patrick Légitimus became influential as well.

The turn of the century was difficult: an economic crisis led to strikes and social unrest, and in 1902, the Pelée volcano erupted, wiping out most of Saint-Pierre, then the largest city in Martinique. In the first half of the twentieth century, rum in Martinique and bananas in Guadeloupe became the backbones of their respective economies. After World War II, in 1946, both islands officially were transformed from colonies into French departments. This completed their total integration into the French administrative, educational, political, and economic system.

The Four Study Sites

The four colonial sites in Basse-Terre examined in this book span most of the pre-plantation and plantation phases of Guadeloupean history. Roughly half of the sherd sample came from Palais de Justice, the cemetery of Guadeloupe's oldest hospital (Paya and Romon 2001). This establishment operated for more than a century, from 1664 to 1788, and was managed, like its twin establishment in Martinique, by a religious community called the Brothers of Charity. Based on descriptions from Martinique, hospitals like these had a large space used communally by average patients and smaller quarters for people of higher status, like army officers. The number of patients could be large; for example, the hospital at Fort Royal in Martinique listed 750 to 800 beds in 1778. They were equipped not only to treat but also to feed and house these patients, sometimes for stays lasting weeks or months.

The Brothers of Charity lived on-site with their domestics and the medical staff they hired to treat the sick and injured. The adjacent cemetery was where the most destitute patients were buried, along with very few clothes or personal possessions. Most individuals buried at Palais de Justice would have been interred naked or wrapped in a light gown or shroud. They were placed face-up in a simple grave dug into the ground, and sometimes covered with a wooden lid. Only a few of the most recent burials received a full coffin, and there were no grave markers. The anthropological profile fits what hospital records described for this population: most were young, low-income, transient men who worked as soldiers or sailors. In particular, quite a few skeletons showed on the leg bones old injuries, consistent with dangerous and physical occupations.

Artifacts such as pipes and ceramic sherds were scattered in the fill layers inside and around the graves, in no apparent relation to the skeletons. The lack of complete or even near-complete objects confirmed that these were not grave goods. Space management practices such as the creation of ossuaries and the use of secondary as well as multiple burials created a complex stratigraphy. Two undated major cleaning events took place, however, after which the general orientation of the graves changed. In addition, there was some evidence that extra soil was laid down over the old burials and that this soil came from other parts of the cemetery, of which only about 15 percent was excavated.

It appeared that the Brothers of Charity used the cemetery grounds as a dumping site for their trash. An unusual find supported this interpretation: two epiphyses of an ulna and a metacarpal bone that were perforated with copper wire must have belonged to an articulated skeleton used for anatomical study at the hospital. Also, the quality and variety of the vessels found at the site pointed to a long-established local community as the owners of the ceramics, rather than transient or destitute patients. Most of the ceramics found at Palais de Justice must have been used by the Brothers of Charity themselves.

Another ceramic collection came from the altered and complex stratig-raphy of a colonial cemetery, this one at the Cathedral of Basse-Terre (Bon-nissent and Romon 2004). Before this church was elevated to a cathedral, it belonged to the Catholic order of Capuchin Franciscans. They arrived in Basse-Terre in 1673 and dedicated their first church to Saint-François, which in turn became the name of the surrounding neighborhood. Some-time between 1675 and 1695, the Capuchins built a stone church in the cur-rent location of the cathedral. They also opened an adjoining cemetery for the interment of primarily white Basse-Terre residents. According to church records, a few people of color were buried there too. A document from 1769 mentioned that the cemetery for nonwhites, both freed and enslaved, was located right next to the cemetery for whites and was enclosed by a wall.

This burial ground fell out of use some time in the beginning of the nine-teenth century, before 1817. An 1817 document listing all the cemeteries of Basse-Terre noted that the Capuchin cemetery had closed. The site was transformed into a small cobblestone plaza called Place des Capucins. In one spot, a thick fill layer was deposited on top of the cobblestones to install the pedestal of a cross of Calvary. Later on, the cross was removed and the plaza paved over with asphalt.

Unlike at Palais de Justice, the population buried at the Capuchin cem-etery included women, adolescents, and children in addition to adult men. These residents were also in better health and their skeletons showed fewer pathologies. Most skeletons were in their primary context, and three-quar-ters of the individuals had been buried in coffins, some wearing clothes and jewelry.

Although unlike the men interred at Palais de Justice these Guadelou-pean residents would have had the means to afford religious objects or burial markers, such objects are completely absent, suggesting this might be a typi-cal practice at French colonial cemeteries. Just as at Palais de Justice, how-ever, the ceramics and artifacts recovered in and around the burials were not burial goods, but rather trash discarded in the cemetery grounds. Further, the religious community in charge of the church, the Capuchin Franciscans, might have owned these ceramics. A recovered pipe inscribed "Père (Father) Buren/v" suggests this.

The third site is a large military fortress at the southern end of Basse-Terre that expanded out of the fortified house of Charles Houël. Known today as Fort Louis Delgrès, it was originally Fort Houël and at other times was called Fort Richepance, Fort Saint-Charles, and several other names. In June

1995, the Service régional de l'archéologie conducted a small excavation at the fortress prison, where the Monuments Historiques had scheduled some restoration work (Bonnissent 1995). Historical maps showed that the prison was built between 1765 and 1766, but more importantly, that it was probably located directly on top of Charles Houël's original mansion.

The archaeologists located some remains of this house. In one of their units, the oldest wall belonged to the corner of a building that was paved inside. Because it was also right on top of the natural ground, it represented the earliest phase of occupation and seemed to have been part of Houël's first building, described as a *donjon* (keep or main tower). According to contemporary observers like the Dominican brother Jean-Baptiste Du Tertre,[2] this donjon had a square plan and, perhaps, four small bastions in its corners. The exact date of its construction is unknown, but it must have been sometime between 1649, when Houël took full possession of the island, and 1654, the date of Du Tertre's visit.

By 1656, Houël had added four triangular bastions to the sides of his square keep, creating an octagon that was relabeled a house. This phase was captured in several historical maps. At the excavation site, two other walls were uncovered oriented at 45° angles to the oldest one, as were the triangular bastions to the original square.

Some other features seemed to date from after Houël's departure in 1664 but before the fort was destroyed in 1703. Houël's successors focused on expanding the fortifications and defensive works around the house. Then the British navy attacked Basse-Terre twice: in 1691 they were not able to approach the fort, but in 1703 they laid siege to it and the French destroyed Houël's house before retreating. The more recent features found at the site, such as the paving of a gun platform, dated from the end of the eighteenth century.

The provenience of the ceramics excavated during this project was not recorded very precisely, and artifacts from different features were bundled. Yet the site yielded two unequivocally seventeenth-century objects: a Dutch delftware barber's bowl in the Wan-Li style, traditionally dated from the second quarter of the seventeenth century (Ray 2000: 8); and a green lead-glazed coarse earthenware drug pot called an *albarelle*, usually found in sixteenth- and seventeenth-century French contexts (see Arcangeli 2000; Bresc-Bautier 2001; Goy 1995; Guilhot and Richard 1995; Henigfeld 2005; Régaldo-Saint Blancard 1988) (both pictured in figure 6.2). The assemblages also contained a mix of eighteenth- and nineteenth-century ceramics.

Between 1649 and 1664, the fort was the military and political center of Guadeloupe as well as Charles Houël's personal residence (Desmoulins 2006; Pérotin-Dumon 2000). Houël convened official meetings with planters and received important visitors and emissaries here. Small separate buildings nearby housed the kitchen, offices, and barracks for the eight soldiers and sergeant who lived at the fort. After Houël's departure in 1664, Guadeloupe had three more leaders who might have lived on-site; namely, Claude François Du Lion (1664–77), Pierre Hinselin (1677–91), and Charles Auger (1691–1703). The seventeenth-century artifacts found at the site may have belonged to any of them, but it is just as likely that Charles Houël himself discarded them. In this case, his use of a delftware barber's bowl would be a strong symbol of the integration of Guadeloupe into the Dutch colonial world during his administration.

The fourth collection came from 28 Rue Amédée Fengarol, a lot that runs between Rue Amédée Fengarol and the former shoreline of Basse-Terre. This street used to connect the center of Basse-Terre to Fort Houël; first merchants built their warehouses along it, and in the second half of the eighteenth century, some housing appeared. At that time, this neighborhood, called Mount Carmel, attracted free men and women de couleur who wanted to become homeowners (Pérotin-Dumon 2000: 470). The early history of the site reflects this, and the family of Mathieu Oplas, a free *homme de couleur* (man of color) who worked as a carpenter, left a lasting impact. They lived there for 17 years (1789–1806), longer than anybody before them, and built the main part of the house that stands on the lot today. They might also have owned the eighteenth-century ceramics that were excavated in the yard.

There was no enforced spatial segregation based on race in the city, and houses often changed hands between white families and families de couleur. In 1806, a white middling family headed by Veuve Paragot, a widow from Martinique, bought the lot at 28 Rue Amédée Fengarol. Paragot and her relatives lived there until at least the 1880s and would have used some of the nineteenth-century ceramics found inside the two units that were excavated in the backyard. This family did not belong to the planter elite, but they owned their house and a few slaves. Starting in the 1830s, they made a living by growing tobacco on a small plantation in nearby Gourbeyres and later renovated a room on the first floor of their house into a tobacco shop. Two features were therefore consistent in the history of this site: it was a residential household, and it attracted Creole families of moderate wealth.

Together, these four sites cover a long time span, reaching back into periods when historical sources are rare. Fort Houël offers a glimpse of the types of objects available in the early years of the colony. The Palais de Justice, Cathédrale, and part of 28 Rue Amédée Fengarol allow us to view the eighteenth-century world when Guadeloupe's Creole society matured. Finally, two excavation units at 28 Rue Amédée Fengarol illustrate what happened later, during the Revolutionary era and after the abolition of slavery in 1848.

Demographic Information in the Inventories

In Guadeloupe as in France, probate inventories are not a reliable source of demographic data, because individual notaries did not systematically record the same kind of information and did not treat men, women, and children with equal importance. Nevertheless, it was possible to determine that 66 percent of the sample inventoried the belongings of couples, and 33 percent those of individuals. Individuals who had married at least once greatly outnumbered the people who had never married at the time of their deaths. A greater proportion of households had minor children than had either adult children or no children. From all the evidence, it appears that families in Guadeloupe were slightly younger when their belongings were inventoried compared to families in Paris, where Daniel Roche (1985) estimated that the heads of households were on average between 40 and 50 years old.

The sample also reflected the feminization of the Guadeloupean population during this period: women became as numerous as men in the eighteenth century, sometime between 1733 and 1783 (Gautier 1985: 33). Pérotin-Dumon (2000: 334) confirmed that the population of Guadeloupean cities also feminized greatly in the nineteenth century and that this trend started in Basse-Terre in the 1800s. In my sample, about 60 percent of the total testators were men and 40 percent were women, but the ratio changed over time. Women were in the minority before 1800, accounting for only 29 percent of the inventories, but after that date they represented 53 percent of the sample. As women became more numerous in society, the number of inventories conducted in their homes also increased.

Almost 85 percent of the inventories mentioned the profession of the head of household, particularly for men, whose occupation was recorded in 90 percent of cases (see table 2.1). Fortunately, notaries were consistent in labeling

Table 2.1. Occupations recorded in the inventory sample, with corresponding number of households

Job title	Occupation	Count
Aide-major	Major's aide-de-camp	1
Arpenteur	Surveyor	1
Aubergiste	Innkeeper	1
Boulangère	Baker (female)	2
Bourgeois	Gentleman	1
Capitaine de cavalerie	Cavalry captain	1
Charpentier	Carpenter	5
Charpentier de navire	Shipwright	1
Entrepreneur de bâtiment	Contractor	1
Forgeron	Blacksmith	1
Gérant/Administrateur d'une habitation	Plantation manager	2
Habitant	Planter	62
Interprète, Anglais et Hollandais	Translator, English and Dutch	1
Maître en chirurgie/Chirurgien	Surgeon	8
Marchand	Merchant	12
Marchand orfèvre	Goldsmith	1
Marchand perruquier	Retail wigmaker	1
Menuisier	Joiner	1
Navigateur	Sailor	2
Navigateur-Commerçant	Sailor–retail trader	1
Négociant	Trader	6
Notaire	Notary	2
Propriétaire	Landlord	4
Soldat	Soldier	1
Tailleur	Tailor	2
Tonnelier-Commerçant	Cooper, retail	1

occupations, with some minor variations due to the fact that men sometimes had multiple jobs and titles. Often a man might be a planter as well as a land-lord of a plot of real property, or might be engaged in trade in addition to practicing another profession. Anyone who was solely a planter falls in the planter group, and the same is true for the landlords.

Anne Pérotin-Dumon (2000: 493–574) produced a comparative list of occupation frequency based on a census of Basse-Terre residents in 1797. The main discrepancy between her data and this sample resulted from the difference in historical context and the locations of the inventories. Because the census she used was conducted during a period when slavery was officially halted (1794–1802), many slaves were recorded in it as domestics. She also focused on urban households, whereas my sample came from both the city and the surrounding countryside. Outside of Basse-Terre, the primary way to make a decent living was through agriculture, meaning that planters were more numerous in my sample. Also, surgeons tended to distribute their practices geographically to cater to different populations, and were therefore also more numerous. Finally, some villages specialized in particular activities. For example, three sailors lived on Îles des Saintes (Archives Départementales de la Guadeloupe [ADG], Notariat, Basse-Terre: Mimerel, 2E 2/198, 2/20/1781; Jaille, 2E 3/6, 8/7/1788; Barbier, 2E 3/75, 3/9/1789), and both female bakers worked out of Trois-Rivières (ADG: Nesty, 2E 2/79, 5/6/1829, 5/25/1829).[3] These types of occupations did not make Anne Pérotin-Dumon's list. Yet if one isolates the inventories for Basse-Terre alone, the data agree with her record of the most frequent occupations for white men.

To learn more about the many planters in the inventory sample, an effort was made to determine what crops they grew. This type of information was not readily available in the inventories themselves and could be inferred from stored harvests and equipment in only 52 percent of the cases. As expected, there were very few sugar planters, since the climate of this half of the island was not well suited to its cultivation. A few planters grew cotton, but coffee was by far the most common crop, which fit the fact that coffee production peaked in the area in the 1780s.

Occupations alone do not make for a complete story. Some large social differences existed between people who shared the same profession; for example, among the many planters. More useful for the purposes of this work is a classification based on household wealth, measured by the amount and quality of material culture present in the inventory. Land, real estate, chattel, or crops were less relevant, and in order to calculate the actual net worth of the households, all pending debts and credits would have had to be taken into account, which would have required too many complex calculations, and in the case of missing data, assumptions.

Based on material culture, this population was divided into three groups. The poorest households ($n = 31$) owned very few pieces of furniture and rarely any expensive objects. The inventory of their material possessions typically had fewer than 30 entries. In comparison, elite households ($n = 45$)

owned many expensive objects and pieces of furniture, and the inventories of their houses often had 100 or more entries. Middling households ($n = 69$) fell between these two groups.

In her in-depth study of Guadeloupean cities, Anne Pérotin-Dumon warned that Basse-Terre and Pointe-à-Pitre housed a large transient population that might not be captured in the written records. As in most Atlantic ports, this transient population was composed of men who worked as sailors on trading vessels or as soldiers. The length of their stay depended on the economic and historical situation, but typically they owned very little, particularly not any local real estate. Another segment of French colonial society with high turnover was French administrators temporarily assigned to the colonies (Pluchon 1982). In Guadeloupe, these administrators usually lived in Basse-Terre, but they tended not to mix with the white Creole elite, whom they often regarded as inferior. They usually returned to France as soon as their assignment ended. By definition, probate inventories would be most useful to people with established roots who had possessions to pass along to local heirs. So, unsurprisingly, there were no French administrators and only one French sailor who fit the profile of the transient population.

Like the other French Caribbean colonies, Guadeloupe started out as a land of immigration for French colonists and poor white engagés (Debien 1951). In the eighteenth century, however, the situation changed dramatically. The island retreated to a marginal position in the French empire, and immigration from France stalled, mostly in favor of Saint-Domingue (Butel 2002). Saint-Domingue had become by far the richest French colony and was perceived as a land of opportunity. In addition, much of its planter elite consisted of absentee owners who needed managers and employees to oversee their plantations. As a result, newly arrived immigrants (*transplantés*) from Europe tended to outnumber white Creoles (Weaver 2006: 15). Pierre Pluchon (1982: 171) estimated that, at most, only 22 to 27 percent of the white population in Saint-Domingue was island born.

By contrast, absentee plantation ownership did not occur in Guadeloupe and Martinique, where planters usually lived on their land (Butel 2002; Pluchon 1982; Vanony-Frisch 1985). Of the families in the inventories, 42 percent lived off the land as planters and another 5 percent owned a plantation in addition to practicing a profession. Moreover, many of the wealthiest households belonged to or had ties with the Creole elite. Together these facts offer good evidence that most of these individuals were Creoles not recent transplants. Similarly, the free gens de couleur who needed inventories done probably all had local roots, especially since half of them were married and several were planters.

Guadeloupe had a three-tiered caste society, where castes were defined by race and legal status. There were whites, free gens de couleur, and slaves. White men and women constituted the "default" group in the inventories, the one to which people belonged when notaries did not mention the race of their clients. Slaves appeared in the documents only as possessions, and free gens de couleur made up only 7 percent of the sample (10 inventories).

The population of free gens de couleur in Guadeloupe grew over the time frame of the inventory sample, from 1 percent in 1778 to 3 percent around 1790 and 7.7 percent in 1822 (Pérotin-Dumon 2000: 328). The relative proportion of free gens de couleur in the inventories increased too, from 6 percent of the sample in 1778 to 28 percent in the years 1829–33. Yet because the count was so low, these inventories can hardly be considered representative of the entire free population of color. Indeed, Pérotin-Dumon estimated that free gens de couleur originated 20 to 25 percent of all the notarial acts in Guadeloupe, which is a far cry from the 7 percent that these inventories together represent.

Six women and four men de couleur were inventoried in Basse-Terre, Capesterre, Vieux-Habitants, and Trois-Rivières. Because the majority of these inventories dated from the nineteenth century when Guadeloupe's population was feminizing, it is logical that women dominated this subgroup.

In terms of occupation, free men of color were carpenters or planters, and the women either bakers or not employed. According to Pérotin-Dumon's study, both carpenter and planter were common jobs for free hommes de couleur, but baker was less so for free *femmes de couleur*, at least in Basse-Terre, where almost all were either seamstresses or shop owners. In Pointe-à-Pitre, however, a few women happened to bake and sell pastries for a living, which was not unlike being a baker in Trois-Rivières. In sum, the occupations represented in the sample were not unusual for free gens de couleur.

For the entire sample, half of the testators were married and half were not. Some of the single women had children, but the only single man in the sample did not. Indeed, matrifocal families de couleur were typical, since married people represented at best 20 percent of this group. Pérotin-Dumon also demonstrated in her survey from the second half of the eighteenth century that married free gens de couleur formed the urban elite of this population. The households in the sample were distributed equally between the poor and middling groups, but four of the five couples were classified as middling households, confirming that couples de couleur fared a bit better than others.

In this sample, all middling and wealthy households had slaves, and a quarter of the poor ones did as well. Probate inventories have already been used extensively to study the slave population during the colonial period in Guadeloupe (for example, see Gautier 1984; Pérotin-Dumon 2000; Régent 2004; Vanony-Frisch 1985). At minimum, notaries recorded the name, age, and market value of each slave. The slave's origin and race, as well as other qualities, specific skills, and physical or character "flaws" that could affect his or her value might also be recorded.

Like their masters, most Guadeloupean slaves were Creole. In her authoritative analysis of 8,820 enslaved individuals between 1770 and 1789—which represented about 10 percent of the slave population at the time—Nicole Vanony-Frisch (1985: 40) concluded that the vast majority was island-born. Only 20.8 percent of her sample were African-born slaves, 14.3 percent were of mixed race, and 44 percent were both black and island-born.[4] Other authors have estimated that only one-quarter to one-fifth of slaves in the late eighteenth century were African-born (Dubois 2004: 6). This trend lasted until slavery was abolished. Based on the 1848 registers of new citizens, between 12 and 14 percent of former slaves were African-born (Fallope 1983). Moreover, African-born workers were concentrated on a few large sugar plantations in the eastern half of Guadeloupe rather than in the Basse-Terre area. Once again, eighteenth-century Guadeloupe contrasted sharply with Saint-Domingue, where the bulk of the slave population was African-born and recently arrived (Moitt 2001: 21).

Just how many slaves lived in Guadeloupe when these inventories were made? In the 1790 census, slaves accounted for 85 percent of the island population of about 107,000 (Dubois 2004: 51). That proportion remained stable until the early 1800s, then slowly decreased over the rest of the period surveyed in the sample, which runs through the early 1830s. In 1818 the percentage fell below 80 percent, reaching 67 percent just before slavery was permanently abolished in 1848 (Fallope 1987: 190; Pérotin-Dumon 2000: 329). Another important statistic was that the proportion of slaves in urban areas was much lower than on plantations, fluctuating between 45 and 50 percent for both Basse-Terre and Pointe-à-Pitre (Adélaïde-Merlande 1985:

4; Pérotin-Dumon 2000: 329). Pérotin-Dumon estimated that 65 percent of households in Basse-Terre, and 75 percent in Pointe-à-Pitre, owned only one or two slaves. Households with more than four were extremely rare. French authorities taxed urban slaves at a much higher rate than rural ones, and the urban slave capitation tax rate (tax per head) rose exponentially: the first four slaves cost the same amount, but the rate increased by 50 percent for slaves five and six, and by another 33 percent for any additional slaves (Adélaïde-Merlande 1985: 21–22).

Women constituted an important part of this population. In the transatlantic slave trade men generally outnumbered women, making up 64 percent of the human cargo that arrived in the French Antilles (Moitt 2001). As a third-rate destination in the slave trade, however, Guadeloupe received proportionately more female slaves than either Saint-Domingue or Martinique. As Moitt also pointed out, creolization tended to equalize the sex ratio among slaves, and Guadeloupe was notably creolized. Further, in her demographic study of Guadeloupe from 1770 to 1820, Anne Pérotin-Dumon (2000) observed that male slaves made up half, or perhaps less, of the total slave population.

The slaves who would interact most often with ceramics were the domestics, which was the most common occupation for both male and female urban slaves (Pérotin-Dumon 2000: 549). Still, women dominated the domestic workforce; for example, in the census of 1797 there were 357 female versus 120 male domestics in Basse-Terre. Other authors have reported that mixed-race Creole women were considered the ideal domestic (Moitt 2001; Vanony-Frisch 1985). In Saint-Domingue Creole domestics even fetched 25 percent higher prices than African-born ones (Moitt 2001: 59, citing Médéric-Louis-Élie Moreau de Saint-Méry).

Enslaved domestics were ubiquitous in the Antilles, but even more so in Guadeloupe, because wealthy families there were resident on the island (Vanony-Frisch 1985). In Nicole Vanony-Frisch's extensive sample, these domestics worked—in order of decreasing frequency—as unskilled female servants, (mostly male) cooks, laundresses, male valets, male wigmakers, and seamstresses. This list corresponds very well with the inventory sample: most domestics appear to have been unskilled, and some of these unskilled female domestics were referred to as "servants." The few skilled domestics included six cooks, three wigmakers, two valets, two seamstresses, a laundress, and a nanny. Naturally, they all worked in wealthy homes. The merchant and surgeon Antoine Belost and his wife, Marie Steel, had by far the most extensive domestic workforce, with a cook, laundress, valet, nanny, wigmaker, seamstress, and several unskilled domestics (ADG: Mimerel, 2E 2/195, 12/7/1775).

Along with its three-tiered caste organization, interracial libertinism and concubinage defined French Caribbean society (Garraway 2005). French colonial authorities frowned upon interracial unions and marriages, which they dubbed *mésalliances* and regarded as threats to the white community. Nonetheless, in Guadeloupe, just as in Saint-Domingue and Martinique, some white men lived with free femmes de couleur or with enslaved women who acted as de facto spouses and managed the household. These concubines became what contemporaries called *ménagères*, or literally, housewives. The inventories imply that a few single men lived with one of their slaves or with a free femme de couleur whom they manumitted (ADG: Mimerel, 2E 2/196, 9/23/1777; Mimerel, 2E 2/198, 11/26/1781; Roydot, 2E 3/11, 1/30/1806; Nesty, 2E 2/84, 1/21/1833). Married men who had illegitimate families were harder to identify, but there was at least one possible case (ADG: Nesty, 2E 2/79, 8/4/1830).

Conclusion

The bulk of this inventory sample is concentrated in the 1770s and 1780s, when Guadeloupean society was thriving and its Creole culture was well advanced. Much of the data extracted from the inventories therefore relate ceramic uses to the typical domestic life of Creole households during that time. The archaeological sites offer a longer-term view than the documents do, because they not only reveal the kinds of ceramics used throughout the eighteenth century but also yield sporadic data for the seventeenth and nineteenth centuries. Given the lack of precise dating and careful excavations at these sites, however, the ceramic assemblage is not adequate for precisely delineating each historical phase and does not add detailed information about the development of Guadeloupe's colonial society. The ceramics confirm major trends in, for instance, water management and health and hygienic practices but do not show precisely how other important aspects of Creole domestic life (for instance, cooking) arose or changed over time. Because no inventories exist before 1774, more excavations would be needed to clarify how Guadeloupe's colonial society evolved and transformed.

Fortunately, analyzing ceramics lets us study a larger than usual segment of this society, including the slave population that lived alongside free Guadeloupeans. Enslaved domestics or concubines worked—and sometimes spent all hours of the day—in close proximity to their masters. Consequently, they left subtle traces of their presence in Guadeloupean houses, which notaries recorded. More significantly, slaves handled some of the ceramics that are studied here on a regular basis, so these objects yield rare and essential information about certain aspects of slave life. Water-storage ceramics—an important staple of Guadeloupe's ceramic culture—are a prime example of this.

CHAPTER THREE

Just Add Water

Domestic Water Reserves and Water-Storage Ceramics

Water-storage ceramics were an important component of Guadeloupe's ceramic culture, and procuring a good supply of water was a critical domestic issue in the early modern period. In Daniel Roche's (1984) words, this was "le temps de l'eau rare" (the time of scarce water). The difference between that time and today is striking, as now we need only to turn on the tap to get an unlimited, clean, and safe supply of water. Yet some similarities also exist. First, in many developed countries, the public is losing confidence in the quality of their water supply, just as people did in early modern societies. Our distribution systems are aging and in need of expensive upgrades. New kinds of contaminants have appeared and are raising concerns about the adequacy of our purification techniques. In response, many households have reverted to buying home water filters or carting bottled water home from the supermarket. So, now as then, steps are taken at the household level to improve the quality and taste of water. Meanwhile in developing countries, millions of people lack access to clean water, and traditional methods of collecting and storing water may still be relevant.

Naturally, people's views on water have evolved. There was no concept of waterborne diseases before the second half of the nineteenth century. For instance, yellow fever and cholera were not linked to fecal contamination in water until after 1850, and the microbes responsible for these infections were identified only in the 1880s (Hamlin 2000: 52). Yet there had long been a tradition of assessing the quality of water based on sensory judgments and assumptions about its health effects (Goubert 1989; Hamlin 2000). In Western societies, rainwater was generally the best on the water-quality scale. Water from mountain streams was favored over water from streams in hot plains or well water, and running water was always preferable to stagnant.

Early modern European towns showed very limited "hydraulic consciousness" (Hamlin 2000). Their water management strategy often involved little more than providing access points throughout the city. In Paris, for example, water was secured via the Seine River, public fountains, and some wells. But directly piping water into individual homes had not been on Parisians' minds since Roman times (Coleman 2001). Water quality was poor and people were aware of that fact, so treating water at home was a common practice. Worldwide, known purifying techniques ranged from removing impurities through sedimentation to decanting the water, adding purifiers (like wine or vinegar) and coagulants, or boiling the water before use (Hamlin 2000).

Carefully managing one's home water supply was therefore crucial, and this was probably particularly true in the tropical environment of Guadeloupe. How did people obtain their supply there? Assessing Basse-Terre's water sources and distribution system will help answer this question. Then, analysis of the water-storage ceramics listed in the probate inventories and found at the archaeological sites will show exactly how Guadeloupeans dealt with their domestic reserve.

Sources of Water in Basse-Terre

For more than a century before the French colonized Guadeloupe, European ships had been visiting the future site of Basse-Terre. Its advantages and drawbacks as a place for settlement were well known. Its roadstead had waters deep enough for ships to anchor close to the coast, though it did not adequately protect them from bad weather. High grounds near the coast and at one end of the site could be used to build a fort, according to the recommendations of the Compagnie des Isles d'Amérique for new settlements (Desmoulins 2006: 40; Pérotin-Dumon 2000: 97). Above all, Basse-Terre had excellent sources of freshwater, thanks to the three permanent rivers and several seasonal creeks that flowed down to the sea— waters running downhill from mountains were in general thought to be very healthy (Hamlin 2000). The last feature was rather rare in the French Antilles. When building new settlements the French usually preferred locations with good harbors, even when these places were not well suited for human habitation. For example, the towns of Fort Royal, Martinique, and

Pointe-à-Pitre, Guadeloupe, were built in swamplands characterized by relentless heat, swarms of mosquitoes, and dire lack of freshwater (Boucher 2008: 20, 271).

In Basse-Terre, the declivity of the terrain also made it possible to build a rudimentary but efficient water distribution system. Water was diverted from the rivers upstream of town and brought down in canals using gravity and low pressure. Religious communities, who were among the earliest landowners in the city, created the first water catchments (Desmoulins 2006: 73). The Jesuits, the Carmelites, and the Brothers of Charity managed to extract water from the Ravine de l'Espérance, and the Capuchins drew from the Rivière aux Herbes (figure 1.2). In Baillif, a town west of Basse-Terre, Father Jean-Baptiste Labéat also built a 2,800 m canal to irrigate the sugar plantation of the Dominican brothers (Desmoulins 2006: 74).

Most canals in this water distribution system were simple unlined earthen ditches, though a small number were built in masonry (Desmoulins 2006: 74). A few reservoirs helped clean the water and regulate its flow. The system also used connecting pipes, which were initially made of lead but after 1850 were of cast iron. Both canals and reservoirs were usually uncovered, and small wooden bridges provided crossings over the numerous little streams that transected the city (Pérotin-Dumon 2000: 371).

As Basse-Terre grew, new connections were simply added to the original network. Though an easy way to develop a distribution system, this process came with obvious pitfalls. Every water distribution point in the city tapped the same few river sources, and the supply available at any one point was contingent on the condition of the upstream network.

Cisterns and wells were rare in Basse-Terre, especially before the nineteenth century. In her survey of the city's notarial archives, Marie-Emmanuelle Desmoulins (2006: 205) found only a single mention of a well, dating from 1822. Anne Pérotin-Dumon (2000: 429) cited the presence of a well in the courtyard of a merchant's house in the newest part of Saint-François at the end of the eighteenth century. The military had cisterns both at Fort Delgrès and at their infantry barracks by the mid-eighteenth century, but very few private houses had similar setups. Desmoulins identified only one private cistern, near the Champ d'Arbaud and dating from 1855. In the 1820s, a visitor named Longin (penname for Le Manceau Félix Langin) also recalled drinking water from a cistern in a house near the center of town (cited in Pérotin-Dumon 2000: 761).

The first public fountain in Basse-Terre was erected in Saint-François, the wealthiest neighborhood, in 1749. By the end of the 1780s, four more fountains had been installed (Pérotin-Dumon 2000: 373). One of them was a fountain at the shore, designed by a city planner named Mallet around 1788. It was accessible not only to individuals but also to ships' crews that needed to replenish their water supply. Other neighborhoods of Basse-Terre, even old ones like Carmel, were not as well equipped as Saint-François (Desmoulins 2006: 77).

Mallet was also commissioned to inspect the entire city's water supply network and presented his findings in a detailed 1788 report.[1] Mallet stressed the need for public water access outside of Saint-François, including in the neighborhood where 28 Rue Amédée Fengarol is located. He proposed that a fountain be built at the entrance to the former military hospital across the street from that site, but this project was not completed until much later, sometime after 1825. In 1842, a Basse-Terre inhabitant sought to install a fountain in a nearby street called Rue Saint-Ignace, because there were still no sources of potable water in the area. Many Basse-Terrians who lived outside of Saint-François did not have convenient access to water until late in the nineteenth century.

Visitors, though, were impressed by the sheer quantity of fountains. Some recorded their impressions, praising Basse-Terre's freshwater sources and describing how they cooled the city and made its tropical climate more bearable. For instance, Paul Erdman Isert, a German doctor, painted this picturesque portrait of the city in 1787: "One sees here and there gushing fountains that distribute fresh and crystal clear water. There are many gardens inside and outside the city that are nearly all watered with running water and that provide local people with the most delicious vegetables" (Isert 1972: 318; translation mine).

In the nearby uplands another traveler, Baron de Montlezun (1818: II. 45), found the air fresh and the waters limpid and delicious. In the 1820s, Longin admired two pyramidal fountains downtown that yielded "a very beautiful water." He also noted that this water was good for "drinking, domestic use, and cooking" (cited in Desmoulins 2006: 77). Eugène Édouard Boyer-Peyreleau (1823:1.180) lauded the quality of Basse-Terre's waters and the numerous public and private fountains he saw. He stated that many of the houses he visited had running water. Another visitor, Joseph Leggins, commented in 1830 on the many "plain" but "neat" fountains of the city (cited in Pérotin-Dumon 2000: 371). He noted that these fountains contained water that was "conveyed through pipes" from an "inexhaustible" source streaming down from the neighboring hills.

Idyllic descriptions of Basse-Terre's fountains and waters represent a trope in the travel literature of the Antilles. In most of these accounts, Basse-Terre was also sharply contrasted with Pointe-à-Pitre, which was deemed favorable for trade but very unhealthy. The Baron de Montlezun (1818: II.76), for instance, deplored the latter's unhealthy climate, unbearable heat, scarcity of shade and breeze, and lack of clean water.

The visitors' descriptions were perhaps overly idyllic. In Basse-Terre canals and gullies tended to foster chronic epidemics of malaria (Pérotin-Dumon 2000: 318). The canals leaked water into stagnant puddles that supported mosquito breeding. As explained later, the water that spouted out of Basse-Terre's fountains was also often very polluted, and it caused regular typhoid fever and cholera outbreaks. Yet eighteenth-century doctors and early nineteenth-century hygienists believed fresh air was the most important prophylactic element against all diseases. Thus, Basse-Terre's cooling sea breeze created the illusion that it was the healthiest place to live in Guadeloupe (Jennings 2002: 239). This belief persisted even despite evidence to the contrary. In 1823, for example, Boyer-Peyreleau noted that the death rate of soldiers was higher in Basse-Terre than in Pointe-à-Pitre (cited in Pérotin-Dumon 2000: 318). He surmised the difference was due to the fact that Basse-Terre attracted many more newcomers, who were naturally more susceptible to tropical diseases, rather than to Basse-Terre's environment or water supply.

The 1788 Mallet report laid out some systematic and recurrent problems with Basse-Terre's water system. First, the canal system was very unequally distributed. As in other early modern cities, priority was given to administrative buildings, religious communities, and military installations (Desmoulins 2006; Pérotin-Dumon 2000). The elite could enjoy fountains in their courtyards and even indoor running water while everybody else had to fetch their supplies.

The correlation between direct water access and wealth or status was a common feature of early modern urban life. It was the case in colonial cities like Santiago, Chile, as well as in major European cities like Paris and London (Roche 1984; Webre 1990). In general, public fountains received their water last, after administrative buildings, elite households, military installations, and religious communities. Stephen Webre (1990: 74) estimated that as little as 4 percent of Santiago's population received 62 percent of the water supply at the end of the seventeenth century. Daniel Roche (1984: 389) noted the same glaring inequalities in Paris: religious communities, important administrators, court members, and nobles used about half of the city's water. Similarly, Basse-Terre's water topography matched its social geography. Saint-François, the wealthiest neighborhood, had the most public and private fountains.

The better real estate in Basse-Terre came with specific water rights that were recorded in sale documents. Since these rights have not been studied in detail yet, it is unclear how much they cost or exactly how they were allotted (Desmoulins 2006: 77).[2] The flow rate that a landowner could expect was however precisely described as anything between a trickle and a steady rivulet. Holes were sometimes drilled in stone regulators to control the amount of water that was delivered to a property (Desmoulins 2006: 78). Naturally, water rights often spurred disagreements between neighbors, especially when the amount of water each expected could not be delivered (Blandin-Pauvert 1986: 62).

The length of time that water flowed throughout Basse-Terre was also very uneven. As late as the 1870s, water flowed for only a few hours each day. Natural shortages were common as part of regular seasonal variations. Mallet, for example, pointed out that canals and fountains remained empty for weeks at a time during the dry season (cited in Pérotin-Dumon 2000: 775). Because canals and reservoirs were crudely built and left uncovered, a great deal of water was also lost to evaporation and ground absorption (Desmoulins 2006: 78).

Fraud and tampering also hampered the distribution system. Mallet observed that in some areas of Basse-Terre so many illicit ditches had been dug into the canals that their original contour was disappearing. Slaves were often blamed for diverting water for their own uses, especially on Saturdays and Sundays. On the other hand, Mallet pointed out that many plantations located upstream stole water from the rivers for sugar production and irrigation of their gardens, thus depriving inner-city landowners of their share (cited in Pérotin-Dumon 2000: 775).

Still, the overriding problem with Basse-Terre's water supply was the lack of a sewage system. Latrines were rare in private houses before the late nineteenth century. Marie-Emmanuelle Desmoulins found only one mention, dating from 1783, of a "cabinet d'aisance" (indoor privy). She also cited a military report that described the scarcity of outhouses and privies as late as 1863. A few military and religious communities were exceptions. For convenience, they built their latrines directly over the canals and streams, so that waste would flow away (cited in Pérotin-Dumon 2000: 776). For everybody else, dumping chamber pots in the streets, canals, and rivers was common practice. The city passed numerous bans against such behavior, but to no avail.

The rivers also provided an expedient means for disposing of industrial waste from the plantations. In addition, washerwomen did their laundry in the rivers, releasing soaps and scum that encouraged alga growth and deposition of silt in the pipe networks. Finally, canals and rivers could simply become obstructed with solid waste. In the 1820s, Longin recorded that the Rivière aux Herbes was littered with all kinds of domestic trash (cited in Pérotin-Dumon 2000: 778). Seasonal storms tended to exacerbate this chronic pollution and littering by dislodging trash and pollutants and moving them throughout the whole system. Although water was plentiful during stormy periods, it was also less clean and not necessarily fit for human consumption. In his 1788 snapshot survey, Mallet judged that Basse-Terre's waters were dangerous and unhealthy in several spots, including at the Ravine de l'Espérance, where he found the water muddy, murky, and unsafe for drinking.

The maintenance of the canals was a constant burden to a city that apparently lacked funding for repairs. In France, public fountains were usually free, but private water access was taxed to pay for the maintenance of the common supply. In Basse-Terre, such taxes probably never existed. Because all relevant municipal records have disappeared, it is unclear exactly how the supply was managed at the city level (Desmoulins 2006: 77). It seems, however, that officials repeatedly asked citizens for help to clean up canals and streams. They also often called upon civic spirit in sharing the use of the rivers. If nineteenth-century attitudes reflected those of earlier periods, Basse-Terrians were generally incapable of pooling their resources to improve the situation. In 1844, for example, they outright refused to finance the pressing project of bringing water from the Rivière aux Herbes to the Champ d'Arbaud (Desmoulins 2006: 79). During the nineteenth century, many cities in the metropole managed to upgrade both the quality and availability of water supplies (Roche 1984), whereas Basse-Terre's aging water system was decaying. A terrible cholera outbreak in 1865 served as a wake-up call and finally created the political will to clean up and modernize the system (Desmoulins 2006: 80).

Overall, the problems that plagued Basse-Terre's water supply, such as regular shortages, inequitable access, and pollution, were not unusual for the time (Roche 1984; Webre 1990). Although somewhat crude, Basse-Terre's water supply must have been a functional and valued amenity. Otherwise, visitors would likely have been less impressed with what they saw and people would have tried to get water through other means. For instance, they would have dug more wells, like their neighbors in Pointe-à-Pitre, or would have taken steps to systematically harvest rainwater at home, which only a handful of people did.

Water-Storage Ceramics

As mentioned, only Basse-Terre's wealthiest households were directly connected to the city's water supply. Because of shortages, pilfering, and tampering with the canals, water delivery was not reliable, however, and even well-off households must occasionally have had to hire water carriers or send their servants to the rivers. Anyone who could not afford a personal water connection had to fetch their supply from the rivers or, after 1749, from the public fountains. Similarly, outside of the city, people would travel to the nearest source of freshwater.

In the early twentieth century, several local publishers printed postcards portraying stereotypical images of Creole women and children gathered around public fountains. These images appear to show women using wooden buckets as carrying containers. Inventories document that wooden buckets already served that purpose in the eighteenth century. Called *quart à l'eau* (a maritime term), these buckets almost always stood near the household water reserves. Such buckets were also common in eighteenth-century France. Historians have found mentions of them in probate inventories from Paris (Pardailhé-Galabrun 1988; Roche 1985), from rural areas such as Perche ornais (Cailly 1998), and from provincial cities like Toulouse (Dousset 2003: 47).

The water fetched in these buckets was then stored in large coarse earthenware jars referred to as *jarres à l'eau* (water jars) in the inventories (figure 1.1). Seventy percent of the households had at least one such container, for a total of 169 vessels. In a few cases, jars like these held other goods, but at least 90 percent served for water storage.

The provenance of most models was recorded. Precisely half came from Provence, France, and the rest were made locally. There is strong evidence that the French jars came from Biot, a pottery that specialized in this kind of vessel at the time. First, Biot jars have been found at most contemporary archaeological sites in Guadeloupe, including the four sites in Basse-Terre selected for

Figure 3.1. *Top*: sherd of Biot water jar with typical gritty, buff paste. *Bottom*: rims of local coarse earthenware drip jars reused for water transport and storage. Photograph by author.

this study (figure 3.1). Further, whole specimens still stand in the gardens and courtyards of historic Creole houses. I have seen a very well-preserved Biot jar at the house of the Némausat family in the center of Basse-Terre.

Biot began producing these jars during the first half of the sixteenth century (Amouric et al. 2006). Originally, they were designed to hold olive oil produced in Provence mills, but they were quickly adopted for storing and transporting many other dry and wet goods, such as olives, salted fish, dried fruits, and dried vegetables. These jars made excellent shipping and storage containers: they came in several sizes and could be sealed with a piece of terracotta, a cloth, a wooden lid, a dish, or even with lime.

Biot's success also stemmed from its location near the ports of Antibes and Marseilles. In the sixteenth century, its ceramics were already being shipped along the Mediterranean coast at least as far as Genoa, Italy. Analysis of the archives of the port of Marseilles illustrates that Biot ceramics traveled all over the French Atlantic and beyond in the eighteenth century. On this side of the ocean, Biot sherds have also been found at sites outside the French colonies. For example, according to the Historical Archaeology Type Collections of the Florida Museum of Natural History, they have been found at Santo Domingo in the Dominican Republic and in Monroe County, Florida. With regard to Guadeloupe, Biot jars must have arrived there as containers for flour and olive oil. Even though Biot dominated the colonial market, at some point in the late nineteenth century, this type of jar became known in the French Antilles as the *dobann* (or *dobanne*), a name that derived from a rival pottery in Provence called Aubagne.

The Biot jar sherds unearthed at the four sites in Basse-Terre had a buff body, were both thick and large, were slipped in white, and were glazed with a classic yellow lead glaze inside (figure 3.1). (Biot jars sometimes have a green lead glaze, but none of the sherds in Basse-Terre exhibited this variation.) For this type of large ceramic vessel, it is interesting to note that the number of rims unearthed greatly underrepresented the number of sherds or vessels. Only two rims were excavated, though 36 sherds and a minimum of seven vessels were identified.

The inventories also mentioned locally made water jars. A small and "very old" example was present in one of the wealthy households inventoried in 1778. This jar was so old that it was worth only 4 livres, 10 sols, but it documents that local potteries were making water jars well before the 1770s. After 1780, some local jars were even said to come specifically from the archipelago of Les Saintes, where the Fidelin pottery was active; this pottery had opened on the islet called Terre-de-Bas sometime in the 1760s (Gabriel 2004).

Local jars were obviously designed specifically to store water, as they sometimes came with a tap (*champlure*). Unsurprisingly, jars with taps were more expensive than jars without. In the 1775 inventory of the Belost house in Saint-François, a locally made medium-sized jar in fairly poor condition with a tap was valued at 12 livres, while another one of the same size and in good shape but without a tap was worth only 9 livres.

Unfortunately, the inventories recorded few other formal attributes of these jars. An anthropological study of the last potters at work in Martinique confirmed that handmade jars still belonged to the local repertoire in the first half of the twentieth century (De Roo Lemos 1979: 34). Water jars were also part of St. Lucia's ceramic tradition (Vérin 1967: 476). On average, these *jè* were 52 cm high and had a rim diameter of about 15 cm. They were handmade by coiling, had no handles, and had a thumb-pressed decoration around the rim. Sometimes the top was incised with a banana tree stipe (a part of the stalk of the banana tree). Unfortunately, no similar study occurred in Guadeloupe before the local potteries closed down, so we do not know for sure what Guadeloupean models looked like.

Some of the thick, unglazed, local coarse earthenware sherds found in Basse-Terre might have come from such vessels. They all belonged to large hollowware vessels and tended to be decorated with molding or impressions (figure 3.2).

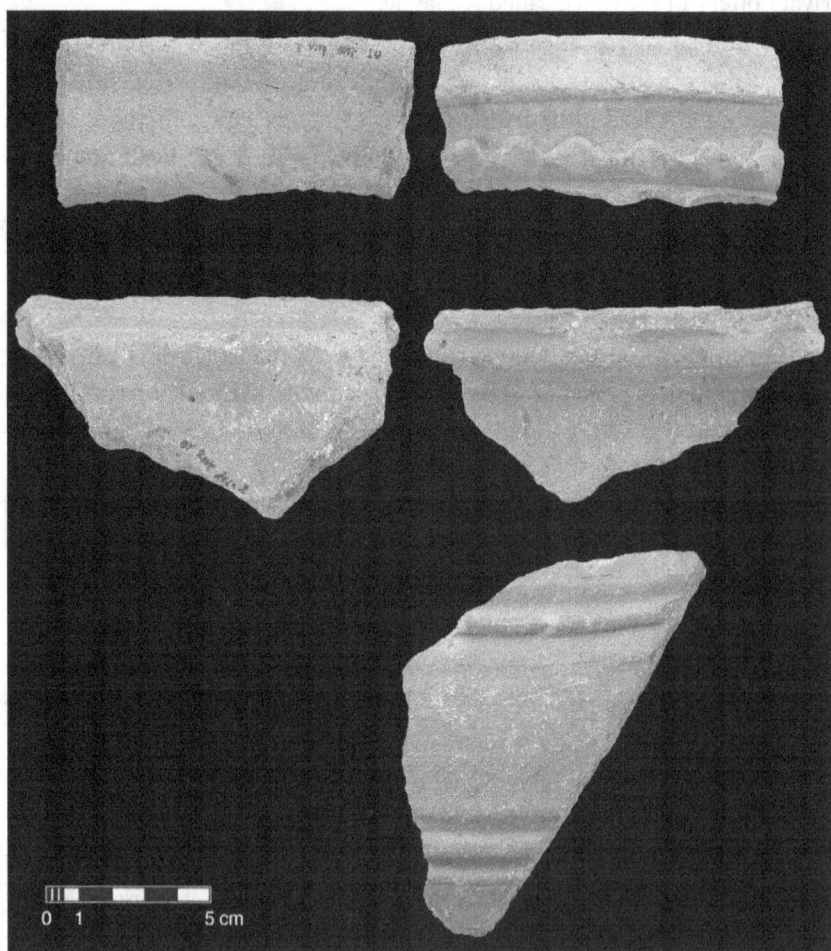

Figure 3.2. Possible sherds of local coarse earthenware water jars. Photograph by author.

The entries in the inventories listed small, medium, and large sizes for both the local and Biot jars. Capacity was rarely recorded, but one of the jars was able to hold 80 pots, or about 149 liters. Despite this substantial volume, it was not labeled as a large jar, which illustrates the fragmentary nature of information about size and capacity.

In the archaeological sample, all of the sherds had very large dimensions. A historical illustration from 1830 signals that the size of Biot jars varied significantly (Amouric et al. 2006: 65). It shows that these jars could contain anywhere from 50 to 600 livres—the livre being the equivalent of a pound or half a kilo—so roughly 25 to 300 liters. The biggest models were most likely reserved for the storage of water. Henri-Louis Duhamel du Monceau (1777: 300) mentioned that the stoneware jars that imitated them were almost as large, and held half a *muid*,[3] or about 130 liters. Water jars in Basse-Terre must have been the most massive ceramic objects around.

Inventories confirmed that the price of water jars increased with their size: a medium jar cost twice as much as a small one, and a large specimen more than double the medium size. They also showed that local jars tended to be less valuable than imported ones. Yet both Biot and local jars were distributed equally between poor and wealthy households, suggesting their origin and formal differences did not have practical importance.

Comparing their average value versus those of other ceramic objects indicates that water jars were costly. In fact, they were among the highest priced ceramic objects in each wealth group: they accounted for the five most expensive ceramics that the poorest group of inventories yielded; 13 jars were among the 15 most expensive ceramic objects owned by middling households; in wealthy households, these jars represented about half of the most valuable ceramics: there were 37 jars among a list of 68 ceramics that were worth more than 10 livres. In many instances, the water jar was one of the most—if not the most—valuable ceramic objects around.

Certainly in part because of their monetary value, many jars were kept in service even after they were well worn or damaged. In the inventories, about 10 percent of the total sample was described as "cracked" (*fêlé, fendu*), "old" (*usé, ancien*), "broken" (*cassé*), or even "destroyed" (*défoncé*). For all other ceramics used in Guadeloupean houses, only about half as many, about 5 percent, were in poor condition. Other factors can also explain the longer life span of water jars. They were large and bulky objects, which made disposal cumbersome. A cracked jar could also still be useful, as long as the break was not so low as to affect its functionality. These objects were crucial for storing water, and a cracked vessel was certainly better than none at all.

Perhaps the site at 28 Rue Amédée Fengarol directly illustrates why water jars disappeared. Water jar sherds at that site came from backyard contexts dating from the nineteenth century. The site's history revealed that a reservoir and a drainage system were built there between 1856 and 1888. We can hypothesize that its residents used Biot jars to store their water until they were able to build this reservoir. The spread of such features in Basse-Terre during the nineteenth century could have hastened the decline of water jars. Private cisterns also became affordable around midcentury, as the Champ d'Arbaud neighborhood illustrates (Desmoulins 2006: 206). Ultimately, wider access to running water rendered the water jars obsolete.

Jars served as the main water reserve in most houses, but evidence from the inventory demonstrates that drip jars (*pots de raffinerie, pots de sirop*) also played a role in the transportation and storage of water (figure 1.1). Eleven households had drip jars that they reused for domestic purposes. In most cases, these objects were closely associated with other water-related objects. An inventory listed a drip jar that "helped carry water upstairs" from two small sources located in front of the house. In a merchant's shop, a drip jar was also sold in tandem with a water bucket.

There was no discernible pattern in the 11 households that reused drip jars in this way. They spanned the 1770s to the 1830s and all three wealth groups. The occupations of their heads of household ranged from craftsman to surgeon to planter and to a successful merchant whose house was particularly well furnished. One head of household was of mixed race, whereas all of the others were white. Hence, reusing drip jars for domestic purposes, and especially for water, seems to have been a convenient solution not dictated by sheer necessity. The only apparent commonality between these households was that most were located outside of Basse-Terre.

Previous archaeological studies have established that potteries in Guadeloupe produced both industrial sugar wares and domestic utilitarian objects (Gabriel 2004; Gibson 2007; Kelly et al. 2008). Plantations also tried to make their own sugar wares as soon as they started producing clayed sugar: Jean-Baptiste Labat mentioned a pottery at the Dominican plantation in Marigot as early as 1703; the historians Denise and Henri Parisis (2010: 19) found an enslaved potter working for the Marre family at Trois-Rivières by 1716. Each plantation or pottery probably used its own source of clay (Kelly et al. 2008; Parisis and Parisis 2010).

Reusing drip jars made perfect sense in the countryside, but evidence from the urban sites proves that this practice was common inside the city as well. The rims of local drip jars were found at 28 Rue Amédée Fengarol, the Palais de Justice, and the Cathédrale. These vessels were of wheel-thrown coarse earthenware with various body colors and rim shapes, probably because of their heterogeneous origins (figure 3.1). Certainly, these industrial wares were not aesthetically standardized, and individual potters produced their own varieties.

This phenomenon was also visible among an assemblage of imported sugar molds and drip jars that was excavated in a test-pit survey of the Embouchure de la Rivière site in Baillif, near Basse-Terre (Bigot 2005). The vessels came from a layer of refuse that contained sugarcane slags and dated from the second half of the seventeenth century. They had white bodies with green lead glaze inside and on the rims, and were probably made in Sadirac, one of the early modern French potteries that specialized in making vessels for the sugar industry. Notably, there were no local ceramics in the assemblage.

The rim diameters of the local jars in the present sample measured 12 to 20 cm and perfectly matched those of the imported Sadirac ceramics. Apparently, the sizes of the local drip jars were based on the French ones. Pierre Régaldo-Saint Blancard (1986), who studied the Sadirac pottery, estimated that the capacity of those drip jars ranged from about 1.5 to 3 liters.

It might be significant that the two sites in Guadeloupe with seventeenth-century components, the Embouchure de la Rivière in Baillif and Fort Houël, had only imported jars, whereas four more recent sites, including the slave village of La Mahaudière sugar plantation in Grande-Terre (Gibson 2007), had only local ones. In his memoirs Jean-Baptiste Labat (1722: III.286–94) reported that both imported and local drip jars were present in Guadeloupe at the end of the seventeenth century.[4] The fact that there was no mention of the provenance of the drip jars used for either domestic or industrial purposes in the eighteenth-century inventories suggested that these jars were locally made. By the 1770s, then, the use of imported drip jars had declined. A relative chronology can be described as follows: Imported jars were more frequent in Guadeloupe during the seventeenth century. Sometime before the end of the century local potters started to copy the imports. Over the next century, they managed to take over the market, and imported drip jars became rare.

Both drip jars and sugar molds (together called *formes à sucre*) were sold for the same price, so it is possible to estimate the value of the former using data from sugar molds. Jean-Baptiste Labat (1722: 3:289) noted that at the beginning of the eighteenth century the cost of sugar molds averaged around 3 livres but fluctuated a great deal with supply and demand. In the inventories, sugar vessels were valued between 0.75 livres and 1.5 livres, but they peaked at 3 livres around 1806. Compared to water jars, this was rather inexpensive.

Although drip jars were present in only 11 inventories, they were found at three of the four domestic sites studied in Basse-Terre, as well as at the slave village of La Mahaudière. Thus they seem to have been even more common than the documents suggest.

They were convenient for several reasons: they were made locally, throughout the countryside, and in large numbers, so they were readily available. They were also cheaper and smaller than water jars, but still large enough for carrying a useful quantity of water around the house or back to the house from a river or fountain. Many of the recycled drip jars found in domestic contexts in the Caribbean must have served as water vessels. At the very least, Gabriel Debien's (1974: 232) description of typical slave housing confirms the existence of this practice in Saint-Domingue. Drip jars were one of the objects that slaves used to store their water.

Whereas drip jars and water jars were widespread, the ceramic water vessels called fountains (*fontaines*) were present mainly in the homes of affluent families (figure 1.1). These objects consisted of three parts: the main body (a reservoir that often had two handles and a tap), a lid, and a basin. The back of the reservoir was usually flat, so that it could be set against or hung on a wall. Some fountains stood on wooden stands, as did one example at the house of Antoine Belost, which rested on a stand nailed to a post in the courtyard.

The surveyed inventories cited a total of 12 fountains, all from the eighteenth century. Two of them were made of tinplate and the rest of faience, so the ceramic type was more common, and all were imported from the metropole. The shop of Antoine Belost revealed that a small, old, undecorated white fountain with a broken basin and no lid was still worth 3 livres in the 1770s. A fountain in good shape could fetch more than 16 livres. Thus, even a subpar fountain was worth as much as many drip jars, while the best models were as expensive as regular Biot jars.

Four sherds of faience and one of faience fine that could be the remains of wall fountains were recovered (figure 3.3). The three faience sherds all came from the Palais de Justice, which suggests that this site was wealthier than the others. Stylistically, the sherds bear rather common decorations, which

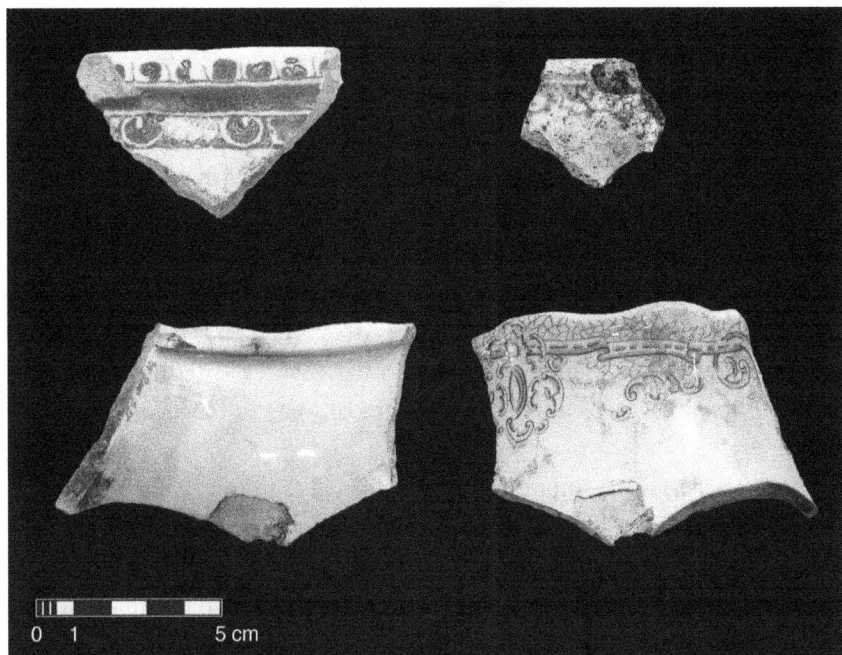

Figure 3.3. Sherds from probable wall fountains. *Top*: two possible rims of faience basins; *top left*: Rouen-style pattern in *camaïeu bleu* (blue and black); *top right*: Faint Moustiers-style pattern in blue. *Bottom*: green transfer-printed rim of a faience fine fountain. Photograph by author.

might indicate that Guadeloupean customers had access only to run-of-the-mill fountain models. The faience fine was found in a nineteenth-century context of 28 Rue Amédée Fengarol. Contrary to what the inventories would suggest, its existence indicates that fountains did not disappear completely after the eighteenth century but remained available to middling households in the nineteenth century.

By design, these fountains would provide extra water storage. Some were also used for cleaning purposes: one example in a storeroom was described as "used for washing" (ADG: Mollenthiel, 2E 3/79, 9/29/1778), and another was found in an outdoor laundry area at Antoine Belost's house. The bulk of these objects were however located in the social and dining areas of Creole houses: the parlors in four cases, and the gallery in two other instances. In these spaces faience fountains would serve as decorative water containers where a thirsty guest could refill his glass, or have a glass brought to him, during a meal. The basins of the fountains also configured them for social hygienic practices: people could use them to wash their hands before dinner, which was common polite behavior in the Antilles, or to rinse their glasses. Their high price combined with their utility help explain why fountains were the appanage of elite households.

Fountains might have been even less common in other parts of the French colonial world. There were no fountains listed in the lavish 1785 inventory of Marianne Lelièvre, a resident of the French colony of Ile Bourbon in the Indian Ocean (Jauze 2006: 131). Nor were such objects present at Place-Royale in Quebec, either in the inventories or among the scores of ceramics excavated there (Genêt 1980; Lapointe and Lueger 1997). Importing fountains from the metropole seemed optional, rather than essential to the French colonial lifestyle. It was a particular choice of wealthy Guadeloupeans and their merchants.

Pitchers (*pots à eau*, literally "water pots") were the last class of ceramics designed to contain liquids; they could often have been used for water service (figure 1.1). In the inventories this single label designated several types of objects made from different ceramic materials and used for different purposes. Overall, pitchers were not very popular: they appeared in a modest 14 percent of Guadeloupean houses.

Two-thirds of the pitchers in use were faience, one example was porcelain, and the rest were coarse earthenware. Their distribution revealed little: all types of households had both coarse earthenware and faience pitchers, and the porcelain example was in a wealthy home. Faience pitchers were valued between 0.75 and 3 livres, and coarse earthenware ones between 1 and 3 livres. Since these ranges overlap, it was impossible to infer the material of the ceramic pitchers based on price alone. Yet the material of the pitcher determined its function, and did so in a similar way for all Guadeloupean houses.

Coarse earthenware pitchers were usually kept in the kitchen, where they must have been used for household chores. Servants could take them to fetch water from the water jar or could use them to keep a small reserve of water at hand for preparing meals and drinks. Faience pitchers, on the other hand, were located in offices, parlors, or bedrooms but never in kitchens. In most instances, they were inventoried with the tableware, which suggests that they were serving vessels. These were present in only 3 percent of houses, because other serving containers, such as glass and crystal carafes, were vastly more popular. Traditionally, faience pitchers were also drinking vessels, but most households had glasses, cups, or bowls for that purpose. Serving drinks in faience pitchers seemed to have fallen out of fashion.

In a few rare instances faience or porcelain pitchers appeared to serve a hygienic purpose, in that they had a matching washbasin, were stored with non-tableware objects, or both. At maximum though, there were five houses in Guadeloupe (about 3 percent of the sample) that used or could have used a pitcher for washing. This number is unexpectedly low for such a common early modern object. By comparison, for instance, in her study of 2,783 Parisian inventories, Annick Pardailhé-Galabrun (1988: 356) noted that 21 percent of houses after 1750 were equipped with a wash set. Given that houses containing a simple wash pitcher were not even included in that figure, the discrepancy between Paris and Guadeloupe is notable and significant.

As was true for the other ceramic water vessels, the archaeological evidence was corrective and complementary. A total of 147 sherds that could be pitcher parts were unearthed, for a minimum of 45 vessels. They were of French faience, both white (*blanche*) and brown (*brune*), and local coarse earthenware, but never of imported French coarse earthenware, as the documents indicated.

Because faience pitchers were used as dinnerware, their style is analyzed in chapter 5 (figures 1.1 and 5.8). Their size was fairly typical. Their rim diameter fell between 9 and 12 cm and their base diameter between 7 and 9 cm. One lid with a diameter of about 6 cm was also recovered, indicating that several examples may have existed. At the sites in Basse-Terre, a few handles but no spouts were found. One vessel had a hole in its upper part to fit a lid.

The dimensions of the local pitchers were similar, except that they had a comparatively larger base, maybe for stability: the rim diameters measured between 8 and 10 cm, and the base diameters ranged from 9 to 13 cm (figures 1.1 and 3.4). These were wheel-thrown coarse earthenware, but with a much less coarse body than for the drip jars. The sherds were more consistently a bright red, and their walls thinner. The treatment of their surface was also distinctive, with tool marks and burnishing on the exterior. Some recent compositional analyses indicate that these ceramics were probably made in Guadeloupe (Kelly et al. 2008).

Both faience and coarse earthenware pitchers were present in large quantities at the four sites, suggesting that they were more numerous than the documents would imply. Certainly, some of the faience sherds could have belonged to coffeepots, hot-chocolate pots, or teapots, many parts of which are undistinguishable from water pitchers. Yet this does not explain the large

Figure 3.4. Locally made coarse earthenware pitchers from the 28 Rue Amédée Fengarol site. Four of the bases show incised marks. Photograph by author.

number of coarse earthenware pitchers at the sites, which are unmistakable because the local pitchers had a unique shape.

Pitchers nearly disappeared from the inventories by the end of the eighteenth century: only one specimen dated from 1830. But the sites tell a different story, as a few faience pitcher sherds and many coarse earthenware ones were present in the nineteenth-century contexts of 28 Rue Amédée Fengarol. Local pitchers were even found in the topsoil. These objects were so essential that they probably never really went out of use. A historical postcard also proves that pottery peddlers in Guadeloupe continued to sell them after the 1830s.

In sum, faience pitchers were popular items early on but fell out of favor as glassware became more common. The inventories from the 1770s and 1780s document 16 faience pitchers in use, but almost four times that number were for sale in shops, indicating perhaps that supply exceeded demand. Meanwhile, coarse earthenware pitchers might have been convenient, popular, and also prone to breakage. If they were used to draw water from the household reserve, to transport water throughout the house, and for household chores, they may have been subject to frequent mishaps. They could have accumulated in the archaeological deposits as a result, which would explain their relative abundance at the sites.

Patterns in Ceramic Water Containers

In Guadeloupe, then, one of the functions of pitchers, fountains, and drip jars was to serve as water containers, while water jars housed the main domestic reserve. The fact that local potteries started producing almost all of these vessels proves that they were important in residents' lifestyle. A significant proportion of the local domestic production was devoted to water-storage ceramics. Water jars, pitchers, and drip jars repurposed for water-related tasks represented a prodigious 68 percent of the local ceramics listed in the inventories.

These objects must have met the water management needs of households, otherwise local potters would have created new and better designed models. Data are not available for Guadeloupe itself, but some regional potteries made additional types of ceramic water vessels during the nineteenth and twentieth centuries, and possibly earlier. On St. Lucia, the *krish* was the local equivalent of the French *cruche,* or water jug (Vérin 1967: 476). It had a double handle, a spout, a lid, and often some incised decoration and was useful for storing a small quantity of water. The *goglet* or *karaf* had a similar function and was even more popular. The former name stemmed from the French *gargoulette* (a type of water vase that was made in the south of France), and the latter from the French word *carafe.* In twentieth-century Martinique, ceramic water vessels seemingly resembled the ones used in eighteenth-century Guadeloupe (Beuze 1990; De Roo Lemos 1979; Victor 1941). Surveys cited the presence of jars (De Roo Lemos 1979: 31) and pitchers, called *pott l'eau* (Victor 1941: 36). Other evidence suggests however that gargoulettes and carafes existed from the mid-nineteenth century, because such items are pictured in the first catalogue of the Musée National de la Céramique at Sèvres, published in 1845 (Brongniart and Riocreux 1845: 75, 96).

During the colonial period, other types of water-storage ceramics could also have come from the metropole, in particular the cruche or one of its many regional variations, such as the *dourne, kanti, orjol,* and *gargoulette.* These objects were all specifically designed for the transportation, storage, and consumption of water and were, a priori, available to French colonial merchants. Gargoulettes had reached Ile Bourbon in 1785: 14 were present in the inventory of Marianne Lelièvre (Jauze 2006: 131). At Place-Royale in Quebec City, no less than 149 cruches were listed in the 77 inventories analyzed by Camille Lapointe and Richard Lueger (1997: 224). Yet neither the word *cruche* nor any of its equivalents appeared a single time in the sample of Guadeloupean inventories. Likewise, Guadeloupeans seemed to lack the stoneware pots and stoneware water jars that existed in the metropole and at Ile Bourbon.

As an alternative, Guadeloupeans might have repurposed non-ceramic objects that were perfectly suited for storing water. In particular, *dame-jeannes,* large glass bottles usually enclosed in wickerwork, were present in great quantities in their houses. According to the documents, these objects held a great variety of drinks and foods, but there was never any indication they held water. On the other hand, Albert Jauze (2006) believes that dame-jeannes were used both to transport and to store water at Ile Bourbon. Describing slave housing in Saint-Domingue, Gabriel Debien (1974: 232) also reported that slaves who could not afford cruches used dame-jeannes and drip jars instead. Finally, a twentieth-century postcard shows young water carriers in Guadeloupe using a dame-jeanne to transport their load.

These containers could have been a natural complement to Guadeloupe's ceramic equipment, but the inventories provide no evidence of their use during the colonial period. As far as water management was concerned, in Basse-Terre water jars, pitchers, reused drip jars, and a few fountains for the wealthy, seemed to suffice.

A spatial analysis of water ceramics in the inventories uncovered some other interesting patterns. Guadeloupeans kept their main water reserves in a variety of spaces, apparently based on convenience: in many cases, the jars were located under the gallery, in the courtyard, or in the backyard. Yet they also appeared in parlors (*salles*), pantries (*offices*), storerooms, and kitchens.

A few elite homes—four cases in the sample—had another option: a water-storage shed (*case à eau*), which is today considered part of the vernacular Creole architecture. These freestanding sheds were usually built in the courtyard or a backyard of an urban house. For instance, in her study of eighteenth-century housing in Basse-Terre, Anne Pérotin-Dumon (2000: 426) reconstructed the plan for a typical merchant's house, depicting a water-storage shed in the courtyard adjacent to the detached kitchen.

Alternatively, wealthy families might have an indoor water storeroom (*magasin à l'eau*). One such room inventoried held several water-storage ceramics and was located near the parlor and the pantry. The differences between these specialized rooms and the water-storage sheds were both architectural (inside versus outside) and functional. Unlike storerooms, water-storage sheds could be designed to collect rainwater from the rooftop. Some of the sheds preserved today are still equipped with pipes and taps serving such a function (Desmoulins 2006: 109). Moreover, in her novel about nineteenth-century Creole life, the author Arlette Blandin-Pauvert (1986: 15–16) highlighted this particular role of the outdoor shed.

What was striking about the various storage options was that water vessels almost never appeared inside master bedrooms. Water jars, fountains, and drip jars were seemingly banished from these areas. Wash pitchers, present in about 20 percent of Parisian bedrooms, made only a few exceptional appearances in Guadeloupe. Taken together, this evidence indicates that Guadeloupeans avoided keeping water in the room where they slept.

There could be a number of reasons for this practice, but one obvious hypothesis is that they wanted to avoid attracting insects or perhaps breeding mosquitoes near their beds. On average, mosquitoes breed in standing water in about ten days, but the process speeds up when the water remains above 80°F. Some species' life cycle can even be as little as four days. Keeping even a small reserve of water indoors in Guadeloupe certainly increased the risk of encountering this pest. Meanwhile, mosquito nets were rare luxury items—only three wealthy households in the inventories could afford one. Most people slept without any mosquito protection beyond good air circulation.

Water Quality

Some of the houses with water-storage sheds or water storerooms also had a stone water filter or dripstone. The filters described in the inventories were made of a large, hollowed-out piece of porous stone supported by a wooden frame, which corresponds to models in use in Europe at the time (figure 3.5). In France, using sandstone filters and adding wine to drinking water were the most common water treatment practices (Baker 1981; Hamlin 2000). In their encyclopedia, Denis Diderot and Jean Le Rond D'Alembert (1751–72: 809) noted several reasons why stone filters were relatively unpopular. First, the quality of the stones varied greatly, and it was a costly mistake to buy a filter that did not work properly. Second, the filtering process was very slow. Finally, the filter could give water a bad taste, because it retained solid impuri-

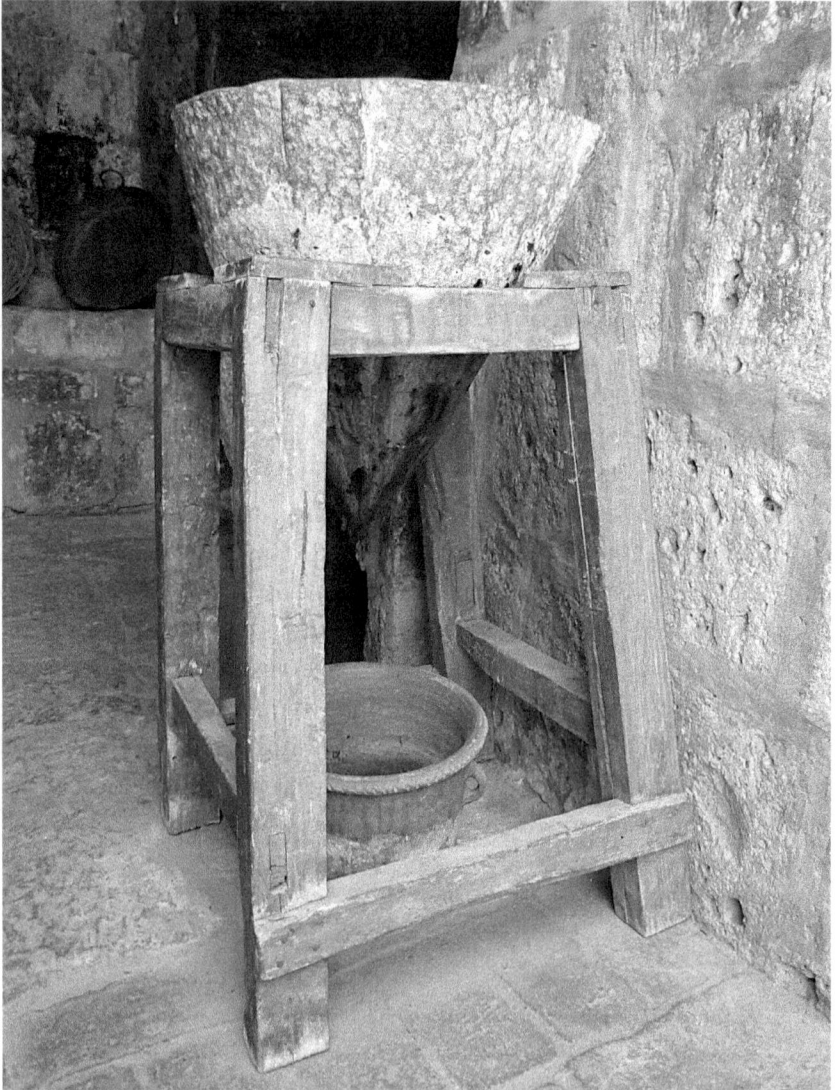

Figure 3.5. Traditional water filter from the monastery of Santa Catalina in Peru, similar to the models described in the Guadeloupean inventories. Photograph courtesy of Pethrus (available at http://commons.wikimedia.org/wiki/File:Water_filtration_stone,_Santa_Catalina_monastery,_Arequipa,_Peru.jpg).

ties and was difficult to clean, even by vigorous brushing. Indeed, all types of porous filters require regular if not daily physical cleaning to prevent both clogging and the growth of biofilms (Sobsey 2002: sec. 4.7).

Spaniards introduced dripstones to the West Indies as early as the sixteenth century (Coleman 2001). The first filters were imported, but later Barbados started producing local models made of coralline limestone. These were probably exported to other Caribbean islands, such as Jamaica. In Guadeloupe, filters were at least as expensive as the water jars, if not more so, so only wealthy households could afford them. They appeared more frequently in the 1820s and 1830s than in earlier periods; only one eighteenth-century house was equipped with a dripstone. So, although these objects remained expensive and rare, their popularity increased over time. A few well-off Guadeloupeans seemed particularly keen on improving the quality of their water supply: they installed rainwater harvesting systems on the roofs of their water-storage sheds—rainwater being deemed the healthiest in general—and bought costly stone filters to further purify it.

Most households did not take these extra steps, but they might still have tried to improve the quality of their water through the simple act of storing it. If water is kept undisturbed and unmixed for a few hours, the larger particles of sand and silt settle out by gravity (Sobsey 2002: 4.2). If it rests overnight or for a couple of days, the larger microbes will do the same. When water was eventually drawn out of the container, this was done carefully, so as not to disturb the sediment. It was also necessary to regularly clean the storage container, if not to rinse it with freshwater after each use. In Basse-Terre, this decanting method could have been applied intentionally or not. Regardless of the motivation, the general habit of storing water at home in water jars helped improve the quality of the domestic water supply.

The Role of Female Servants

Nowadays, 20 to 30 liters of water per day per capita is estimated to be enough to cover basic human needs. Guadeloupean inventories did not record the size of the water jars very well, but Duhamel du Monceau (1777) gave a capacity of about 130 liters for the average model. Such a reserve could sustain six people for a day or a couple for about three days. Therefore, even large vessels serving small households must have required refilling at least several times per week. Managing the water supply was an arduous, repetitive chore.

Who was in charge of these tasks? If historical postcards are accurate, fetching water was mostly the provenance of women. Today, women and children are often in charge of this chore worldwide. Other Guadeloupean postcards portrayed water carriers for hire, who were either men or children. In her survey of urban jobs in Guadeloupe in 1797, Pérotin-Dumon (2000: 510–11) found that professional water sellers were black men and that they all worked in Pointe-à-Pitre. Given that Basse-Terre had more water access points, maybe water carriers were not as common there.

Having a healthful water supply was vital to a household, but managing the domestic reserves came without any title or job description. It was a nameless task probably most often assigned to unskilled female servants. Whether they bought water from carriers or hauled heavy buckets themselves, these servants must have done so at least every few days. Their other tasks would have included monitoring the level of the reserves; refilling the water jars and fountains; sweeping the water-storage area; and maintaining all of the equipment, in particular emptying, rinsing, and scrubbing the water reserves and stone filters on a regular basis.

Domestics who lived with their masters might have been able to tap from the house's main water supply, just as servants of rich employers did in Paris (Roche 2000: 157). On plantations, however, field slaves had to go some distance to fetch their own supply. At Ile Bourbon in 1844, planters argued that it was important to repair the Lancastel Canal, which they used to irrigate their plantations, for this very reason (Prosper 2000: 52): "Then [the slave] is not done yet, because . . . new fatigues must start for him. He needs water for his family, and whatever the time he must go to the nearest river to get some. He gets back only at around seven or eight o'clock to prepare his dinner" (cited in Prosper 2000: 52; translation mine).

The Ile Bourbon planters' argument was that fieldworkers needed to get water at the end of their shift, so it would be charitable to rebuild the canal and spare them a long trip to the river. Of course, this description must be taken with a grain of salt, since the authors wanted the canals repaired for their own purposes. Yet it demonstrates that slaves were responsible for fetching their own supply. Savvy planters probably understood that it was in their interest to provide their workers with convenient water access. Gabriel Debien (1974: 219) even argued that the location of slave quarters on plantations depended on both prevailing winds and proximity to a source of clean water such as a creek, canal, pond, or well.

Interestingly, it seems that enslaved women who managed the water reserve shaped part of Guadeloupe's ceramic water equipment. Perhaps as the individuals who handled these ceramics most often, they had a say in which objects were most suitable. At any rate, that locally made, utilitarian pitchers and drip jars were typically used in place of other more specialized French-made ceramics, such as water jugs, proves slaves' involvement. If masters were more hands-on in that domain, they would probably have chosen fewer plain and more imported objects for these tasks.

Comparison with Paris

A comparison between Guadeloupe and Paris is instructive. First, it highlights the universal need to keep water reserves in early modern homes. In a typical Parisian house the largest reserve was stored in the fountain (Pardailhé-Galabrun 1988: 349). Initially, fountains were made of copper, but by 1780 cheaper models in faience and stoneware appeared, effectively replacing the metal ones. As a result, more low-income households than before could buy a fountain (Roche 1985: 157). People who lacked fountains tended to use whatever they had on hand, such as jugs, pails, or even small jars or pots.

Annick Pardailhé-Galabrun (1988: 349) found fountains in 68.5 percent of Parisian households. In Guadeloupe, water jars appeared in 70 percent of the overall sample and in 77 percent of households before 1790—the date when Pardailhé-Galabrun's survey stopped for Paris. These numbers, taken from two very different locations, appear both high and strikingly similar. Both in the tropical colonial environment of Guadeloupe and in one of Europe's largest cities, around three-quarters of households kept a large container of water at home. This proportion could have been similar in other early modern places situated beyond the French colonial world.

Annick Pardailhé-Galabrun also noted that the average capacity of Parisian fountains was 65 liters, but around 40 percent of households could store less than 45 liters, and half of the fountains held less than 90 liters. Only about 10 percent of Parisian households had fountains holding more than 130 liters, which was the size of the average Guadeloupean water jar. It is probable that typical households in Guadeloupe were able to store somewhat more water than their Parisian counterparts could.

The apparent concern of Guadeloupeans about the quality of their water supply was mirrored in France. The large majority of Parisian fountains were made of copper. Henri-Louis Duhamel du Monceau (1777: 300) reported that people grew suspicious of this metal during the eighteenth century. A lawyer and physician named Joseph Amy (1759) made a detailed study of common contemporary water-purifying techniques in relation to health issues. He blamed copper fountains for potentially poisoning hundreds of families and stated the models that were galvanized with lead were no better. Glass or ceramic fountains, on the other hand, tended to be too small in his view. Amy claimed that the elaborate tin fountains of his invention were the best, but even in his biased opinion, water jars appeared to have an edge. Not only did they work well for purifying water by decantation, but they also did not impart a bad taste to the water, as most other options did. Believing that quality and taste went hand in hand, people went to great lengths to improve the taste of their supply. They tried to filter it with all kinds of materials: sand, natural sponges, cotton cloths, wool, and silk are some of the media cited by Amy. Some households even macerated their water-filtration sponges in alcohol and orange blossom water beforehand. Amy claimed that his fountains did a good job of keeping water fresh, but to do so they required constant maintenance, including daily washing and emptying of the reserve along with regular filter changes. In comparison, the maintenance of water jars was less laborious, and Duhamel du Monceau noted that their popularity was on the rise, even though they could be difficult and expensive to procure in some areas. On that point, Guadeloupeans were relatively lucky and even proved proactive when they started to produce these vessels locally.

Conclusion

For an eighteenth-century city, Basse-Terre had a good water supply. Simply having access to running water, whether via rivers, fountains, or canals, already put its residents ahead of most of their contemporaries, including Parisians. It also made other water acquisition methods, such as collecting rainwater or digging wells, almost unnecessary. Nonetheless, storing water at home was as essential in Basse-Terre as it was elsewhere, because even the best water supply faced chronic problems of shortages and pollution.

The sheer necessity of keeping a substantial amount of water at home explains why Biot jars, the largest ceramics around, were initially chosen for this role. They proved so practical that local potters made their own copies. The common practice of reusing drip jars for carrying or storing water also seems logical. Drip jars were appropriately sized, inexpensive, and attainable by almost everyone, including some enslaved individuals. As far as water management was concerned then, reusing existing objects was a prevalent, logical, and common solution. Many other societies or cultures may have applied a similar strategy in their domestic settings.

At first glance, wealthy people appeared the most proactive in trying to improve the quality of their supply, as they had the means to buy expensive stone filters. Yet whether people realized it or not, storing water in jars had a similar effect through simple sedimentation. This means that in reality most households were engaged in some kind of water storage and purification activities, and such interesting practices in premodern times deserve further attention.

In general, ceramics must have been only part of the array of objects used for domestic water management, though in Guadeloupe they were all that was needed. In the context of a tropical colony far away from the metropole, ceramics seemed particularly adequate. They were readily available through trade or local production, and as an added benefit unglazed coarse earthenware tended to keep water cooler. In his review of water jars in France, Duhamel du Monceau (1777: 300) mentioned their durability and longevity as reserves, as long as the water inside was not allowed to freeze. Certainly, Guadeloupe's climate met that requirement.

Guadeloupeans' choices made sense in their particular context, but they were not far removed from those of their contemporaries in the metropole. Whatever solutions early modern households employed, managing the domestic water reserve was an important and physically demanding chore rarely recorded or acknowledged in documentary sources. In Guadeloupe the material traces of water management spoke of the subtle but essential contribution of enslaved female servants, a theme that the next chapter explores further.

CHAPTER FOUR

A Canari in the Kitchen

Creole Cooks, Foods, and Cuisine

An important part of Guadeloupe's ceramic culture arose out of its kitchens, where enslaved cooks developed what is today considered the traditional Antillean cuisine. The sites and inventories together provide an in-depth and complementary perspective on this topic. First, they help shed light on the population of enslaved cooks and explain Guadeloupe's gender-based hierarchy, which aligned with early modern French customs as well as colonial social order. Second, they illustrate the specificity of Creole kitchens. Documentary evidence of foods and food-storage ceramics combined with a brief review of the history of food sources in Guadeloupe reveal what kinds of ingredients were available during the colonial period. A detailed analysis of colonial ceramic cookware and a review of modern Antillean cookbooks then give us an idea of what dishes these cooks might have prepared.

Servants versus Chefs

In historical sources, enslaved cooks formed a very special group. First, they stood out for their notably high value. In Nicole Vanony-Frisch's (1985: 90–92) study, the median estimated price of 40 Guadeloupean enslaved cooks in the 1770s and 1780s was 2,600 livres. Cooks were second in value only to overseers, at 3,000 livres. Moreover, the record price paid for a single slave was for a cook, Céladon, who was sold in 1783 for 8,000 livres. On the plantations that Frédéric Régent (2004: 92) surveyed, cooks were worth even a bit more, 2,986 livres on average, second only to tailors. Similarly, five of the six cooks recorded in the Basse-Terre–area inventories were worth an average of 2,700 livres; the sixth had a markedly lower value, 1,200 livres, because he was "very crippled."

These numbers are all the more noteworthy given that nearly half of the cooks in Vanony-Frisch's study—and four out of the six in the inventories I surveyed—were Africans. In fact, along with sugar refining, cooking was one of the rare professions not dominated by Creole slaves and relatively open to African-born individuals (Vanony-Frisch 1985). Theoretically, African origin should have lowered the value of a cook, since Régent (2004: 102–8) demonstrated that in Guadeloupe African-born slaves were consistently worth less than both black and multiracial Creole slaves. For cooks, however, race or origin seemed to matter less than skill, and being born in Africa was not an impediment to becoming a highly sought-after professional. Cooks were worth more in part because their services could be leased out for extra income (Fourniols 2000: 62n18).

Another important characteristic of enslaved cooks in historical sources was that most were men. Many examples in the francophone Caribbean travel literature and in the diary of Martiniquais planter Pierre Dessalles indicate as much. Men constituted more than 90 percent of Vanony-Frisch's sample, and all six cooks mentioned in the Basse-Terre inventories were male. Enslaved women who officially worked as cooks did exist, but they were rare. Incidentally, the situation was identical at another French island colony, Ile Bourbon, in the Indian Ocean. Ève Prosper (2000: 47) observed that cooks on the plantations in the Saint-Pierre area were male, and Albert Jauze (2000: 76) noted that cooks were among the most valuable slaves. As a result, Prosper (2000: 47) described this profession as typically male in Ile Bourbon, just as Gabriel Debien (1974: 87), Arlette Gautier (1985: 215), and Frédéric Régent (2004: 94) did for the Antilles.

In reality, the profession of cooking was segregated less by race or origin than by sex. It seemed that both enslaved men and women cooked, but in very different contexts. Male chefs in historical sources worked for well-off households or for hospitality and food businesses. The six cooks in this study's sample belonged to wealthy households and to the innkeeper Jean-François Bernier. Frédéric Régent (2004: 92) indicated that cooks were mostly present on plantations with more than 100 slaves, and Albert Jauze (2000: 76) noted the same phenomenon for the largest estates of Ile Bourbon. As a result, households with professional cooks appear to have represented a minute portion of colonial society—just 4 percent of the households surveyed in Basse-Terre and 1.3 percent of those in the south of Ile Bourbon had them (Jauze 2000). Likewise, chefs amounted to less than 0.01 percent of the 8,820 slaves studied by Vanony-Frisch in Guadeloupe, and 0.16 percent of the 1,325 individuals studied by Prosper for Ile Bourbon.

The small numbers of cooks reported stemmed from the fact that historical sources only recorded the existence of professional chefs, as opposed to average domestic slaves who cooked as part of their daily chores. Specialization and training must have set the chefs apart from everyday cooks. It is probable that chefs were not expected to have as many responsibilities as other domestics and that cooking was their main activity. Chefs also seemingly came to the profession in two ways: through apprenticeship or previous experience. The four African chefs from the Basse-Terre inventories were quite young, between 16 and 23 years old. Since they were already in charge of their kitchens, they must have learned their skills through apprenticeship. In his diary, the Martiniquais planter Pierre Dessalles mentioned that his cook's new apprentice was 13 or 14 years old (Dessalles and Frémont 1980: entry for Jan. 24, 1837). Other island-born chefs seemed to be valued for their experience (Vanony-Frisch 1985: 90–92). For instance, Roch, Jean-Baptiste Marre's cook (ADG: Fontaine, 2E 3/5, 7/28/1779) was 58 years old, and at 2,500 livres, was worth more than typical men of his race and age, who hovered around 2,100 livres (Régent 2004: 103). Both of the older chefs in the Basse-Terre–area inventories were born in Guadeloupe.

Most households did not have a chef and must instead have assigned cooking tasks to one of their domestic slaves. Because a majority of these were women, female cooks must have been the norm. These women left more tenuous but just as real documentary evidence of their existence as their male counterparts did. For example, they surfaced in newspaper sale ads. Advertisements in the *Journal politique et commercial de la Pointe-à-Pitre* stated that one female servant was "suited for the kitchen" and that another "could cook a little."[1] A lot of these servants who could cook had other specialties as well, as did a 30-year-old black female slave who was described as "a merchant, a bit of a cook, and a very good housekeeper,"[2] or a 32-year-old mulatto woman who was "a cook, a washerwoman, and a housekeeper."[3] Clearly, women cooks were expected to have other talents in order to be able to manage all of the basic needs of a household.

A modern legacy of the historical role of women in daily cooking can be seen in the annual Fête des Cuisinières (Festival of [Female] Cooks). This event, one of the five main festivals in Guadeloupe, takes place every mid-August. During the festivities, about 250 cooks from the Woman's Cooking Association wear traditional costumes, parade throughout the streets of Pointe-à-Pitre, prepare a large banquet, and go to a special mass where their dishes are blessed. It was during the nineteenth century that these female cooks started to organize in a professional association: they held liturgical events, elected a queen, and wore an insignia made of violet braids (Ovide 2002: 17).

Slave women already cooked for their families, relatives, or communities (Brunache 2011). From the very beginning of the plantation era, both Jean-Baptiste Labat and Jean-Baptiste Du Tertre described how elderly women were in general put in charge of cooking for the *atelier* or enslaved fieldworkers (cited in Debien 1964: 8; Gautier 1985: 204). According to a well-known depiction of plantation work in Du Tertre's book (1667–71), preparing manioc cakes was a task assigned to the *négresses* (black women).

It was a reflection of the social norms and values of colonial Guadeloupe that women typically did the cooking whereas men were appointed as professional chefs. Women scholars in particular have pointed out the strong dichotomy between male and female tasks in the French Caribbean (Gautier 1985; Pérotin-Dumon 2000: 515). This division even transcended caste lines: what was true for enslaved cooks also applied to free individuals. Men who chose to be cooks were regarded as professional caterers or chefs, but there were few free women in this profession (Pérotin-Dumon 2000: 507–8). Cooking was only one of the numerous skilled jobs open to male slaves. Female slaves, on the other hand, had more limited options. The majority worked as seamstresses, laundresses, or nurses (Gautier 1985: 215). In 1797, when all actively employed women were listed in a census—there were no slaves at the time since slavery had been temporary abolished—domestics were by far the most numerous (57 percent of working women in Basse-Terre), followed by laundresses (18 percent) and seamstresses (15 percent) (Pérotin-Dumon 2000: 847–48). In theory, women worked (at best) with needles, whereas men handled the most advanced tools of the time, including those for carpentry and blacksmithing (Gautier 1985: 219). Men monopolized the superior technologies, just as chefs had access to better cooking equipment.

The same gender division existed in the metropole. Noble and wealthy households preferred to employ a *cuisinier* (male cook), whereas bourgeois households that could not afford a cuisinier hired instead a *cuisinière* (female cook) (Figeac 2007: 161). Male chefs needed several kitchen assistants, one of whom was often a female servant. Reproducing this male-dominated system in the colonies was all too easy because enslaved women already occupied the bottom of the social pyramid (Pérotin-Dumon 2000: 515). Even enslaved cooks likely benefited from some kitchen help. When the latter was not a child apprentice or an assistant, it must have been a house slave, often a woman. For example, Marre's chef Roch was probably assisted by his wife, Rosine, and their three daughters, who were the only other slaves in the house. In sum, although historical sources tended to portray cooking as a male-dominated profession, women were very much involved in it. While faithfully reflecting the values and structure of French Caribbean colonial society, in which they had the lowest status, enslaved women also managed to transcend both the French preference for male cooks and African customs that placed women in charge of food preparation (Carney and Rosomoff 2009: 74; Gautier 1985: 46–47, 204).

Dessalles's diary implied that enslaved cooks had some creative leeway in deciding how to prepare the foods they had on hand. At the very least, they were accountable for the execution of dishes and for the quality of meals during social events. On many occasions, Dessalles praised the skills of his cook Philippe, and felt gratitude to him for being instrumental in the success of a party (Dessalles and Frémont 1980: entries for Sept. 20, 1840; Sept. 1846, May 1846 and Aug. 1815 in 1842; and March 1812, Dec. 1814, and Dec. 1828 in 1843). Philippe was also blamed when his cooking did not meet expectations, as were the cooks of other households when Dessalles did not like what they served.

The position of cook, either male or female, came with the power to influence the health and general well-being of the masters. An anecdote recounted by Jean-Baptiste Labat (1722: IV.486) illustrates this point: A wealthy Martiniquais planter hired a caterer for his daughter's wedding, fearing that his enslaved cook would not be up to the task. The latter decided that "harm had been done to him." To exact revenge, he poisoned one of the dishes served at the wedding with tobacco leaves. Most of the guests fell ill for a couple of days, and Labat warned his readers against the strong "purgative" properties of tobacco. Along with the usual feelings of satiety and sporadic gratitude, cooks could thus inspire less pleasant emotions, like fear or anxiety. For instance, they were among the leaders of the insurrections that rocked eighteenth-century Saint-Domingue (Pluchon 1987: 129). Amidst waves of criminal poisonings on the northern part of the island, some planters became so wary of their cooks that they avoided eating foods they had not prepared themselves.

Creole Kitchens

Outdoor cooking was an important part of the colonial experience. In Jean-Baptiste Labat's writings, it was part of his "indigenization process" and took the form of outlandish exotic barbecues called *boucans* (Toczyski 2010). Visiting late eighteenth-century Saint-Domingue, Alexandre-Stanislas, Baron de Wimpffen (1993: 115) noted that most people in town did not have a kitchen and did all their cooking outside. Historical sources also often described slaves preparing their meals this way (Du Tertre 1667–71: II.451). Studying Saint-Domingue plantations, Debien (1974: 233) confirmed that the preparation of manioc flour took place in front of the shed or in the adjacent yard. Local archaeological sites have validated the existence of such a custom: at the slave village of La Mahaudière, food-related artifacts, faunal material, and pipes were most concentrated in the yards, where they outlined the outdoor cooking areas (Gibson 2007: 254, 268). The ethnologist Catherine Benoît (2000: 168–71) witnessed the persistence of this custom in modern Guadeloupe, where little cooking sheds are often set up in backyards, even when the houses have indoor kitchens. In general, lunch is prepared in the shed whereas dinner is cooked inside.

During the colonial period, people with the means to build a kitchen did so. In the inventory sample, 60 percent of households were so equipped. The likelihood of having a kitchen increased directly with wealth: 29 percent of the poorest homes listed one, versus 57 percent of the middling ones and 86 percent of the wealthiest ones. A large majority of these kitchens were detached from the main house and their contents were recorded in a separate section of the inventory. Those in the home were usually located at a distance from the rooms where families spent their time, such as the gallery, bedrooms, and parlors. Many other historical sources, such as travel accounts, deeds, maps, and newspaper advertisements, describe similar layouts. Kitchens were rarely integrated into Creole houses (Charlery 2005; Desmoulins 2006; Edwards 2006; Pérotin-Dumon 2000). In general, the kitchen occupied its own separate shed, which inside Basse-Terre was often located very near slave housing (Pérotin-Dumon 2000: 425–30, 462–63).

Today, Creole kitchens are identified as a typical local architectural element, but very few have been preserved and are available for study (see, for example, Charlery 2005; Desmoulins 2006; Edwards 2006). From his stay in the Antilles in the 1640s, Du Tertre (1667–71: II.451) recalled that at that time wealthy planters preferred to build their kitchen sheds of masonry. Most examples, however, were flimsy wooden sheds that could be opportunely joined to existing masonry walls, as was done at 28 Rue Amédée Fengarol. The best equipped of these kitchens contained a built-in hearth and stove (called *potager*) and sometimes an indoor oven.

Detached kitchens did not belong to France's vernacular architecture. French kitchens were usually indoors, because the custom in wealthy households was to combine domestic and service space inside the same building. Less well-off families rarely had a kitchen per se; that is, an entire room devoted to cooking. Instead, cooking was done at the hearth or fireplace that heated the house, and the room around it was used for many other activities, including sleeping and eating (Figeac 2007: 160–62; Pardailhé-Galabrun 1988: 258).

The expressed rationale for having separate kitchens in the Antilles was that it helped prevent fires (Charlery 2005; Pérotin-Dumon 2000: 423). Certainly, fires must have been a problem there, but no more than they were in the metropole at the time. In Guadeloupe, kitchens and houses were probably more often destroyed by hurricanes than by cooking fires. Moreover, building the kitchen away from the main house was not an entirely satisfactory solution, since as late as 1844, local authorities insisted that kitchens be built of masonry, again to prevent fires. Finally, in wealthy Basse-Terre houses, kitchens were not so much architecturally detached as merely isolated from the main residential rooms. In these cases, the separation was more psychological than physical (Stewart-Abernathy 2004). In other words, distancing the kitchen from living spaces had to do with more than mere fire prevention.

In his journal, the Martiniquais planter Pierre Dessalles revealed deeper motives. During a visit to a bourgeois family in the metropole, Dessalles complained that they made him eat in a space that opened to their kitchen, forcing him to endure heat, smoke, and cooking smells (Dessalles and Frémont 1980: entry for July 15, 1838). His remarks carried extra meaning in the context of this meal: his hosts were trying to impress him in hopes of securing a matrimonial alliance between their offspring. As bourgeois, they were already quite wealthy, but they coveted his noble status. Through his critiques Dessalles was expressing more than physical discomfort. He was conveying his aversion for their lower social rank as well as their project. This anecdote shows that having a detached kitchen was intrinsic to Dessalles's way of living and his self-identification as a member of the colonial elite.

Interestingly, American planters expressed their own partiality for detached kitchens in similar terms. They preferred to separate themselves from the "heat, noise, odors, and general commotion" of the kitchen (Vlach 1993: 43). In his study of American southern plantations, John Michael Vlach did not take these explanations at face value either, tying the development of detached kitchens to the rise of large plantations. Like other outbuildings, detached kitchens appeared when the social boundaries between slaves and masters hardened at the beginning of the eighteenth century. The spatial separation between the "big house" and the outbuildings became less a matter of convenience and more a materialization of the social and racial divide. Isolating the kitchen was one way planters exerted absolute control over their slaves as well as reduced intimacy with their servants (Stewart-Abernathy 2004: 5–8; Vlach 1993: 43). Leslie Stewart-Abernathy (2004) observed in Washington, Arkansas, that detached kitchens were so integral to social separation that they disappeared as soon as this form of slavery ended.

Separation could be a double-edged sword. Isolating the housing and working areas of slaves also gave them more independence (Stewart-Abernathy 2004). In Basse-Terre, slaves working in the kitchens were often not under the gaze of their masters. Another benefit of kitchens and slave housing was their separate access to the outside, which meant that servants did not have to cross the main house to exit or just communicate with someone outside. Although this detail has not received much attention, many examples exist in historic houses and yards. I noted that a typical merchant house compound, such as the Némausat house in downtown Basse-Terre, had two entrances from the street: one through the main house and the other at the opposite end of its elongated courtyard. Similarly, at 28 Rue Amédée Fengarol, the backyard maintained a separate exit through a door in the wall. Finally, the same appears true for many houses whose plans have been published elsewhere (Desmoulins 2006: 187; Pérotin-Dumon 2000: 426, figs. 429 and 422, also see figs. 421a and 422a).

The inventories depict kitchens as functional workspaces. It appeared most activities taking place in them were food-related, and they contained only the necessary cookware. They also were a site for the production of manioc flour, an important food source for slaves and a substitute for wheat flour in Creole cuisine. Grinding cassava roots into flour removed the toxic cyanogenetic glycosides. Raw cassava roots were first peeled and shredded with a grater (*grage*)—present in about 30 percent of households in the sample. Though sometimes done in the kitchen, this step was more often done elsewhere; for example, in a separate shed called a *gragerie, case à farine*, or *case à grager*. The roots were then washed in water to remove their juices. Often, this was performed in an elongated tub called a *canot* for its resemblance to the local dugout canoes of the same name. An alternative method was to bag the shredded roots, then compress the bag to extract the juice. Fewer households seemed to have used this method, but in one inventory bags made of *latanier* (a Caribbean fan palm) served that purpose (ADG: Jaille, 2E 3/6, 8/27/1788). Then the shreds were further dried on a hot metallic plate called a *platine* or in a frying pan. *Platines* were not very common in the inventories, appearing in only nine houses (6 percent of the sample). Most households instead used a *poêle à farine* (literally, "frying pan for flour"). There were 36 houses with at least one such pan, which in 70 percent of instances was kept in the kitchen. Though raw cassava roots were not always processed in the kitchen, manioc meal was typically dried and cooked there. This strengthens the argument that women occupied these spaces.

Other types of work occurred in kitchens more sporadically. On a few plantations, the kitchen was used for processing coffee in lieu of a coffee shed. Laundry and ironing were other domestic chores occasionally conducted in these places. Three-quarters of the 19 households that owned some sort of laundry equipment kept it in their kitchen, but less than 1 percent of the 48 houses that had irons did so. It seemed that domestics sometimes did the laundry in or near the kitchen but preferred to iron clothes in other parts of the house, such as the pantry.

As befits workplaces for household slaves, kitchens were sparsely furnished. A few had a kitchen table or some candleholders, but seating was extremely rare. Tableware was stored elsewhere in all but a few cases. This trend was even stronger for silverware: other than the merchant Mottel, who apparently used the kitchen in the back of his shop to entertain customers, only the free femme de couleur Marie Rose kept her silverware in her kitchen (ADG: Jaille, 2E 3/7, 12/14/1790). Obviously, tableware and silverware could have been useful during the preparation of meals. At Place-Royale in Quebec, just like in France, a fair amount of tableware was stored in kitchens: not only plates and dishes but also soup tureens and salad bowls (Lapointe and Lueger 1997: 224, table 225). That in Guadeloupe both silverware and tableware were strictly kept out of the kitchen implies that all of the food preparation occurred without these objects and that kitchens were deemed an unsuitable place to store them. Storing these items in parlors, pantries, or even bedrooms certainly kept them more easily under the direct surveillance of the masters.

Guadeloupean kitchens contained minimal cooking utensils and tools. Within this limited amount of material culture, minor variations were significant. In one case a pair of iron leg shackles appeared as a constant looming threat to whoever was working there. In other houses, kitchen servants were assigned or took on responsibilities that might have procured them extra liberties, for instance, when they kept chickens or other small farm animals. It was not unusual to see industrious slaves take the initiative of raising poultry to earn extra cash in plantation societies (see, for example, Benoît 2000: 110; Moitt 2001: 73; Vlach 1993: 82). Even raising the master's animals must have yielded some advantages, since these animals could be an important source of food and income for the household. Whoever was in charge of their care could potentially derive some benefit from the position by, for example, being able to maintain their own stock on the side. In the Guadeloupean sample, a few kitchen slaves were entrusted with or negotiated the right to keep chickens, pigeons, ducks, turkeys, guinea fowls, pigs, and rabbits.

Colonial Foods

Foodstuffs that were being consumed at the time of a notary's visit were usually excluded from the appraisal. Only six houses and two merchant shops had foods described as *en consommation*. These were mostly kept in a storeroom (*magasin*) or sometimes in a cellar or pantry. Around 20 percent of mostly wealthy households also owned a *garde-manger* (a piece of furniture dedicated to storing food). Based on a few descriptions, a garde-manger consisted of a solid wood frame covered with a cloth. It had to be lightweight because it was suspended from the ceiling in order to store the food in a well-ventilated place that, more importantly, was somewhat protected from bugs and rodents. Garde-manger appeared in a variety of rooms, but pantries were the location of choice.

The bulk of the foods that were not intended for immediate consumption were in six merchant shops inventoried between 1775 and 1833 (ADG: Mimerel, 2E 2/195, 8/19/1775, 12/7/1775, 12/20/1775; Mimerel, 2E 2/198, 2/18/1780; Mollenthiel, 2E 3/79, 12/6/1779; Nesty, 2E 2/85, 4/29/1833) as well as in the inventory of Jean-François Bernier's inn (ADG: Mimerel, 2E 2/196, 9/9/1776). Among these items were imported pastas like vermicelli and macaroni (Pérotin-Dumon 2000: 850); Gruyère and various soft round cheeses; cured meats and animal products like salami, ham, salt pork, salted beef, and lard; cured or smoked fish like herring, salmon, mackerel, and salt cod; "green peas" of some sort (probably split peas), "green peas from Auvergne" (perhaps the gourmet Le Puy green lentils), and common lentils; spices like salt, black pepper, bay leaves, cloves, garlic, onions, and nutmeg; olive oil and butter; white and red wine vinegar; almonds and sultana grapes; rice, corn, wheat flour, and manioc meal; tea and coffee; and an array of alcoholic beverages including hard cider, beer, red and white wines, dessert wines (Muscat, Cyprus wine, and Malaga wine), a flavored barley wine called *orgeat*, gin, anisette and unidentified liqueurs, fruit brandy, tafia,[4] rum; and finally, fruits preserved in alcohol.

Most of these provisions had been shipped across the Atlantic and were still packed in barrels. In a few instances they were also spoiled. Their provenance was sometimes specified: French wines often came from Bordeaux or Provence, and some liqueurs also came from Provence; a small portion of salt cod was from France, which implied that there were other sources; and some rice was described as "English," which indicated that it probably came from America. Although the inventories spanned 1775 to 1833, there was continuity in the kinds of foods and drinks that merchants sold. Even unusual items, such as almonds or anisette, were available in several places.

Taken alone, the inventories of shops and inns offer a very distorted view of the foods eaten in Guadeloupe. Apart from alcohol and staples like salt, oil, and wheat flour, most of these imported products never showed up in private houses, where local foods dominated. The inventoried products that were likely grown in Guadeloupe included all of the manioc flour, coffee, sugar, tafia, and rum; and some of the vinegars, garlic, rice, corn, peas, and spices. Yet this short list does not even start to cover the range of produce that was grown locally.

Because food is critical for survival, the feeding of slaves was more highly regulated than was their shelter and clothing (Debien 1964). Not only the governor but also his administrators, such as *intendants* and militia officers, were allowed to keep tabs on how planters provisioned their slaves. Planters initially distributed Irish salt beef, salt cod, manioc, peas, and cured fish to their slaves. The size of these rations (called *l'ordinaire*) varied considerably by region or plantation, but they were rarely sufficient. In 1685, the Code Noir mandated an increase in the minimum ration (Article 22) and forbade the replacement of foodstuffs with spirits (Article 23). Meanwhile, slaves soon started gardening, hunting, and fishing to procure extra food. By the seventeenth century Jean-Baptiste Du Tertre (cited in Debien 1964: 6) recalled seeing yams (*ignames*), sweet potatoes (*patates*), local squashes (*giraumons*), a cereal called *mil* that could have been sorghum or millet, and various peas and greens in the *jardins de case,* or individual gardens that slaves grew near their housing. Jean-Baptiste Labat (cited in Debien 1964: 6) noted a few years later that slaves were also fond of both sea and land crabs.

Instead of distributing food to their slaves, eighteenth-century planters began to give them Saturdays off to provision themselves, as was done in the Dutch and English colonies. The Code Noir initially forbade free Saturdays, but they were so popular that they were eventually legalized in 1786 (Régent 2004: 121). At the same time, French colonial authorities pushed for the cultivation of more foods on plantations, leading to the development of communal plantation gardens (*vivres en commun*). Planters reserved part of their land for growing food staples such as manioc, sweet potatoes, and yams, and sometimes forced their slaves to work this land on Saturdays (Debien 1964). Hence, many planters fed their workforce through a combination of various subsistence strategies: distribution of rations, free days to cultivate individual gardens, and collective gardens.

Frédéric Régent (2004: 119–20) studied the area devoted to communal plantation gardens in Guadeloupe in 1790. He determined that they took up about 22 percent of the 11,000 ha that were officially under cultivation at the time. That number was probably an underestimate, however, because it did not include individual slave gardens. Anne Pérotin-Dumon (2000: 544–46) also concluded that Guadeloupe produced enough food to support its urban population, which was not necessarily true elsewhere, for example, in Saint-Domingue. According to nineteenth-century writer Adolphe Granier de Cassagnac (1842–44: 175), free Saturdays were also particularly common in Guadeloupe.

Specific crop cultures varied with local climatic zones. For example, fresh vegetables and fruits were concentrated in Basse-Terre's highlands, in the Bouillante, Pointe-Noire, and Les Habitants areas (Pérotin-Dumon 2000: 545). Manioc was the main staple in Basse-Terre, but in the drier climate of Grande-Terre, bananas were more essential (Régent 2004: 120). More importantly, the range of foods available in Guadeloupe was in constant evolution. During the settlement era, visitors to the French Antilles reported Caribs cultivated gardens that already contained many future Creole staples such as cacao, coffee, sugarcane, squashes, manioc, sweet potatoes, Scotch bonnet peppers, and various tubers (Ovide 2002: 187; Saunier 2003: 5). There were also a plethora of edible wild foods. Fruits included avocados, mameys (locally called *abricots-pays*), bananas, cashews, lemons, limes, oranges, guavas, papayas, cainito (*caïmite*), Barbados cherries (*cerises-pays*), sugar apples (*pommes-cannelles*), water lemons (*pommes-lianes*, a variety of passion fruit), yellow mombins (*prunes-mombins*), and *Chrysobalanus icaco* fruits (*zicaques* or *icaques*). Vegetables included sweet manioc (*kamanioc*), arrowleaf elephant ear (*malanga* or *chou-caraïbe*), Guinea arrowroot (*topinambou*); and available spices were achiote (*roucou*), *bois bandé*,[5] and allspice (*bois d'Inde*) (Lebey 1998; Saunier 2003: 4). Bananas and some Old World foods had arrived in the Caribbean on earlier Spanish ships and must have already been present in Guadeloupe; among these were yams, eggplants, watermelons, cucumbers, chicken, pork, and goats. Island game such as the green acouchi (*agouti*)[6] and iguanas; seafood such as the common octopus (*chatou*), West Indian top shell (*burgo*), conch shell (*lambi*), Caribbean spiny lobster (*langouste*), big-claw river shrimp (*ouassou*), and clams (*chaubette*); and local species of fish were part of the common fauna, and probably also the diet. Turtles and manatees were so sought-after by early colonists that they were already overhunted in the 1660s (Boucher 2008: 236). Relishing island curiosities, Jean-Baptiste Labat also described eating some dishes that used exotic ingredients, like wild monkey head soup (in Saint-Domingue) and roasted palm grubs (Garraway 2005: 132–36).

At some point before the end of the seventeenth century, several more plant species became available: coconuts, ginger, soursop (*corossol*), welsh onions (*cive*), and vanilla (Lebey 1998). Many other foods are believed to have been introduced in Guadeloupe after the mid-eighteenth century, including several Old World spices like cloves, cinnamon, nutmeg, and black pepper; fruit trees like châtaigniers-pays (*Artocarpus altilis* var. *seminifera*, a variety of breadfruit whose fruits contain seeds) and later, the classic breadfruit (*Artocarpus altilis* var. *non-seminifera*, whose fruits do not have seeds), mangoes, star fruits (*carambole*), sapotas (*sapotille*), coffee plums (*prune-café*), jocotes (*prune-chili*), ambarellas (*pomme/prune de Cythère*), and grapefruits; and new vegetables like chayote (*christophine*) and taro (*madère*) (Hatzenberger 1996; Huyghues-Belrose 2006; Lebey 1998). Tamarind might have also been imported around that time, but became popular only in the nineteenth century (Lebey 1998: 185–88).

The origins of the vegetables and fruits that entered Guadeloupe during this period ranged widely. Colonists tried with varying degrees of success to cultivate fruits and vegetables from the metropole. Visiting in 1793, Paul Isert commented that green peas, artichokes, and asparagus were growing very well in Basse-Terre (Isert 1972: 318). Judith Carney and Richard Rosomoff (2009: 136–37) identified 30 plants that were transported from Africa to the New World during the plantation era. Of the foods they list, the following appear to have been present in Guadeloupe: rice, millet, yams, plantains, taro, roselle (*Hibiscus sabdariffa* L., or in French, *oseille de guinée*), watermelons, muskmelons/cantaloupes, African spinach (*calalou*), calabash, various hot peppers, and peas (notably *pois boukoussou, pois d'Angole, pois de canne*)

(Carney and Rosomoff 2009; Debien 1964; Lebey 1998). Both European and African varieties of some vegetables coexisted, as did cucumbers from Africa (*ti concombre*) and from Europe (*concombre*) (Lebey 1998).

Tubers played a crucial role in the Caribbean, in part because they grew underground and were less vulnerable to hurricane damage (Carney and Rosomoff 2009: 118). Hurricanes were often followed by food shortages that could be exacerbated by social factors (Widmer 2006). For instance, although manioc flour could be preserved for months, very few planters bothered to maintain reserves (Debien 1974: 217; Widmer 2006). More generally, eating the roots and leaves of tubers was simply a good way for even slaves to achieve a balanced diet. In her study of Gisèle Pineau's novels, Brinda J. Mehta (2005) articulated the lasting connection between tubers and French Caribbean culture. She drew a direct link between the importance of root vegetables in Creole cuisine and the influential *Poetics of Relation* by the Martiniquais writer Édouard Glissant. As evidence, she cited excerpts from a paragraph in which Glissant defines his "rhizomatic" vision of Creole identity, a concept that he borrowed from Gilles Deleuze and Félix Guattari:

> [the rhizome,] an enmeshed root system, a network spread either in the ground or in the air, with no predatory rootstock taking over permanently. The notion of the rhizome maintains, therefore, the idea of rootedness but challenges that of a totalitarian root. Rhizomatic thought is the principle behind what I call the Poetics of Relation, in which each and every identity is extended through a relationship with the Other. (Glissant 1997: 11)

As will be explained later, tubers are used in a great deal of French Antillean dishes, either in the form of root vegetables or as manioc flour.

Naturally, historical sources gave a more Eurocentric view of gardens and other food sources during the colonial period. For example, their authors often overlooked local herbs and spices. Catherine Benoît's (2000) study of modern Antillean gardens showed that they contain many plants other than food crops, including medicinal herbs, ornamental plants, and utilitarian vegetation used for shading and borders. She also inventoried an impressive number of different varieties, close to 600.

Ceramic Kitchen Equipment

The inventories showed that some ceramics were used for storing foods. The most common ceramic containers were *cannes*, present in 19 percent of middling to wealthy households, and the latter had more than one (figure 1.1). Cannes were used to store liquids, especially hard cider, liquor, or vinegar.[7] Their purpose explains why they were kept in the same room as food reserves and why they rarely showed up in poorer houses, which were the least likely to have stored foodstuffs. As far as ceramics go, cannes were also quite expensive: in the eighteenth-century inventories, most were valued around 3 livres.

Cannes were also very consistently described as stoneware ceramics (grès). In the archaeological collections, the most common stoneware vessels were German-style jugs (figure 1.1). They represented about half of the stoneware, in both sherd count and minimum number of vessels (MNV). The inventories described cannes as "ducdalle" in eight houses and "barbu" (bearded) in three others. Whereas the spelling and meaning of the former term remain uncertain, the latter probably referred to the stamped bearded faces that often decorated Rhenish Bartmann jugs. This term also confirmed that the items described as cannes in the inventories and the German stoneware jugs recovered from the sites were in many cases one and the same.

In the archaeological collections, cannes were least frequent at Fort Houël (MNV = 1), which yielded the earliest ceramics. By implication Rhenish stoneware jugs were more prevalent in Guadeloupe during the eighteenth century than the seventeenth, a pattern also true for many North American sites. Based on excavations in Lower Rhineland, jugs and storage jars still dominated the Rhenish production in the eighteenth century, representing about half of all vessels excavated there (Gaimster 1997: 121, fig. 124).

Along with cannes, the 1770s inventories listed some less-well-identified stoneware vessels used for storing foods. With the exception of white salt-glazed stoneware, all of the stoneware in the archaeological collections were potentially food containers, since they corresponded to fragments of pots, jugs, jars, and bottles (figure 4.1). A sherd from the base of a gray salt-glazed stoneware bottle confirmed its food storage function. The liquid content—perhaps hard cider or beer—had pooled around the edge inside the base and formed a solid layer of yellowish and pitted concretions. Whatever was stored inside had remained there long enough to form this deposit. French stoneware from Lower Normandy represented the second largest group of identified stoneware. The site assemblages suggested that French stoneware was used in conjunction with Rhenish objects, and thus both might have been occasionally referred to as cannes in the inventories.

Other ceramic vessels were occasionally used for keeping foodstuffs. For instance, the merchant Antoine Belost had a potiche full of sultana grapes,

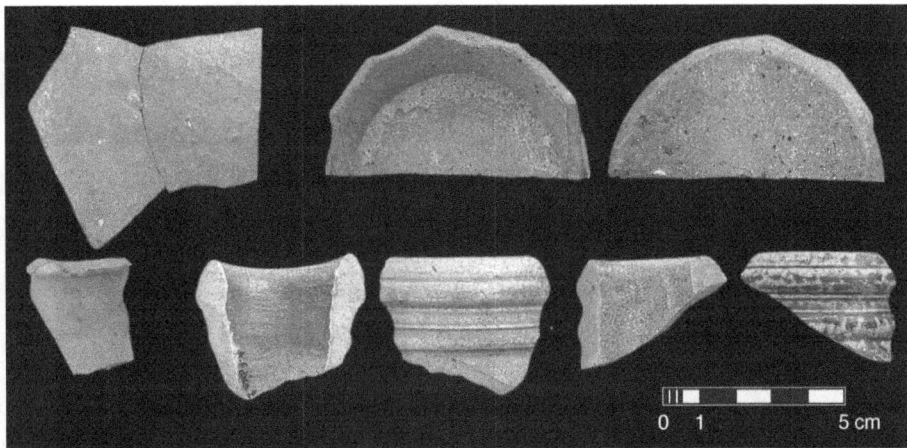

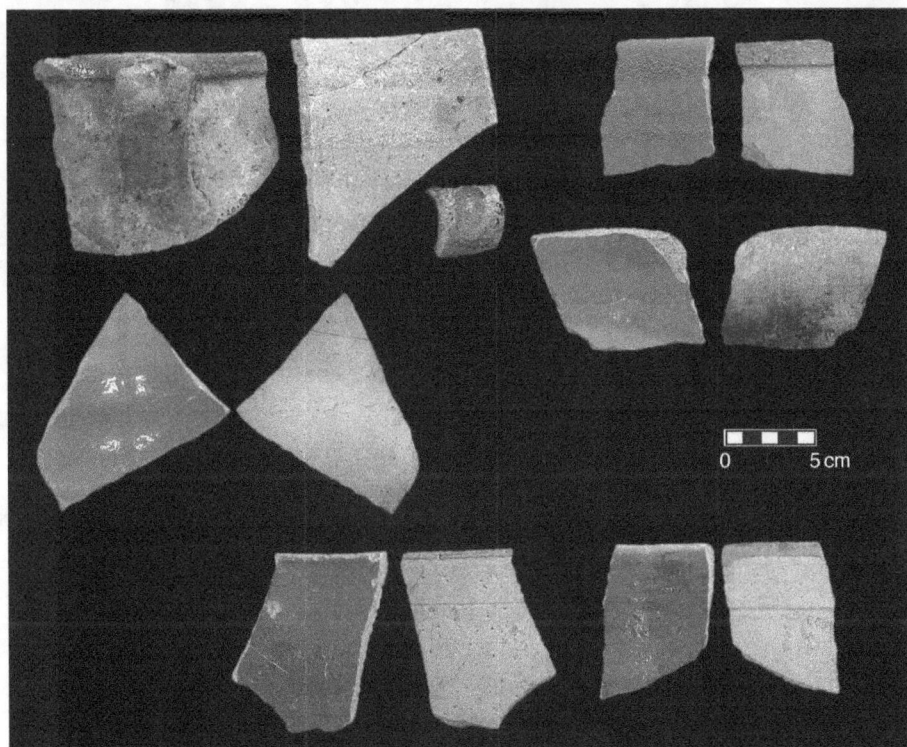

Figure 4.1. **Top series**: examples of stoneware storage pots. *Top left*: body and rim of tall salt-glazed stoneware bottle from Basse-Normandie, France, exhibiting the typical dark brown paste. *Top right*: base of gray salt-glazed stoneware with yellow concretions inside. *Bottom right*: rims of German stoneware bottles. **Bottom series**: coarse earthenware cooking pots from Vallauris, France, organized in chronological order. *Top left*: models with a depressed rim and clear yellowish lead glaze. *Top right*: models with depressed rim, orange slip, and clear lead glaze. *Middle left*: teardrop shape with orange slip and clear lead glaze. *Bottom*: straight-sided models with dark red slip and clear lead glaze. The left example bears a stamped potter's mark: "CONI . . . /VALLAU. . . ." Photograph by author.

which must have referred to a coarse earthenware grape pot from Biot. French archaeologist Jean Petrucci (1991) was the first to identify these vessels. Several vine shoots loaded with grapes could fit inside one pot. The top end of the shoots was sealed with wax, while the bottom end was dipped in a mixture of water and powdered charcoal, which could keep the grapes fresh from the time of the fall harvest until the winter holiday season. (The December 7 date of Belost's inventory fits with this time frame.) In the colonies fresh grapes were a luxury that cost nearly as much as imported cheese: a pound of Gruyère was valued at 18 sols and a pound of sultana grapes at 15 sols.

Beyond food storage, ceramics also were important in cooking. The local name for coarse earthenware cooking pots was the Carib word *canari*, one of the first Caribbean words to be borrowed into European languages (figure 1.1) (Breton 1999: 259). The inventories cited the presence of canaris inside 40 percent of houses, and in most cases, people had two or three of these vessels. Compared to cannes, canaris were fairly inexpensive: they cost about 1 livre on average, but some cheaper models started at around 7 sols. Consequently, compared to cannes, their distribution was less tied to the wealth of a household. Four of 10 middling and wealthy houses, as well as around 15 percent of the poorest ones, were equipped with canaris.

Their single main function also explains their location: more than 70 percent of canaris were located inside the kitchen. The remainder were either merchandise for sale in stores or belonged to houses without a kitchen. Canaris were very rarely used for purposes other than cooking: in one home, they were employed in the processing of cotton (ADG: Mollenthiel, 2E 3/79, 3/5/1778).

These objects had certain attributes that were consistent between the inventories and examples unearthed at the sites. Compared to other ceramics, their provenance was rather well defined in the documents. This information was noted in 33 percent of the listings and for 96 percent of the vessel sample—but the latter included a large merchandise lot of 3,365 units. An overwhelming proportion, about 99 percent of the pots, came from Provence. The data on materials were also quite uniform: 96 percent of the vessels for which this information was recorded were of glazed or unglazed coarse earthenware.

In the archaeological collections, cooking pots accounted for 160 sherds and 47 vessels, representing 5–10 percent of the minimum number of vessels at all the sites (figure 4.1). Like their counterparts in the inventories, all of these pots were coarse earthenware, and the imported ones were also glazed. A majority of the known examples came from Provence, mostly from Vallauris and occasionally from Saint-Quentin-la-Poterie. Even if all of the undetermined vessels had other origins, the Provence region would remain the primary source of imports. The main discrepancy with the inventories was that local pots were more numerous in the assemblages, but inventories tended to minimize the importance of the local ceramics, as they did for ceramic water vessels.

A number of the local sherds came from lids that were possibly used with cooking pots (figures 1.1 and 4.2). They were the rims of flat disks that occasionally exhibited soot or burn marks. Imported lids did not show up in the assemblages, and local potteries might have made these simple pot accessories themselves. The sherds of the possible locally made cooking pots

Figure 4.2. Locally made coarse earthenware cookware. *Top left*: rim of cooking pot similar to the traditional Martiniquais *coco nègue*. *Top right*: two possible lids. *Middle*: saucepan handles. *Bottom*: rims of flanged bowl and bowl with straight rim. Photograph by author.

corresponded to large hollowwares that often had charred exteriors and did not obviously belong to other known local objects. They formed a very heterogeneous group, with some being thrown and others being hand built. One hand-built example found at the Palais de Justice looks like the cooking pot called *coco nègue* that potters in Martinique still made in the 1970s (figure 4.2). More than half of the examples of these possible locally made canaris and lids were unearthed at Palais de Justice.

Vallauris Cooking Pots

Fortunately, the data about the preponderant style of cooking pots, those imported from Vallauris, was more meaningful. Jean Ferdinand Petrucci (1999) has reconstructed the evolution of these vessels from the sixteenth century until the early twentieth century. Although it lacked absolute dates, Petrucci's work established a relative chronology of the pots that applied well to the Basse-Terre assemblages. Firstly, the coating on the pots changed over time. In the sixteenth and seventeenth centuries, it boiled down to a yellowish lead glaze (figure 4.3, top left cooking pot). An orange slip was introduced underneath the glaze sometime around the mid-eighteenth century (figure 4.3, middle series), and then replaced by a dark red one at the turn of the century (figure 4.3, bottom series). The latter lasted until the early twentieth century and is the one that has most often been captured on historical postcards.

In parallel, the morphology of the vessels also evolved (figure 1.1). The first models were what Petrucci called "cooking pots with a depressed rim," which exhibited a rectangular and slightly concave rim. They were discontinued sometime after the orange slip appeared, during the second half of the eighteenth century. The next shapes, "teardrop," developed first with the orange slip, then with the red one. A version of these models was still made in the early twentieth century. Meanwhile, a line of "straight-sided" pots appeared in the nineteenth century and lasted as long as the teardrop versions.

Vessels with a "depressed rim" and a simple lead glaze were found in the earliest context at Fort Houël, and also represented the bulk of the cooking pots sherds at Palais de Justice. The fact that only a few appeared within the later eighteenth-century contexts of Fort Houël and 28 Rue Amédée Fengarol might indicate that they were discontinued after the mid-eighteenth century, as Petrucci proposed. Logically, too, the later teardrop and straight-sided pot models mainly came from the most recent contexts at 28 Rue Amédée Fengarol. The only pot bearing a mark was from there as well (figure

4.1). Vallauris potteries started stamping their ceramics in the 1880s, and Jean-Baptiste Conil was one of the potters who was active at that time (Forest et al. 1996: 67). Since Conil disappeared from the twentieth-century list of potters, this particular mark might have had a short lifespan of a couple of decades at the end of the nineteenth century.

Petrucci's chronology has great potential as a tool for dating French colonial sites. In Guadeloupe, it is particularly relevant: Vallauris cooking pots turned up abundantly at each of the sites in Basse-Terre, with almost 5,500 sherds; moreover, they were the most abundant type of coarse earthenware at La Mahaudière (Gibson 2007: 169). If Petrucci's typology were applied to more sites, it could certainly be further refined. Although the Basse-Terre collections confirmed the applicability of his general framework, they also hinted at the existence of extra types, such as straight-sided pots with an orange-brown slip.

Petrucci further observed that sizes were standardized as early as the early eighteenth century. The nine vessels that could be measured in the assemblages did not cover the whole range of production. Their rim diameters measured between 8 and 33 cm, but clustered in the average sizes of 17 and 18 cm. Based on Petrucci's calculations, they could contain around 5 liters, but larger Vallauris examples existed that could hold up to triple that volume. Data from the inventories support the idea that pots in Guadeloupe were mostly of average size. Less than 1 percent of canaris were described as "small," "large," or "very large."

The sample of measurable pots sometimes seemed to correspond with the nature of the sites. The smallest pot, with a volume of 3 liters, and one medium pot came from the eighteenth-century feature at 28 Rue Amédée Fengarol, which could signify that the family who lived there was not very large, like the family of carpenter Mathieu Oplas. At the other end of the spectrum, the largest pot was recovered in the later contexts of Fort Houël. Whether it was used to prepare meals for the soldiers stationed there or even for the prisoners after the 1760s, its size was adequate for a large community.

After the canaris, the second most frequent ceramic cookware object in the inventories were coarse earthenware saucepans (called *casseroles*, as in French) (figure 1.1). Saucepans differed from cooking pots in having a squat shape and straight handle. They appeared in about half as many houses as the canaris, and almost 80 percent of these houses used only one or two of them.

The term "saucepan" encompassed two categories of ceramics. Six cases were faiences, while the rest were coarse earthenware. Faience saucepans were more often kept in parlors, pantries, and bedrooms of wealthy houses, and coarse earthenware in the kitchen. The distribution of the latter resembled that of the canari. The faiences were thus used as tableware, while the coarse earthenware were indeed cookware. Most Guadeloupeans chose not to use their faience saucepans for cooking. These models were no more expensive—all saucepans cost an average of about 1 livre—and they could sustain heating, as they were made in faience brune, a special type of faience cookware protected by a lead-glazed exterior. Yet enslaved cooks were not allowed to work with them.

No faience saucepans were recovered from the dig sites, which is not surprising given their rarity in archaeology.[8] The origin of the coarse earthenware models fit what the texts indicated: most came from Provence, specifically Vallauris and to a lesser degree Saint-Quentin-la-Poterie (figure 4.3). Others were made locally (figure 4.2). As usual, the latter were quite heterogeneous, some being hand-shaped and others wheel-thrown.

Saucepans were less widespread than cooking pots, so they did not appear in all of the contexts; for example, they were absent from a feature at 28 Rue Amédée Fengarol that yielded a minimum of four cooking pots. Their size was also more uniform. Most saucepans had a diameter of 20 to 21 cm, except for one large model that measured 32 cm.

Compared to canaris and saucepans, the coarse earthenware bowls called *terrines* were very versatile (figure 1.1). In the inventories, they amounted to 178 vessels distributed among 29 houses, most of which owned two bowls. Because of their versatility, these objects were scattered in various rooms. A good many were close to the water jars, but some were stored with the much fancier faience and porcelain tableware. A few appear to have been used for washing laundry, some for personal hygiene, and others for preparing foods. The last case was illustrated in five inventories that recorded bowls stored in the kitchen or elsewhere alongside other cooking utensils.

Appraised at an average of 2 livres in the eighteenth century, bowls were more expensive than the rest of the coarse earthenware cookware, which restricted their distribution in Guadeloupean houses. A minority was locally made while the bulk was imported either from Italy (12 percent) or Provence (83 percent). The local source was the Fidelin pottery, and the Italian bowls were Albisola ware. Imported bowls cost more than local ones.

In the assemblages, coarse earthenware bowls represented 153 sherds and 77 vessels. They tended to occupy a slightly larger share of each site's

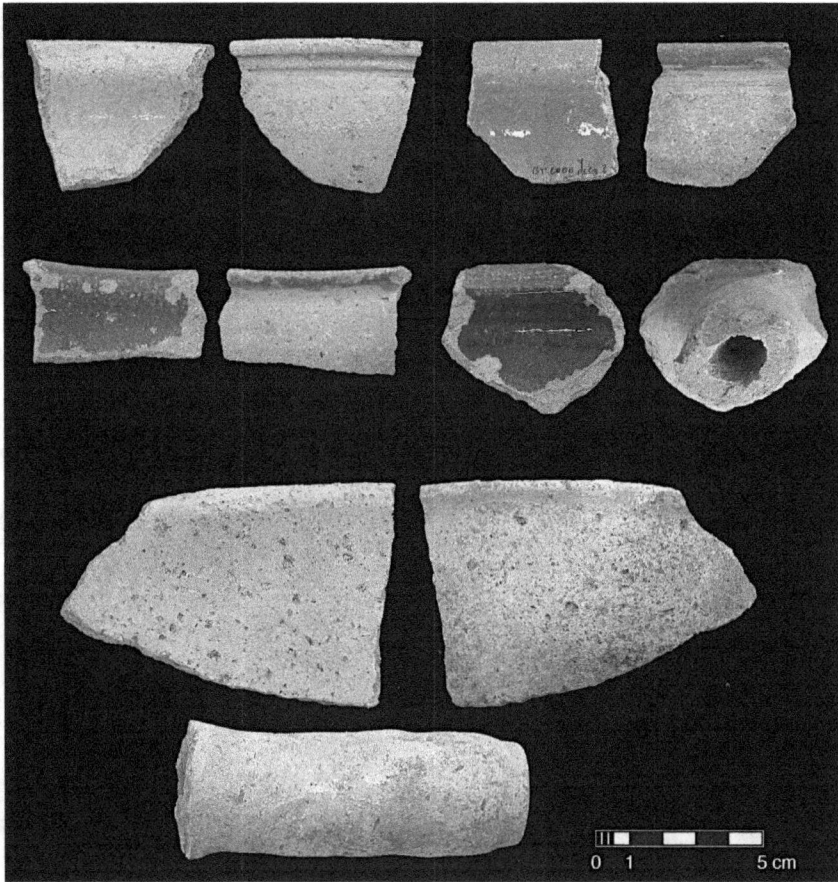

Figure 4.3. French coarse earthenware saucepans. *Top two rows*: models from Vallauris with yellow, orange, and dark red slips. *Bottom*: possible model from Saint-Quentin-la-Poterie with buff paste and yellow glaze. Photograph by author.

minimum number of vessels than cooking pots did. In the earliest context of Fort Houël, their concentration reached 25 percent. Compared to these numbers, the inventory sample was notably low. Guadeloupeans likely used more bowls than the documents indicate.

Among the known imported types, there were no Albisola wares, unlike in the inventories. A large majority, however, came from Provence—78 percent of all French bowls—and in particular from the Huveaune Valley, which does fit the data from the inventories (figures 1.1 and 4.4). Furthermore, bowls from the Saintonge region on the Atlantic coast of France were concentrated in the earliest context of Fort Houël (figure 1.1). All of these imported bowls were either glazed coarse earthenware or slipware, which

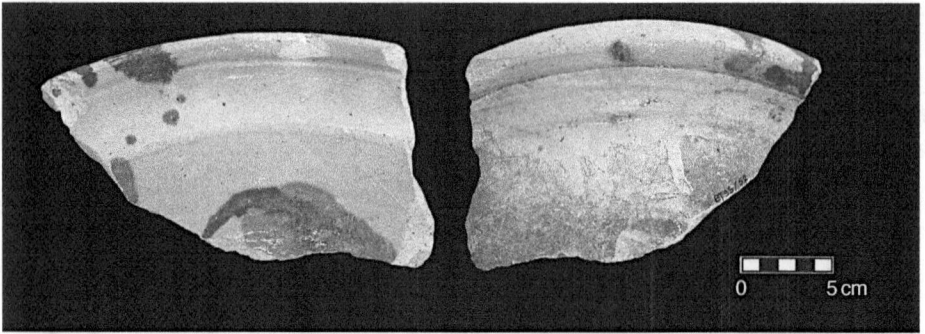

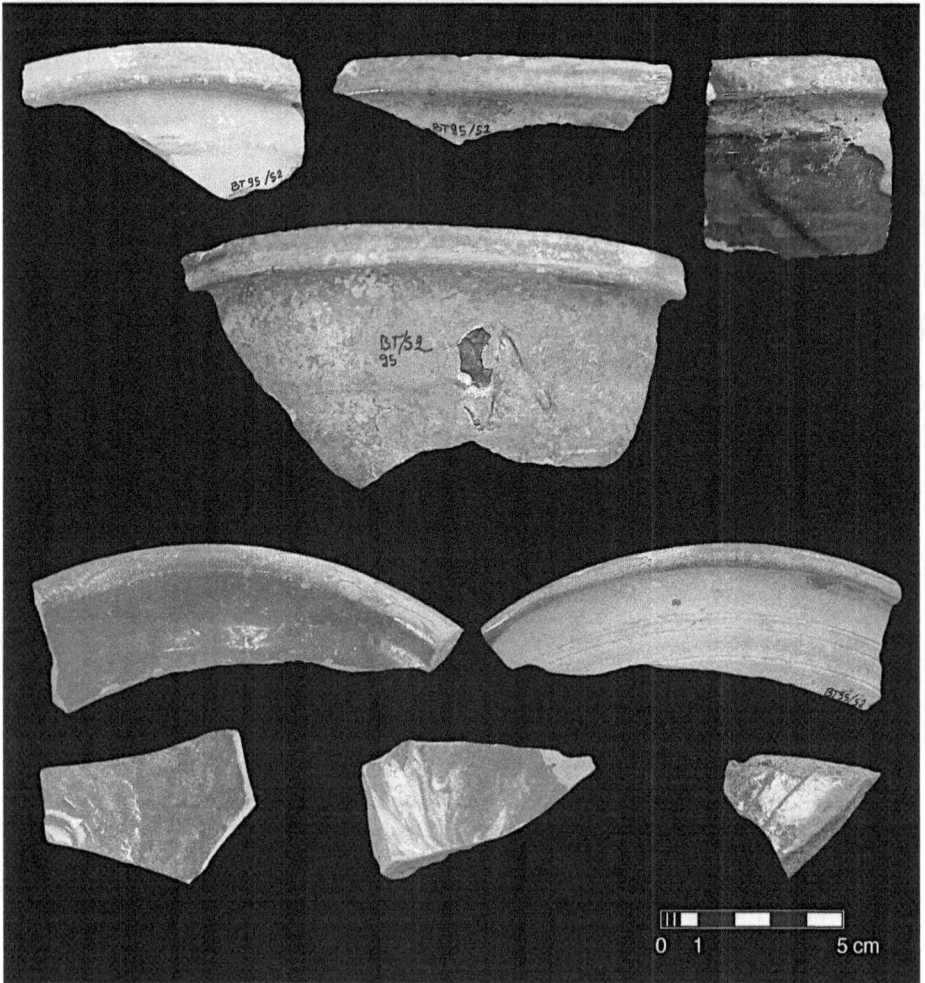

Figure 4.4. French coarse earthenware bowls. *Top*: Saintonge slipware rim with green and brown slip decoration. *Middle*: Saintonge rims with green lead glaze. *Bottom*: Huveaune rim and bases with white on red slip marbled decoration and Huveaune body with a graffito and green glaze on white slip decoration. Photograph by author.

corresponded to the fact that 76 percent of the vessels in the documents were described as "terres vernissées."

Once again, the sherds of locally made bowls showed a variety of shapes, surface treatments, and fabrication techniques. Some rims were straight; others were slightly everted (figures 1.1 and 4.2). Some vessels seemed hand-made and others wheel-thrown. Flanged bowls were an interesting subcategory, as they closely resemble models made in Martinique in the 1970s and are what people today picture as the typical Creole "terrine." On average, local bowls were slightly smaller than the French imports. The rim diameter ranged from 16 to 25 cm, versus 18 to 42 cm for the imported models. They were also most concentrated in the eighteenth-century contexts of Palais de Justice and 28 Rue Amédée Fengarol.

In Guadeloupe, this coarse earthenware cookware coexisted with an array of metallic objects with similar functions. The most common were cast iron or copper kettles (*chaudières*) present in 52 percent of households. Sixteen percent of inventories—sometimes the same ones that listed kettles or ca-naris—also listed cast iron cooking pots (*marmites*). Other metallic cook-ware appeared in one-third to one-quarter of inventories. Metallic saucepans showed up in at least 28 percent of houses, grills in 30 percent, frying pans in 27 percent, and roasting spits in 21 percent. An unidentified object called a *bombe*, perhaps because of its rounded shape, was also mentioned in 22 percent of inventories. It came with a cover and was probably used for roasting coffee beans. A popular non-cookware and non-ceramic kitchen accessory was a mortar. Made of marble or local wood, mortars turned up in 41 percent of households.

Other items appeared less frequently. Casserole dishes with covers were listed in 18 percent of houses, and skillets appeared in 5 percent. Sieves showed up in 11 percent of inventories, skimmers in 6 percent, and strain-ers in 5 percent. Seven percent of households had a kneading trough, and 4 percent a dripping pan. A small minority of kitchens, between 1 and 3 percent, were equipped with one or more of the following objects: a fish poacher, a braising pot, a waffle iron, a meat cleaver, a chopping knife, a kitchen scale, or a chocolate stone. Finally, a billhook and an ax were present in one kitchen. These may have been used for butchering meat.

Some small accessories were inventoried only as merchandise and were never present in homes: pastry implements shaped like fleurs-de-lis that might have been cookie cutters or molds,[9] and more significantly, kitchen knives. Spoons were extremely rare. Either kitchen accessories were scarce in general, or they were not recorded in the documents, which seems more logical. The same phenomenon could explain the glaring absence in the inventories of a classic Creole kitchen tool, the *lélé*. Lélés are pronged wooden sticks made from a local tree, *Quararibea turbinata* (swizzlestick tree), and used as beaters or whisks. They were deemed so essential to Creole cooking that acquiring a lélé was the first thing the cook Larah did after she was hired by the gendarme Georges Bonnemaison in 1900 (Martin 2001: 49). Yet like kitchen knives and spoons, lélés were ignored by notaries. Perhaps these implements were owned by the cooks themselves and were thus not listed as part of their master's estate. Cooks' ownership of their equipment would also explain why in some inventories the kitchens appeared to be nearly empty.

In early modern France, cooking pots were often suspended from a chimney hook, until trivets became more popular in the 1770s (Pardailhé-Galabrun 1988: 288–89; Roche 1985: 144). Up to 79 percent of Parisian houses were equipped with trivets, depending on the neighborhood. In eighteenth-century Toulouse, trivets were present in 22 percent of craftsmen's houses and 50 percent of city officials' homes, while about half of all residents owned a chimney hook (Arcangeli 2000: 29). The picture was very different in Guadeloupe, where there were no pot hangers and trivets were not always associated with the cookware. Apparently the Creole way of using cooking pots started with how the pots were propped above the fire. The seventeenth-century writer Jean-Baptiste Du Tertre (1667–71: 451) mentioned that vessels were suspended from a large stick supported by two smaller forked sticks. Much later, the abolitionist Victor Schoelcher (1842: 2n2) described a method that must have been even more common. He wrote that slaves typically set up their canaris on three clustered stones, a technique that was also popular among the local Caribs.

Another typical French kitchen object was notably absent. Only three chafing dishes appeared in the sample. In contrast, chafing dishes were quite common in the metropole (Wheaton 1983: 101). For example, 28 percent of craftsmen and 53 percent of lawyers in eighteenth-century Toulouse owned these objects (Arcangeli 2000: 29). Chafing dishes became so widespread in Paris during the first half of the century that every house appeared to have had at least one or two (Pardailhé-Galabrun 1988: 291). They were also present in colonial households: in the 1785 inventory of Marianne Lelièvre at Isle Bourbon, much of the kitchen equipment was similar to that in Guadeloupe, except for five chafing dishes (Jauze 2006:

136). The primary function of chafing dishes is to keep food warm or to gently reheat leftovers,[10] and it is noteworthy that Guadeloupean cooks had little use for them during the colonial period. The absence of such a common French cookware object in Guadeloupe might be explained by its lack of utility there. Perhaps Guadeloupean cooks did not often reheat leftovers. Certainly, as explained later, they did most of their slow cooking in other vessels. More interestingly, the dearth of chafing dishes in Guadeloupe echoes that of *cruches*, or specialized French water jugs. In both cases, these objects might have been missing from Guadeloupe's colonial ceramic culture because house slaves were the ones who handled both water-storage ceramics and cookware on a regular basis. Whether or not they had a say in the selection of particular vessels, their role as ceramic handlers put them in a position as intermediaries between the larger ceramic market and what Guadeloupean buyers actually acquired.

There were also considerably fewer kneading troughs in Guadeloupe than in other places. Eighteenth-century Toulousain inventories listed kneading troughs very frequently (Dousset 2003: 47). A typical 1770s household in colonial Ste. Genevieve was also equipped with a large wooden trough and an outdoor bread oven (Ekberg 1985: 299). Just like in the metropole, wheat bread was a crucial dietary staple in this colony. In Guadeloupe, on the other hand, kneading troughs belonged only to professional bakers and a handful of wealthy households. Since wheat did not grow in the Antilles and all of the flour was imported, wheat bread was not common. Manioc flour served as a substitute: mixed with a little bit of water, it made a thick paste that was an accompaniment for many dishes. Several eighteenth- and nineteenth-century writers remarked that Creole men and women of all races preferred manioc to classic bread (Chanvalon 1763: 82; Hearn 1903: 351; Moreau de Saint-Méry 1797–98: I:443; Schoelcher 1842: 9–10). Supposedly, some even continued eating it when they visited France (Granier de Cassagnac 1842–44: 171).

The general impression given by these data is that Guadeloupean cooking required only a few essentials. The most ubiquitous vessels were cooking pots: together, earthenware and metallic models equipped 80 percent of households. Next came frying pans and skillets of various sorts, at 55 percent; saucepans, at 47 percent; and roasting tools, at 42 percent. Excepting mortars, all other vessels or accessories showed up in less than one-quarter of houses.

The sparse paraphernalia of enslaved cooks contrasted sharply with the lavish equipment of enslaved professional chefs. The latter worked with more objects and more of the very specialized ones, such as kitchen scales, fish poachers, braising pots, meat cleavers, and spice graters. A restaurant like Bernier's inn, where the enslaved 20-year-old Pompé was the chef, had two kitchens that contained no less than 114 different cooking utensils, not counting the pieces of furniture. Given that they had access to a much greater supply of equipment, it was also notable that male chefs rarely employed ceramics at all. Only two out of six had canaris on hand, one had an earthenware saucepan, and none seemed to use ceramic bowls. Based on their cookware, chefs were able to prepare a wider range of foods, including more French dishes, but perhaps fewer of the traditional ones that required ceramics.

Creole Cuisine

French Caribbean cuisine has evolved since the plantation phase of its history. In particular, Indian workers brought vegetables such as dasheen (a variety of taro) and spices like turmeric to the islands after 1850. More European vegetables have been acclimated to the Antilles, including spinach, several species of eggplant, and sunchokes (Huyghues-Belrose 2006: 202). Modern cookbooks include popular dishes that are quite recent, such as the famous *colombo* (a curried stew), and make extensive use of modern ingredients, like parsley and thyme (Ebroïn n.d.; Lebey 1998; Ovide 2002). Yet, if these newer additions are set aside, we can get an idea of the kinds of dishes enslaved cooks prepared.

Most authors see Caribbean cuisine as a patchwork of successive influences and try to trace its classic dishes back to their creators. To the Caribs they typically attribute *cassaves* (manioc flat breads); *matoutou* (a stew made with crabs or crawfish and manioc); and *matété* (a similar dish in which manioc is replaced with rice) (Ebroïn n.d.; Querillac 1931). To that list could be added barbecue.

Classic soups are usually seen as inventions of African slaves: examples are *soupe Z'habitants,* where vegetables are cut in large pieces and lightly fried before being added to the liquid; *soupe à Congo,* an eclectic soup with salted meat that can include green bananas, peas, carrots, cucumbers, and any roots or vegetables on hand; and *calalou,* a soup of local greens thickened with okra (Ebroïn n.d.; Lebey 1998; Ovide 2002; Querillac 1931). In addition, *bébélé* (a stew made with tripe and vegetables) and the fritters called *accras* are also thought to be African in origin (Ebroïn n.d.; Ovide 2002). The latter are versatile bite-sized fritters or pancakes that may be flavored with codfish, peas, and vegetables like *malangas* or squashes for savory dishes, or with banana pulp when they are served for dessert (Ebroïn n.d.; Lebey 1998; Querillac 1931). *Blaff* is a dish of fish or crustaceans poached in a stock flavored with herbs and spices, then served with a lime dressing. Together with *dombrés* (little dumplings), *blaff* is thought to be a trace of the seventeenth-century Dutch presence in the French West Indies (Ebroïn n.d.: 15; Ovide 2002: 15). As Vincent Huyghues-Belrose (2006: 213) has demonstrated, however, as traditional as these recipes are, they too have evolved over time. *Calalou*, for example, was originally made with arrowleaf elephant ear, whereas the current version uses Indian dasheen instead.

After centuries of innovation, it is hard to pinpoint the origin and reconstitute the detailed history of each dish. Nonetheless, Huyghues-Belrose (2006: 212) believes that stews and soups were common in Caribbean cuisine in the 1770s. These one-dish meals are still characteristic of much of modern Antillean cuisine. Local cookbooks offer an array of stews (called *daubes* and ragoûts) or braised dishes like *fricassée* that could have been prepared by enslaved cooks (Ebroïn n.d.; Ovide 2002; Querillac 1931). These are made with vegetables, kid (*cabri*), fish, or poultry. One dish, *court-bouillon*, is a stew prepared with local fishes such as *vivaneau* and flavored with tomatoes and the red spice called *achiote* (or *roucou*). Many people consider it to be the "national" dish of the French West Indies (Ebroïn n.d.: 54; Lebey 1998: 321–22; Ovide 2002: 111, 121; Querillac 1931: 162–63).

Vegetable dishes are often based on the peas, beans, and roots that were so crucial to colonial diets (Ebroïn n.d.; Querillac 1931: 193–94). Tubers and breadfruits are made into fries or are cut into chunks and blanched in boiling water. They can then be served as is, with some seasonings, or in purées called *migans*, from a regional French word that describes the same kind of preparation in southwest France. Bananas and plantains are also used for making savory vegetable dishes.

The frequency of some ingredients and the rarity of others seems to be a direct legacy from the colonial period. Codfish, both fresh and salted, is the base for a large number of preparations. It is eaten in appetizers such as *chiquetaille*, in which salt cod is first grilled, then desalted and shredded (Lebey 1998: 319), and in salads such as *féroce d'avocat*, where crushed avocado mixed with manioc flour is served with *chiquetaille* or fresh codfish seasoned with hot peppers and oil (Querillac 1931: 118–19). Codfish can also be used for making fritters or be braised, stewed, poached, or pan-fried with a great variety of flavorings. Land crabs, shellfish, and local crustaceans appear in stews and soups, and are also often stuffed or grilled. Among the meats, pork has a primary role: it is an ingredient in the classic blood sausages called *boudins créoles*, small meat pies (*petits pâtés*), and many stews and soups. Several recipes use a pig's offal parts, like the blood, tripe, tail, and feet, but glazed ham is served at Christmas. Pork shows up in several ways on Christmas tables besides as ham, including in boudins, petits pâtés, soups, and pea-based dishes. Kid and chicken are the other common meats, whereas beef recipes are scarce if listed at all. Similarly, during the colonial period cod, pork, and fowl were more abundant than beef. Salt beef could be imported, but butchered meat—beef, veal, and sometimes lamb, sheep, and horse but not pork—came from the local livestock that was primarily raised for fieldwork, which meant fresh beef was rare and of poor quality. In 1789, Alexandre-Stanislas, Baron de Wimpffen (1993: 115) spent time in Saint-Domingue and noted that the pork was delicious there, but that butchered meat was particularly bad. Around the same time in Martinique, planter Pierre-François-Régis Dessalles (1995: I.184) complained about the rarity of beef and the power of butchers to decide who received which cuts and at what price. Finally, even though manioc meal is often replaced by wheat flour in modern Antillean cookbooks, it is still supposed to be used in many traditional recipes, such as the dombrés, boudins créoles, féroce d'avocat, and cassaves.

Beside stews, fritters, and soups, modern French Antillean cookbooks offer several recipes in three other categories: fresh salads, drinks, and desserts. Cold salads are usually served with a lime-and-garlic dressing, whereas the Creole vinaigrette called *sauce chien* accompanies grilled meat, grilled or poached fish, and cooked vegetables. There are many recipes for sauce chien, but the addition of warm water is what typically distinguishes it from the classic French vinaigrette.

Drinks and cocktails have greatly evolved throughout the history of Antilles. In the settlement years, the colonists discovered the beers favored by the Caribs: *ouicou*, which was based on manioc, and *mabi*, which was made with sweet potato (Huyghues-Belrose 2006: 209; Querillac 1931). Later on, sugarcane inspired a new array of preparations: slaves consumed warm cane juice (*vesou*) mixed simply with lime; more commonly, it was mixed with fruits and syrups to produce flavored wines, or distilled to make liquors such as tafia and rum (Huyghues-Belrose 2006: 209–10). Today, these colonial-era recipes survive in modern fruit punches and rum-based cocktails like the Ti'Punch, a mix of rum, cane syrup, and lime juice (Ovide 2002).

Finally, many present-day Antillean desserts also involve ingredients or techniques that were available to enslaved cooks. These include fruit fritters, fruit salads, jams, candied fruits or candied sweet potatoes, cassaves, and probably also egg-based custards such as *chaudeau*, pies with local ingredients like coconut, and some traditional cakes like *gâteau fouetté*, Guadeloupe's take on angel food cake (Lebey 1998; Ovide 2002).

How Colonial Cookware Was Used

It is striking that many of these traditional Antillean recipes could be prepared with the simple cookware of the colonial period. Soups could be slow-cooked in canaris and stews simmered in canaris or saucepans; salads assembled in bowls; custard slow-baked in casserole dishes; and meat, fish, and shellfish seared on grills. The shape of colonial ceramic cookware would require that foods be chopped in pieces rather than left whole, and many modern recipes still process ingredients this way. A good deal of modern Antillean dishes also require boiling or parboiling foods in water, or frying them in fat, which could have been done during the colonial period in the cookware (both metallic and non-metallic) that servants had on hand. For instance, cooking pots could be used to blanch tubers and vegetables, and saucepans to deep-fry fritters and fries. In early modern France, bowls and casserole dishes were used in the preparation of jams and fruit compotes, so it would not be surprising if bowls were used in similar ways in Guadeloupe.

In the 1880s, the writings of the journalist Lafcadio Hearn confirmed that the local traditional cookware was quite versatile. Hearn insisted on "*mangé-Créole*," or eating only local food, and observed that only a few utensils were necessary to make scores of varied recipes. In "Ma bonne," a chapter about his servant-cook Cyrillia, he wrote,

> She is wonderful as a house-keeper as well as cook: there is certainly much to do, and she has only a child to help her, but she always seems to have time. Her kitchen apparatus is of the simplest kind: a charcoal furnace constructed of bricks, a few earthenware pots (canari), and some gridirons—yet with these she can certainly prepare as many dishes as there are days in the year. (Hearn 1903: 365)

Ebroïn's (n.d.) modern cookbook yields further evidence of the simplicity of cooking utensils, since the author systematically suggests which tools to use when making the Creole dishes she presents. Almost all of her soup and seafood recipes, as well as a large majority of her vegetable, meat, and fish ones, can be prepared with a cooking pot alone. The two other cooking implements she uses most frequently seem to be a grill and a saucepan. She puts together appetizers and serves her food in bowls. The only other cooking equipment she mentions is an oven and its accessories (such as baking dishes), some sieves, and a masher.

The use-wear of the sherds and the entries in the inventories confirmed that coarse earthenware cookware was put through a great deal of stress. An impressive 60 percent of all canari sherds were charred (figures 4.1 and 4.2). In the documents, 13 percent of the entries for canaris mentioned pots that were cracked or old, which was a relatively high percentage given that imperfect vessels usually amounted to only 5 percent of the sample of whole ceramics. Clearly, canaris continued to be utilized beyond their prime.

Extending the lives of their coarse earthenware pots was not necessarily a goal of all cooks. After an in-depth review of ceramic cookware in the medieval and early modern periods, Danièle Alexandre-Bidon (2005: 157) concluded that users were attentive to the tastes that ceramic cookware gave to food. Coarse earthenware pots did not just absorb the odor and taste of their contents, but imparted flavor as well. As a result, brand-new vessels were necessary for some recipes, and pots used with particular ingredients could not be reused with others. In Alexandre-Bidon's view, practical, cultural, or religious considerations of this nature explained the presence of apparently brand-new cooking pots discarded at medieval archaeological sites, sometimes in great quantities. Put simply, some coarse earthenware pots were disposable. This was obviously not the case in Guadeloupe, where most canaris went through extensive and long service before being retired. Because local cookware was not glazed whereas imported pots were, the two types would also have transmitted tastes differently. This difference in taste could have sustained the steady imports of cooking pots and saucepans in the Antilles. Unglazed coarse earthenware might have required seasoning and was also harder to clean (Alexandre-Bidon 2005: 94–100, 189–96).

Compared to canaris, only half as many of the saucepan sherds (30 percent) exhibited charring (figure 4.3). In the inventories as well, saucepans were almost always listed as being in good condition, so they might have been used less extensively than canaris. Interestingly, saucepans in medieval France were also rarely charred (Alexandre-Bidon 2005: 233).

Finally, soot was also present on bowls. Bowls were technically not cookware, but 9 percent of these sherds showed light to heavy charring (figures 4.2 and 4.4). In some cases, sooting occurred in a small area, such as the base or under the rim of a flanged model. On other vessels, however, the sides were extensively charred, suggesting these objects had been used to cook or reheat things. De Roo Lemos (1979: 31) reported that in twentieth-century Martinique acquaintances borrowed terrines from one another when making stews for parties or whenever a great volume of food was required.

Experimental research on soot patterns indicates that soot tends to be high and uniform around the vessel when there is little air movement (Gur-Arieh et al. 2011). Also, the higher the fire's temperature, the less the chance that soot will accumulate. So when sherds are extensively charred, as they are in Guadeloupe, it might indicate that these vessels were used indoors and on a relatively low fire. For instance, the uniform charring seen on some of the cooking pots found at 28 Rue Amédée Fengarol is consistent with the fact that there was a detached kitchen at this site.

Furthermore, soot is both deposited on and removed from pottery walls during each firing event. So the more traces on sherds, the more complex the series of firing episodes must have been. The soot patterns that accumulated on the coarse earthenware cookware in Guadeloupe reveal its extensive and repeated use.

Finally, the rarity of charred faience at the sites proved that enslaved cooks did not use them for cooking, as is also implied by the inventories and other textual sources. This was true even of faiences that were perfectly suited to cooking, like tureens in faience brune. Only two sherds in the entire faience sample showed some alterations due to fire.

In sum Guadeloupean servants prepared meals with very few utensils and relied heavily on their basic cooking pots. These vessels were effectively inseparable from their cooking techniques and the cuisine they prepared. At Place-Royale, bowls rather than pots dominated both the archaeological assemblages and the probate inventories (Lapointe and Lueger 1997; Moussette 1996). Coarse earthenware cooking pots appeared in small amounts or were altogether absent. Similarly in eighteenth-century Toulouse, skillets and frying pans as well as roasting and grilling accessories were the most widespread cookware (Arcangeli 2000: 30–31). In the households of merchants, for instance, even casserole dishes were five times more frequent than cooking pots. Cooks in the Antilles employed more cooking pots than their counterparts in some other parts of the early modern French world. Likewise, mortars seemed more important there than in the metropole, both in Paris and in southern cities like Toulouse, probably because they were used to grind coffee as well as spices (Arcangeli 2000: 23; Pardailhé-Galabrun 1988: 296).

Creole cuisine was therefore varied not because of the sophistication of its kitchen equipment, but rather because of the skill and inventiveness of its cooks. With a minimal and shopworn set of cookware, slave women managed to create a wide array of dishes that took full advantage of the local flavors. They developed a special savoir faire based on the local produce to make dishes that were appealing to their masters' tastes. This know-how is recognized today as an integral part of the French culinary heritage (Lebey 1998).

Since the Antilles could not rely on the staples of the French diet, namely wheat and wine, nor on many other typically French foods, Creole cuisine could at times align with French principles but was never completely governed by them. For example, cooked vegetables became popular in early modern France, and Creole dishes—which incorporated an extraordinary array of vegetables and tubers—fit with this trend. Yet two other important changes in early modern French cuisine did not directly influence colonial recipes: the move away from spicy foods and the strict separation between savory and sweet. With their use of hot peppers and both local and imported spices, Creole cooks never shied away from spicy foods. The division between savory and sweet did occur in the Antilles, but perhaps not as quickly and as completely as in the metropole. Today, fruits and vegetables remain more interchangeable in Creole cuisine than in classic French preparations: some fruits like bananas are used for making savory dishes, and some root vegetables, such as sweet potatoes, appear in desserts. Moreover, according to Lafcadio Hearn (1903: 350), Creole cooks were still adding sugar to many vegetable recipes at the end of the nineteenth century.

Undoubtedly, Guadeloupe was exposed to many influences beyond French cuisine. The range of alcoholic drinks found in the inventories alone demonstrates that Basse-Terre was a cosmopolitan city with wide Atlantic connections. Its merchants imported not just French wines but also drinks like beers and gin that in the metropole were most common in Atlantic ports like Bordeaux (Meyzie 2003: 73–74). Places where the Atlantic culture was less prominent had much less variety as well as more staid tastes. Parisians, for example, mostly consumed a lot of French wines (Pardailhé-Galabrun 1988: 297–300).

The typical capacity of canaris was around 5 liters, which in the average French household yielded enough food for one meal (Alexandre-Bidon 2005: 181). That fact coupled with the absence of chafing dishes suggests that cooks in Guadeloupe did not serve many leftovers. If any foods were left after a meal, they could not be stored for long because of the heat. During his mid-nineteenth-century visit to the French Antilles, Granier de Cassagnac (1842–44: 117) noted that the mistress of the house or her daughter usually left the table early to dole out the leftovers to the servants. Granier de Cassagnac was strongly prejudiced and had ideological motives for emphasizing that the apportioning had to be supervised by the mistress of the house. In most situations, it must have been easier to simply entrust the servant who did the cooking to deal with the leftovers. Of course, not everyone could afford to avoid eating or serving leftovers. Even a wealthy planter like Dessalles did so at times to save money (Dessalles and Frémont 1980: entry for July 25, 1843). During one of these periods, his wife complained that the same dishes as the day before reappeared at her table and that the same meats were eaten over two or three days.

Conclusion

In the Antilles, cooks served a variety of functions. They prepared several meals and snacks a day and handled the leftovers as their masters saw fit, which might sometimes have involved the redistribution of foods to the other slaves. Cooks also raised some animals for the table, like poultry and pigs, and probably had to manage the household food reserves. In Guadeloupe, any stored foods would need to be closely monitored for signs of spoilage, and protected from insects and rodents. Cooks likely had dealings with street vendors who came to the back entrances of urban houses, and also did some shopping in markets. Perhaps they owned some of their equipment and influenced the type of cookware that was deemed acceptable or most useful in the Antilles.

More certainly, cooks appear to have been in charge of their workspaces, which they shared only with other servants. Besides metallic cookware, nothing of value was stored in Creole kitchens, which meant that the masters did not have to keep those spaces under constant surveillance or visit them often. Because the social life of the planter Dessalles revolved around dinner parties, he brought up the topics of food and cooks quite often in his diary. Yet he mentioned visiting his kitchen only once, to scold his chef for a particularly bad dinner (Dessalles and Frémont 1980: entry for Feb. 15, 1838).

Most significantly, enslaved cooks made an extraordinary contribution to modern Antillean culture by developing a rich and varied cuisine under very restricted material and social conditions. The role of women in particular needs to be acknowledged. Studying slave diets based on the ceramics and faunal remains at La Mahaudière, Peggy Brunache (2011) concluded that slave women participated the most in island markets, did most of the maintenance of provision grounds and slave gardens, and cooked for their families. Their contribution to Antillean cuisine thus took two forms: the cooking they did at home to feed their families, and the cooking they did as enslaved servants in the kitchens of their masters. The sherds of the cookware they used are evidence of their incredible labor, creativity, and spirit. Cooking might have represented one of the means by which enslaved women could regain a small degree of control over their lives, as well as try to nurture themselves, their loved ones, and their community. Their function as cooks was all the more crucial since events organized around food were integral to Guadeloupe's Creole culture.

CHAPTER FIVE

The Creole Art of the Table

Tableware is a special class of ceramics in Guadeloupe. It dominates archaeological assemblages and demands attention by its sheer quantity. In addition, its most frequent users were not slaves, and none of the vessels were made locally. The task is thus to figure out the role it played in Guadeloupe's colonial culture.

The attributes of the objects that were part of table or beverage services help clarify this role, in terms of both functionality and aesthetics. A quick review of Creole hospitality and of the domestic spaces dedicated to socializing provides context for understanding the commensal practices supported by this group of ceramics. The inventory records begin a few years after the English occupied the island (1759–63). They document a period of great prosperity when urban life in the Atlantic world was becoming increasingly refined (Pérotin-Dumon 2000: 639). In Basse-Terre, a series of new services and cultural resources appeared from the 1760s onward, including newspapers, a postal service, printing presses, theaters, medical research, and scientific associations. In parallel, the material culture of Guadeloupeans reached heights of comfort they had never seen before. More specialized and highly qualified craftspeople advertised their services, and more luxury goods arrived by ship. The sampled inventories were recorded after early modern table manners had been completely transformed. Place settings were fully individualized, and the use of forks and glassware was quite common.

The Tableware of Guadeloupeans

According to the inventories, Guadeloupeans set their tables with glassware, silverware, and ceramics. Objects for drinking or serving liquids were usually made of glass or crystal. The serving utensils[1] and individual place settings were made of silver in the best houses, pewter or cast iron in others, and copper in a few rare cases. More importantly, pewter tableware existed but was not consequential. Its quality was average and its quantity trivial: the sample included a mere 82 plates and 15 dishes, versus at least 8,165 and 2,635, respectively, for ceramics. In the earliest days of the colony, pewter was probably the most common tableware, just as it was in seventeenth-century France. In his table of the principal merchandise imported to Guadeloupe from 1666 to 1670, the historian Maurice Satineau (1928: 204–5) listed 2,000 pounds of pewter tableware and no other kind. After faiences were invented however, pewter must have started to lose its popularity relative to ceramics. Both the sites and inventories make clear that tableware constituted the lion's share of the local ceramic objects. Plates and dishes alone represented close to 11,000 out of about 20,000 ceramics listed in the inventories and one-third of the sherds in the collections.

Plates (*Assiettes*) and Dishes (*Plats*)

The sample included at least 8,165 plates and 2,669 dishes—a few entries grouped both objects (figure 1.1). Plates were about three times as numerous as dishes and were present in nine more houses. Flatware (in reference to plates and dishes) was also a constant at the archaeological sites. Their concentration hovered at around 40 percent of the minimum number of vessels in all of the eighteenth-century contexts, and about half as much in the older and more recent contexts.

In Guadeloupean inventories, these objects showed up in 71 percent of the poorest houses, 94 percent of the middling ones, and 96 percent of the wealthiest. Economic differences were not expressed through their presence but instead through their quantity. The wealthier a household the more flatware they bought: the poorest group owned around 5 percent of all of the plates and dishes; the middling one, 37 percent of the plates and 22 percent of the dishes; and the wealthiest bought 57 percent of the plates and a whopping 73 percent of the dishes.

Faience flatware was the most common type in both sources, representing around 57 percent of the inventory sample and 65 percent of the flatware vessels in the archaeological collections. The rest of the flatware in the inventories was made of coarse earthenware—mostly Albisola ware—porcelain, and a few delftware vessels imported from England or the Netherlands. The sites yielded similar data, with the addition of materials that would not be separately identified in the inventories, such as creamware, pearlware, whiteware and, in the most recent contexts, faiences fines. An interesting pattern was that faience (both blanche and brune) was more common for dishes than plates: the faience types represented 50 percent of the archaeological plate sample versus 80 percent of the dishes. Perhaps wealthy households, which could afford to buy most of the dishes in Guadeloupe, preferred French faiences. Plates, on the other hand, were more widely distributed throughout Creole society and came in a greater variety of materials.

Plates of unusual sizes or that were specialized for soup or dessert constituted about 13 percent of the inventory sample. These were concentrated in the wealthiest houses. The situation was similar for oval dishes: they encompassed 9 percent of the sample and the wealthiest group owned almost 90 percent of them. In the collections, oblong dishes were the most numerous at Palais de Justice, the site with the most lavish collection of tableware. Sizewise, the inventories described 13 percent of dishes as "small," 11 percent as "large," and another 19 percent as belonging to sets containing several sizes. In terms of value, this categorization based on size mattered more for dishes than for plates: the average appraisal of small faience dishes in the eighteenth century was about 12 sols, medium ones were around 18 sols, and large ones were 34 sols.

Regarding the functions described in the documents, dishes used for soups were the most frequent and appeared in seven houses. The *entremets*[2] and the dessert were served on other small types of English refined ceramics (called *grès* or *grès blanc anglais*). A few examples were reserved for meats, stews, or appetizers. A dish of openwork porcelain was also used for presenting fruits. These specialized dishes were slightly more widespread than the specialized plates. In a few instances, they even showed up in middling houses.

The price of plates was fairly consistent. On average, faience plates in the eighteenth century cost around 12 sols, and their appraisals ranged from 5 to 25 sols. Porcelain plates tended to be more expensive, being worth 40 sols on average in the eighteenth century. In general, there was little fluctuation in the pricing of plates made of the same material. In comparison, the price range for faience dishes was very wide, at least 5 to 240 sols. Given this wide range, factors other than size and shape must have influenced their value, and quality must have mattered too. The average appraisal of eighteenth-century porcelain dishes was also quite a bit higher than for any other tableware, reaching 220 sols.

Interestingly, expensive faience dishes showed up in all kinds of houses, even in the eighteenth century. The average appraisal of the dishes owned by each wealth group did not correspond with their income; for instance, the dishes of the poorest houses were worth 37 sols on average, versus 28 sols for both the middling and wealthiest ones. This implies that Guadeloupeans who did not belong to the elite chose to splurge on faience dishes. The dishes of well-off Guadeloupeans were not systematically deemed superior either. To set themselves apart, the elite could therefore buy more of these objects or invest in other materials, such as porcelain. All but 4 of the 22 households that had porcelain plates were among the elite, and so were 9 out of the 10 that had porcelain dishes. None of the poorest households owned any porcelain dishware.

Among imported flatware, French faiences tended to be less expensive than either English or Dutch delftware. Also, flatware that appeared new had a much greater value. Unsurprisingly, the proportion of flatware that was noticeably worn or used was greater for poor households: it amounted to 16 percent of the plates and dishes they owned, versus 10 percent for middling houses and 4 percent for wealthy ones.

Tureens (*Soupières*)

After flatware, tureens were the most widespread type of tableware objects (figure 1.1). The inventory sample recorded 152 vessels present in 42 percent of households in the 1774–1833 period. The wealthier a household, the more likely notaries were to find a tureen: 16 percent of the poorest houses were so equipped, compared to 38 percent of the middling ones and 67 percent of elite ones. It was also not uncommon for a house to have more than one example. Both middling and poor households averaged two tureens, while the wealthiest households owned three. The fact that some types were round and others oval could in part explain why households would need more than one of these vessels.

Most tureens were made of faience brune, but they also existed in Albisola ware, glazed coarse earthenware, porcelain, and some English refined earthenware that appeared to be white salt-glazed stoneware.

The average value of the faience tureens in the eighteenth century was higher than for dishes. Their price range was also more extensive: at 360 sols, the highest appraisals were 25 times greater than the lowest ones, at 14 sols.[3] Faience brune tended to be more affordable than faience blanche, and the Albisola models were by far the cheapest of all, at around 10 sols. Porcelain examples, as expected, were rare and worth much more than faiences: 21 livres, or 420 sols, in one case; and 66 livres, or 1,420 sols, in another.

In the archaeological collections, tureens turned up in small amounts at all of the sites and main contexts. The majority of the tureen sherds were of faience brune: this type represented 78 percent of the sherds and 68 percent of the minimum number of vessels (figure 5.1). Next most frequent was Albisola ware, accounting for at least 16 percent of the vessels, and the rest was

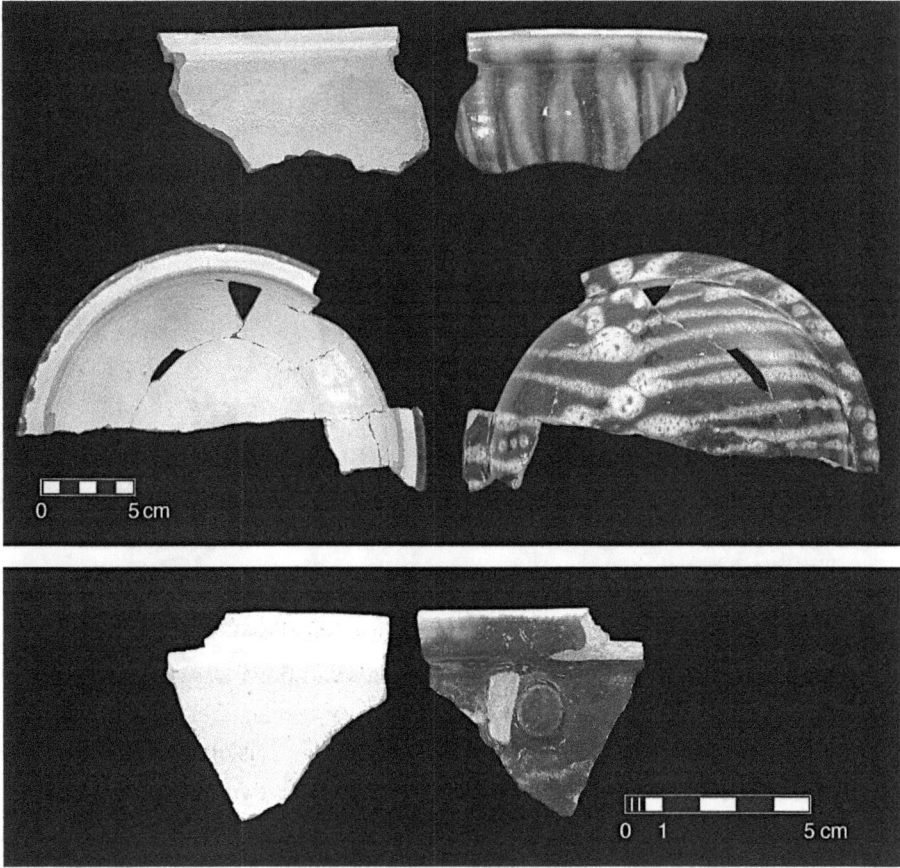

Figure 5.1. Rims and a lid of faience brune tureens. Photograph by author.

made of faience blanche or refined earthenware. Faience brune vessels were easier to identify than tureens made of other ceramic materials, so this might partially explain their preponderance.

The diameter of the typical tureen models measured between 20 and 24 cm. Three lids were smaller, around 16 cm, and one larger bowl had a diameter of 27 cm. The inventories confirmed that small numbers of smaller and larger models existed: they represented about 11 percent of the sample.

Salad Bowls (*Saladiers*)

Salad bowls (figure 5.2) were less common than tureens (figure 5.1). In the inventories, they amounted to 71 vessels, distributed among 24 percent of households. Only 6 percent of the poorest households and 22 percent of the middling ones owned such an object, whereas 40 percent of the wealthiest households did. The wealthy group also possessed almost three-quarters of

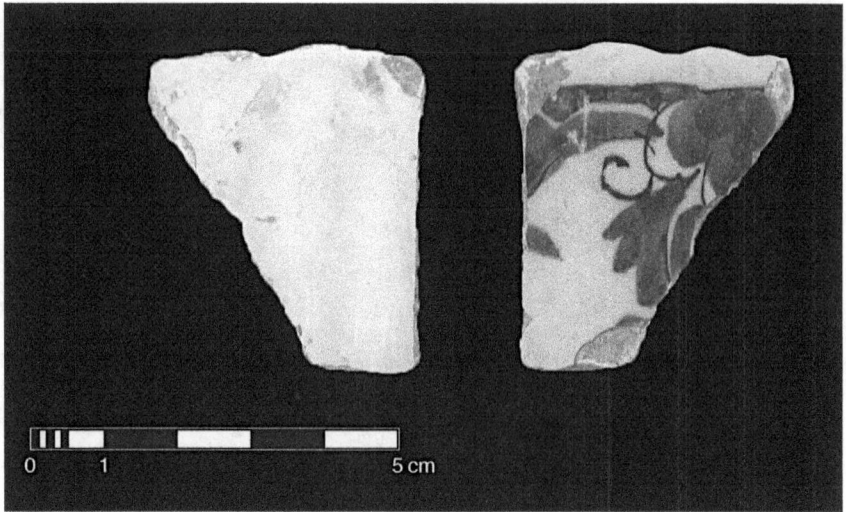

Figure 5.2. Rim of a faience salad bowl with *camaïeu bleu* (blue and dark blue) decoration. Photograph by author.

the sample, indicating that ownership of a salad bowl was a more powerful marker of wealth than ownership of flatware or tureens. Yet salad bowls were not particularly expensive: faience models cost 34 sols on average, and their price range was fairly limited, from 15 to 90 sols; two porcelain examples were appraised at 45 sols. At least 80 percent of salad bowls were made of faience (figure 5.2). The absence of salad bowls in cheaper materials, like coarse earthenware, was consistent with the fact that wealthy households bought the bulk of these objects.

The archaeological data corroborated these results. Salad bowls were present at the Palais de Justice, the Cathédrale, and the nineteenth-century contexts of 28 Rue Amédée Fengarol. They were less widespread than other tableware objects. The first two sites yielded faience examples, like those described in the inventories, but the more recent contexts at 28 Rue Amédée Fengarol contained faience fine examples.

Ceramics for Condiments

The ceramics used for condiments constituted a very small group of vessels in a minority of eighteenth-century households. Ceramic sauceboats (*saucières*, 12 vessels), mustard pots (*moutardiers*, 10 vessels), and saltcellars (*salières*, 13 vessels) appeared in six or seven houses each (figure 1.1). Oil and vinegar sets (*huiliers*) showed up in six houses as well, and included oil and vinegar cruets (*carafes* or *burettes*) and the base that held them (*porte-huilier*).

Except for the sauceboats, these objects came in other materials as well, often glass or crystal, and were thus much more frequent than the ceramic tally would imply: mustard pots were actually present in a total of 10 inventories, oil and vinegar cruets in 25 percent of households (37 inventories), and saltcellars in 38 percent (55 inventories). Consequently, mustard pots and sauceboats remained the least common objects, mostly accessible to wealthy households. Oil and vinegar cruets and saltcellars were however more widely distributed: most were present in wealthy and middling households and a few were in the poorest households. Finally, two faience olive dishes (*vases à olive*) and a possible olive saucer (*soucoupe à olive*) of unknown ceramic material were recorded in two wealthy houses.

In general, ceramic condiment vessels were made of faience. Porcelain sauceboats and mustard pots also existed, while the merchant Antoine Belost owned a set of English refined earthenware—perhaps white salt-glazed stoneware—that included a sauceboat, a mustard pot, and four saltcellars. The price of these objects ranged between 10 and 60 sols, with the exceptions of two cheaper faience saltcellars in a middling house that were worth 7 sols 6 deniers each, and two very expensive porcelain mustard pots in a wealthy household appraised at 165 sols each. In general, it seemed that function, rather than price, limited the diffusion of these objects.

The archaeological collections barely registered the presence of this ceramic group. The evidence amounted to a possible creamware sauceboat rim from Fort Houël, and a more probable brown glazed coarse earthenware saltcellar from one of the nineteenth-century contexts at 28 Rue Amédée Fengarol. The latter, in particular, postdated the inventories and had little in common with the condiment ceramics described in the inventories. Its existence suggested only that cheap, coarse earthenware varieties of saltcellars were still in use in the nineteenth century.

Ceramics for Water, Wine, and Other Cold Drinks

The ceramic tableware included faience pitchers in a mere 3 percent of households, and it seemed that Guadeloupeans were phasing these objects out of their services by the time the inventory sample started. In fact, faience pitchers were absent from nineteenth-century inventories, though a few faience fine and coarse earthenware carafes probably had a roughly analogous function. Overall, Guadeloupeans preferred to consume water, wine, and other non-heated beverages from glass or crystal. For example, individual glasses showed up in at least 45 percent of households, and glass or crystal carafes in 32 percent.

The presence of wine glasses and bottle coolers (*seaux*) in an eighteenth-century house was slightly more meaningful (figure 1.1). Coolers were filled with cold water and used to rinse drinking glasses during a meal or to keep bottled drinks cool. Most were large enough for a bottle or several glasses, but others belonged to individual sets consisting of a single wine cooler and its matching glass. In Guadeloupe, coolers were often of glass or crystal, but both the noble Hureault de Gondrecourt and the innkeeper Bernier had faience models. Bernier's were worth 7 sols 6 deniers each in 1776, which corresponded to the price of many glass or crystal versions. These objects appeared in only seven wealthy houses and two middling ones, or about 7 percent of the sample. Though the coolers were not very expensive, they helped elevate the refinement of a few select tables.

No sherds from the archaeological collections could be identified specifically as coolers, though sherds of faience and faience brune pitchers that could have been part of the tableware represented a small portion of the vessels at each site. They seemed most concentrated inside the eighteenth-century context of 28 Rue Amédée Fengarol (a middling house) and the earliest context at Fort Houël, which seemed to confirm that ceramic pitchers were in fact not especially popular.

Bowls (*Bols*) and *Écuelles*

According to the inventories, bols were used for soup, punch, coffee, or tea (figure 1.1). The sample listed 162 bowls, 20 percent of which came with matching saucers, and 5 percent with lids. Wealthy households were more likely to own them (51 percent did) than either middling (16 percent) or poor (23 percent) households.

The poorest houses had faience bowls exclusively. Middling households frequently bought stoneware models as well. Wealthy ones possessed faience and porcelain in roughly equal numbers. This distribution of ceramic materials accorded with appraised values. The highest valued faience models, at 90 sols, were nine times as expensive as the cheapest ones, at 10 sols. Therefore, the great range of size and quality among faience bowls explained why they were present in all kinds of households. Stoneware types were slightly more expensive than faience ones: they were worth 25 sols on average, but none were cheaper than 15 sols. This would make them slightly more affordable for middling than for poor households. Finally, porcelain bowls cost a lot more: small vessels were worth 40 sols on average, but medium and large ones, respectively, reached 495 and 660 sols.

More than one-third of the vessels were of unusual sizes, and most of the "small" (31 percent of the sample) and "large" (3 percent) examples were in wealthy houses. One of the large porcelain bowls was "for punch" and must have been a serving bowl rather than an individual drinking vessel.

Écuelles constituted a small group of 13 vessels that shared some characteristics and functions with bols (figure 1.1). These shallow bowls with two flat handles were traditionally used for eating soups and similar foods, but Guadeloupean inventories made clear that they were used there as part of tea sets. Like the metallic écuelles found among the silverware, ceramic ones often came with a lid, and sometimes a saucer. They were mostly in faience, except that the merchant Belost owned one in porcelain, and occurred with similar frequency in middling households (7 percent) and wealthy households (11 percent). Their appraised values were comparable to bols, but unlike the latter, écuelles disappeared from the sample after the 1780s.

In the archaeological assemblages, the sherds of large bowls would have been classified as salad bowls and thus do not appear in this section. Nevertheless, the sites yielded at least 21 individual-size bowls that could have had the functions of bols or écuelles. These vessels were absent from the earliest and most recent contexts, but their presence was not negligible in eighteenth-century assemblages.

This group included two "posset" bowls made of Staffordshire slipped coarse earthenware, one from 28 Rue Amédée Fengarol and the other from Palais de Justice. Fort Houël yielded mostly creamware and pearlware examples, while porcelain was present everywhere else. Palais de Justice showed the greatest variety: in addition to the Staffordshire bowl, it yielded some Batavia ware, several blue underglaze porcelains, a porcelain from the pink family, an English delftware in the Fazakerley style, a pearlware with a Chinese house pattern, and a nineteenth-century faience fine. A few sherds had the right dimensions and shape to have belonged to either écuelles or bowls: one such was an Albisola rim from Fort Houël (both objects have been found at eighteenth-century French sites; Foy et al. 1986); others included a faience brune rim and two coarse earthenware sherds from Palais de Justice, which probably came from France. However, the bulk of the bowls were not manufactured in France.

Beverage Services

This category included all of the other ceramics used for serving tea, coffee, or hot chocolate: cups (*tasses*) and saucers (*soucoupes*), teapots (*théières*), coffeepots (*cafetières*), services (*déjeuners, services*), sugar bowls (*sucriers*), cream pots (*pots à lait*), butter dishes (*beurriers*), and "tea vases" (*vases à thé*). Together, these objects were present in about half of the households.

Cups and saucers were the most common and amounted to 909 vessels (figure 1.1). They appeared in 6 percent of the poor households, 32 percent of the middling ones, and 64 percent of the wealthiest one. Although they were not systematically paired in equal numbers, they often showed up together, which suggested that cups and saucers were normally bought together. The sample was about equally divided among middling and wealthy homes, and there was not a marked difference in terms of number of vessels per household—22 for the middling houses and 30 for the wealthy ones. When middling households acquired cups and saucers, they did so in comparable quantities as their well-off counterparts.

Teapots were the second largest ensemble, with 47 ceramic items and two examples where the material was not specified but was likely ceramic as well (figure 1.1). Fewer houses were equipped with teapots: 3 percent in the poor group, 13 percent in the middling category, and 36 percent among the elite. Unlike with cups and saucers, middling households owned far fewer vessels than wealthy ones did.

Coffeepots stood apart because they were often made of metal as well as ceramic (figure 1.1). All materials included, they showed up in 9 percent of middling houses and 36 percent of wealthy ones, which was comparable to teapots. The ceramic sample was only a subgroup of coffeepots, but it was significantly concentrated in wealthy households. Although ceramic coffeepots tended to be less expensive, they were mostly sought-after by wealthy buyers.

Only two ceramics in the whole sample were clearly designed for drinking chocolate rather than coffee or tea: these were two porcelain cups with matching saucers in an inventory from 1833. Drinking hot chocolate could of course have been more widespread than this finding suggests, since any cups or bowls could serve this purpose. The presence of chocolate grinding stones confirmed the consumption of this beverage in at least a few, mostly wealthy, houses.

In the nineteenth century, a new type of tableware appeared: the matching tea or coffee sets that were called services or, more often, déjeuners. They first appeared in 1829, and seemed to become immediately popular with all three categories of households. A total of six houses were so equipped in 1829–33, whereas seven other households owned the classic separate cups and saucers, teapots, and coffeepots. Almost half of the houses preferred to purchase these matching services. One of these sets specifically contained a sugar bowl, a cream pot, a coffeepot, and a dozen cups and saucers.

Sets existed before 1829, but they were inventoried vessel by vessel rather than as a whole, which makes them harder to identify. Several ceramic accessories facilitated this task. Sugar bowls were explicitly listed in a total of 19 houses (13 percent of the sample)—one example was made of silver, but the rest were of ceramic. Three of these houses also used cream pots. Butter dishes were part of three sets. A service owned by merchant Antoine Belost contained an unusual array of vessels: six cups and saucers, six handleless cups, one teapot, one cream pot, two bowls and saucers, one large cup with handle, one écuelle, and two "vases" that might have been used for storing tea leaves.

In ten different houses, sets and déjeuners were associated with a piece of furniture called a *cabaret* (a small chest of drawers with a cupboard). Some of the earlier examples were probably of lacquerware imported from China, which had been popular in France since the 1730s. After 1780, however, the designs changed: they were made of metallic sheets that were either "painted" or "glazed" and had no particular provenance. Cabarets could be located in bedrooms, pantries, or parlors. The associated ceramic sets tended to be in porcelain and to have service for 12 people. As luxury items, cabarets naturally were mostly found in wealthy households.

At least half of the tea and coffee drinking vessels were in faience, a third to a quarter, depending on the object, in porcelain, and a few in what notaries called "stoneware," which probably referred to refined earthenware or fine stoneware.

The appraised value of cups and pots depended on their composition. In the eighteenth century, the average price of a faience or stoneware cup was around 11 sols, whereas porcelain models cost five times as much, or 54 sols. The best faience cup, at 15 sols, was worth a lot less than the least expensive variety in common porcelain, at 25 sols. The trend was similar for teapots and coffeepots (both had similar average values): faience teapots were worth 23 sols on average; faience coffeepots, 28 sols; and stoneware teapots, 30 sols. The only porcelain example that was individually appraised cost three times as much, or 90 sols. Finally, as was true for the tureens, the pots that were made of faience brune were among the cheapest options.

The quality of cups and teapots or coffeepots corresponded with the wealth of the owners. Porcelain was expensive and chiefly owned by wealthy households. Compared to middling households, wealthy individuals also bought more stoneware than faience objects.

As the very appearance of déjeuners implied, the pressure to buy services augmented in the 1820s and 1830s. Before this period, only about 40 percent of the households with evidence of coffee or tea drinking owned both the cups and brewing pot that were needed to constitute a minimal coffee or tea service. The number of houses with additional vessels was even lower: a mere 18 percent of these households also owned a sugar bowl, which was the most common accessory. After 1820, however, more than 60 percent of the houses equipped for coffee or tea drinking owned at least some cups and a pot, and close to 50 percent had a complete service.

Chronologically then, it seems that wealthy households pioneered the use of tea and coffee services in the 1770s. At that time, middling households equipped themselves for coffee or tea drinking, they focused on acquiring a lot of cups. It was not until the 1780s that the poorest households either became interested in or were able to afford these objects. By the 1820s the relative weights of ownership were equalizing. The proportion of households using tea and coffee ware had grown to about 50 percent or 60 percent of the sample, and the equipment of poor and middling households had come to resemble the belongings of the elite.

At the archaeological sites, the share of tea and coffee ware in relation to other vessels was quite constant, around 7 percent. Objects consisted mostly of pots and cups. One saucer was found, at the Palais de Justice, compared to at least 29 cups, so more saucer sherds must have existed but not been iden-tified as such; perhaps they were bundled with the plates, and the smaller pieces might not even have been retrieved from the sites. Similarly, if sherds of uncommon accessories like sugar bowls or cream pots were collected, they were not recognized.

The percentage of cups and pots recovered (7 percent) was significantly greater than their share in the inventories, where they represented only 4.8 percent of the entire ceramic sample. This was an unusual finding, as the reverse was generally true for tableware. In the case of the flatware, for ex-ample, its concentration at the sites ranged between 16 and 43 percent, but its share in the inventories was as high as 54 percent. Perhaps tea and coffee services had a particularly high breakage rate, due to the fact that they were repeatedly filled with hot liquids. Certain other factors, such as fashion and style, might also have created incentives for replacing these vessels on a regu-lar basis.

The composition of the sherds was quite varied at every site. They included Albisola ware, faience blanche and brune, white salt-glazed stoneware, creamware, pearlware, porcelain, whiteware, and faience fine. This could be further evidence that coffee and teaware tended to be replaced often. This large array of materials also mirrored the variety of the entries in the inventories. Beverage objects came in "white," "yellow," "yellowish," "common," "fine," or "varied" faiences; in "painted" and "plain" stoneware; in "coarse," "common," "normal," or "gilded" porcelain; and in faience brune. These entries also contained more information than usual about decoration, suggesting that the style of tea and coffee ware was varied and important.

How Did Tableware Compare among Guadeloupe and Other Places?

Plates and dishes were tableware essentials in Guadeloupe. Plates revealed socioeconomic differences less by their presence or value than by their sheer numbers. Well-off households owned more of them, and sometimes further distinguished themselves by buying a few specialized items, like soup or dessert plates. Little comparable data about ceramic tableware in French inventories or at archaeological French sites is available. In the Atlantic port of Bordeaux, Philippe Meyzie (2003: 75) reported an average of 130 plates in the houses of noblemen and 104 in those of merchants and traders. These two groups formed the elite of the city in the eighteenth century. In comparison, the wealthy households in Guadeloupe owned more plates, 155 on average, whereas the middling group owned an average of 22 plates, and the poor group around 6. Among the fabric makers in the French rural area of Perche after 1750, only about 17 percent of households had faience plates (Cailly 1998: 759). In Guadeloupe, the percentages for middling households (94 percent)—which would be the closest equivalent—and even for the poor homes (71 percent), were remarkably higher. To the extent that data are available, they indicate that more people in Guadeloupe bought ceramic tableware, and they bought more of it, and that the richest Guadeloupeans had services that rivaled those of noble French households in terms of size.

The shapes of dishes varied, and their value increased with their size. Less than 15 percent of the dishes, in both the archaeological collections and inventories, were oval, so their presence at any given site should be interpreted as a small sign of refinement. Indeed, oval dishes were absent from the assemblages of the middling household at 28 Rue Amédée Fengarol and were most numerous at the Palais de Justice, which yielded the fanciest tableware. Also, since a few non-wealthy households bought some of the very expensive ceramic items, one should not be surprised to find some finely decorated dishes at middling household sites.

Tureens were not as common, but they still played a very important role in all kinds of households. They were the complement to flatware in an ideal service. It seemed that only their relatively high price prevented them from being as widespread as flatware. Salad bowls (saladiers) were optional for most households but less so for the elite. Individual bowls for drinking from (bols) were more popular, almost as widespread as tureens. At some point, Guadeloupeans decided that bols were convenient for soup, and that they could use them to supplement their scanty soup plates or even rarer écuelles. This was remarkable given that salad bowls were part of the classic French faience production, but bols were not. Most of the bols found in the Guadeloupe collections were foreign made, and came from China or England. Bols were not the easiest ceramics to acquire, but Guadeloupeans put a premium on using them.

Other objects could be considered luxuries, not because of their value but because only the wealthiest households bothered to acquire them: they included all of the condiment dishes as well as the table coolers.

When everyone from the wealthy planter to the femme de couleur working as a baker used ceramic tableware, status had to be conveyed in some other way. Consequently, the elite bought large quantities of essentials, acquired rare objects, and focused on better materials. This partly explains the sheer concentration of porcelain tableware at the top of the wealth spectrum: well-off households owned 100 percent of the porcelain tureens, sauceboats, and mustard pots; 90 percent of the dishes; 81 percent of the plates; and 66 percent of the salad bowls (though the data for salad bowls are based on a very small sample). They also bought 100 percent of the porcelain coffeepots, butter dishes, and cream pots; 92 percent of bowls; 85 percent of cups; and 75 percent of teapots and sugar bowls. They tended to own more of the most expensive objects (tureens, dishes, bowls), while their less well-off counterparts made do with relatively cheaper essentials (plates, cups).

In seventeenth- and eighteenth-century Paris, Annick Pardailhé-Galabrun (1988: 307) observed that the wealthiest households used porcelain tableware services while the rest of the population could afford only decorative objects and some ceramics for tea and coffee. In Toulouse, tea and coffee services in porcelain made their appearance in elite households only at the very end of the eighteenth century (Dousset 2003: 40). These studies also pointed to one major difference with Guadeloupe regarding provenance. Porcelain in Paris was imported from Saxony in Germany, China, Japan, "India,"[4] and the Netherlands, and also came from several French potteries: Saint-Cloud, Sèvres, Chantilly, and Rouen (Pardailhé-Galabrun 1988: 307). In Toulouse, foreign porcelains came from Saxony, China or Japan, and French ones from Limoges (Arcangeli 2000: 37). In contrast, 80 percent of the porcelain vessels in Basse-Terre came from China. A few European porcelains were retrieved from relatively recent, nineteenth-century contexts. The sources for porcelains were therefore much less varied and did not include European potteries in the eighteenth century. Much Guadeloupean porcelain resembled what was found onboard the *Machault,* a French ship that sank in 1760 in the Restigouche River of New Brunswick (Sullivan 1986)—which may indicate that colonies in general received the same restricted porcelain selection.

For the most part, Guadeloupeans chose objects that were commonly made by French faience potteries. In Parisian inventories, faience tableware encompassed most of the same vessels—that is, in no particular order: plates, dishes, tureens, sauceboats, saltcellars, mustard pots, pitchers, coolers, sugar bowls, salad bowls (called *jattes* instead of saladiers), and cups and saucers—plus a few more like ewers, eggcups, casserole dishes, and fruit bowls (Pardailhé-Galabrun 1988: 307, 296). The 1792 inventory of Beaufort Castle in Jura, eastern France, yielded a similar list of 547 tableware objects in faience and refined earthenware: 237 plates, 79 dishes, 35 fruit bowls, 32 milk and cream pots, 19 undefined pots, 8 salad bowls (saladiers), 8 sugar bowls, 8 terrines, 7 coolers, 6 small coffeepots, 5 salad bowls identified as jattes, 4 fruit baskets, 2 sauceboats, 2 écuelles, and an oil and vinegar set (Goy and Brossault de Rambay 1995). The early eighteenth-century tableware retrieved at the Sauvage Inn in an eastern French town called Besançon included drinking vessels, plates, saucers, eggcups, dishes, écuelles, salad bowls, and tureens (Munier 1995).

Compared to what was available in other colonies, the faience tableware of Guadeloupeans might have been slightly limited. At Ile Bourbon, the very wealthy Marianne Lelièvre owned 416 plates, 78 soup plates, 12 dessert plates, 124 dishes, 4 écuelles, 14 tureens, 10 oil and vinegar sets, a few bowls, and an unspecified number of salt cellars, fruit bowls, jam pots, and mustard pots (Jauze 2006). At Place-Royale in Quebec, archaeologists recovered faience sherds of plates, soup plates, dishes, écuelles, salad bowls, terrines used for pâtés, tureens, eggcups, oil and vinegar sets, saltcellars, cups, teapots, trays, pitchers, and ewers, all of which might have been part of the tableware (Genêt 1980: 80). There were also plates, bowls, and "gobelets" among the foreign tin-glazed earthenware objects.

Given the uneven quality of these data, it is hard to evaluate in detail how tableware in Guadeloupe compared to other places. Yet some objects appear to have been relatively less popular; examples are eggcups (found in Paris, Place-Royale, and Ile Bourbon) and ewers (present in Paris, Place-Royale, and Toulouse) (Arcangeli 2000; Dousset 2003). The tureens that were so widespread in Guadeloupe were also remarkably absent from other places: they did not show up in Toulouse (Arcangeli 2000: 35), in the inventory of the Beaufort Castle, or in the Perthuis and Estèbes houses at Place-Royale (Genêt 1980: 74–85). Finally, bols were rare not only in the inventories from France but also from Place-Royale (Genêt 1980: 24).

Clearly, Guadeloupeans selected tableware that was functionally adapted to the Creole dishes and drinks they consumed. Tureens or large dishes were ideal for serving soups and stews, and salad bowls for the rice, pea, and vegetable dishes that Creole cooks put together. In the French dining style (*service à la française*), soups, appetizers, and sauces were generally served in the first course (Flandrin 1999: 371). A "roast," which was based on a fish or meat that was not necessarily roasted, a salad, and some side dishes would make up the second course. The meal ended with an optional third course and a dessert. At each course, the main fare was placed in the center, and the side dishes were arranged around it in a geometric pattern of large dishes and smaller plates (Wheaton 1983: 141). An average Guadeloupean household that followed this style of service might, for example, use some of their plates and dishes to arrange appetizers such as fritters (accras), blood sausages (boudins), pork-flavored pies (petits pâtés), and salt-cod-based salad (chiquetaille, féroce d'avocat) around a Creole soup served in a tureen for the first course. The second course might focus on a Creole stew or a barbecued meat or fish, presented in a tureen or one of their largest dishes. It might be accompanied by a salad placed in a dish or salad bowl, plates of manioc cakes or dumplings; or side dishes of fried and pureed vegetables, beans, peas, or rice. In sum, even if Guadeloupeans only had access to the average French tableware ensemble, they still managed to tailor their services to their needs. In particular, they decided which objects were more important and useful (such as tureens) than others (such as eggcups), and turned to foreign ceramics as complements (that is, bols) when necessary.

As far as beverages were concerned, pitchers and other ceramics for cold drinks were rare and outnumbered by glassware. Ceramics for hot drinks, on the other hand, enjoyed growing use. Elite households were well equipped to drink coffee, tea, or hot chocolate by the 1770s. Their sets were the most comprehensive and could include sugar bowls, cream pots, and butter dishes. The elite were also avid buyers of ceramic coffeepots and teapots, even when metallic alternatives existed. They selected expensive sets made of porcelain, but also cheaper "stoneware" ones that might have appeared newer, prettier, or more exotic.

Cups were to coffee and tea wares what flatware was to dinnerware. In Guadeloupe, cups usually came with saucers. The middling households that owned faience cups bought them in similar quantities as their rich counterparts, as if a minimum number of vessels was necessary to enjoy these ceramics. This fact proved that these beverages were imbibed during social events. An individual or a couple at home could easily have consumed these drinks in a variety of containers, but at least a few tea or coffee cups were required to serve them at social gatherings.

Both teapots and coffeepots were remarkably scarce in poor households before the nineteenth century. They subsequently seemed to infiltrate all kinds of households, including low-income ones. The early nineteenth century was also the period when Basse-Terre's population was feminizing and more women began appearing in the inventory sample. It is possible that the two trends were related.

The absence of a teapot, coffeepot, or hot chocolate pot in a given house did not mean that its residents never consumed these drinks. Pots were simply not necessary, as their relative rarity in an area where coffee had been grown for some time implied. Bernier's inn offered a conspicuous piece of evidence. His inventory listed an extensive array of tableware fit for serving hot beverages at his restaurant, including 25 faience cups and saucers and some silver coffee spoons. These items confirmed that Bernier would offer coffee, tea, or chocolate to his customers. His inn, however, was devoid of any coffeepots or teapots.

One of the earliest mentions of coffee in a French probate inventory made clear that coffeepots were optional. An entry dated from February 11, 1692, listed 18 pounds of coffee, a mortar and pestle, and 12 "fingeans" with saucers that were "used for drinking coffee" and were probably imported from

Turkey (Desmet-Grégoire 1994). In these early days of coffee consumption, coffee mills were not yet available and beans were ground in a mortar. In the metropole, coffee mills started to appear in the inventories of the early eighteenth century and became more common after the 1720s (Desmet-Grégoire 1994: 169).

Half a century later, most Guadeloupean households still used the more rudimentary procedure of crushing beans by hand. The kitchen mortars that served for spices, pastes, or sauces functioned for "pounding coffee" as well. In the sample, 41 percent of houses had a mortar. An even greater percentage were equipped with a frying pan that could be used for roasting the beans. Since mortars and pans were usually kept in the kitchen, this meant that coffee was prepared there by the cook or a servant, then brought to the masters for consumption.

In reality, coffee could probably be consumed by any locals who could buy or procure a few ounces of beans. Ultimately, pots and cups were more a sign of refinement than evidence of coffee consumption. In Paris as well, coffee with milk was so popular that it had become a working-class drink by the end of the eighteenth century and could be bought from shops or street peddlers (Desmet-Grégoire 1994: 169; Flandrin 1999: 360). Yet local inventories showed that only a fraction of households owned coffeepots: in the 1760s, their concentration ranged from 20 percent in the lower-class neighborhoods to 40 percent in richer areas (Roche 2000: 246).

In Guadeloupe, tea was imported at apparently great expense. The inventory sample recorded the presence of tea leaves in the shops of three merchants. In one of these cases, half a pound of tea was worth 21 livres, which made the price per pound 42 livres, or 840 sols (ADG: Mimerel, 2E 2/196, 4/5/1777). Although tea was lightweight, this appraisal was far higher than for other imported gourmet foods, and would place the price of a cup at roughly 3 to 4 sols. Tea was thus a rare luxury, and it is doubtful that the 13 percent of poor and middling households that owned a teapot actually drank imported tea very often. Since some of these households also owned faience cups that were designated "for coffee" (*tasses à café*), they might have used their teapot for serving coffee or local herbal teas instead.

Guadeloupe thus provides a cautionary tale against equating the frequency of coffeepots, hot chocolate pots, or teapots in inventories with the actual popularity of each of these drinks. This is especially true for poor and middling households, where the presence of cups would yield a more accurate indication that these beverages were being consumed.

Finally, based on inventory data, the nineteenth century saw a widening in the income level of Guadeloupean families that bought tea or coffee services, but not a revolution in their core demographics. Nineteenth-century déjeuners belonged to married couples or families de couleur such as the Saint-Gérauds who had a stable domestic partnership. In the eighteenth century, accessories such as sugar bowls, cream pots, and butter dishes, as well as matching ceramics in general, were usually listed in the inventories of couples not single individuals. Sets evidently had a particularly strong appeal amongst the most established Creole families.

Style and Decoration

Most of the data on shapes and decorations came from wealthy houses. Flowers were the only decorative pattern recorded by notaries, along with occasional notes about color. Flowered patterns were noted in about 4 percent of the houses, on what represented a minute portion of the total tableware and beverage services. Yellow vessels were the most numerous among the faiences. For the porcelains, blue was the most common color, followed by gilded porcelains. Some porcelain vessels were associated with the color red, either because they had red flowers or because they appeared mostly red. Lastly, merchant Antoine Belost owned a bowl and six cups for drinking tea that were made of "porcelaine brune"(brown porcelain), which undoubtedly referred to Batavia ware. Fine stoneware pieces were often described as "painted," to help distinguish them from common stoneware, as both types were called "grès." Painted stoneware mostly belonged to tea and coffee ware. Finally, 4 faience dishes and 10 faience plates in one house were *façonnés* (shaped), probably indicating that they were scalloped.

Comparing these scant data with the archaeological collections was informative. In the last case, the share of scalloped vessels appeared grossly underestimated by notaries and appraisers. The amount of scalloped tableware varied, but was quite noticeable: it ranged between 40 percent at the Palais de Justice and 10 percent in the nineteenth-century contexts of 28 Rue Amédée Fengarol. Given that notaries and appraisers generally failed to document this detail, it must not have mattered much for appraising the quality of faiences.

Historical texts indicate that flowers were the most common figurative pattern on faience, faience brune, tin-glazed earthenware, pearlware, porcelain, and faience fine. Flowers showed up on both Dutch and English delftware; for example, they were part of the Mandarin pattern and Fazakerley

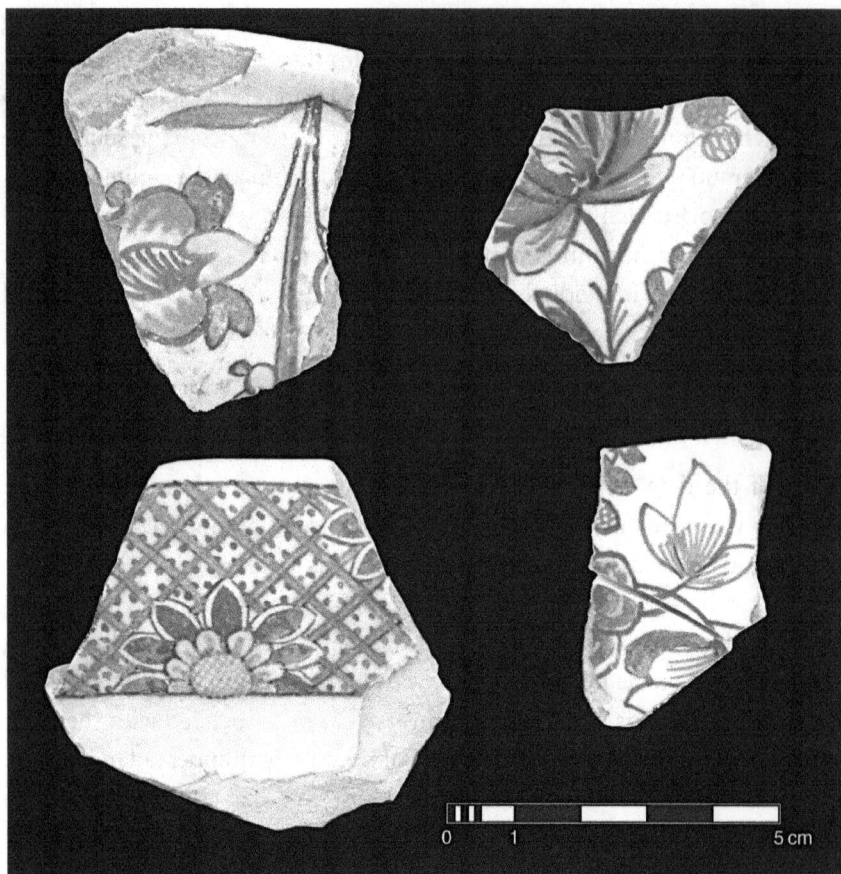

Figure 5.3. Faience tableware with quality polychrome floral decorations in blue, red, green, and yellow. *Bottom left*: rim with a refined Guillibaud pattern from Rouen that was popular in the 1710s–30s. Photograph by author.

decoration on English ceramics. Most of the decorations marketed by the major French potteries contained flowers in their designs (Guillemé Brulon 1997a, b, 1998a, b). Even the Guillibaud style from Rouen, which was inspired by a more geometric design, still incorporated flowers (figure 5.3).

Some floral patterns were recurrent in the collections. One inspired by daffodils appeared on at least five vessels from Fort Houël (figure 5.4). Although it was executed in two different styles—in several hues of blue called *camaïeu bleu* in French and in a polychrome rendering using blue, yellow, and green—it clearly belonged to a set of matching tableware that included cups, saucers, plates, and dishes. Another set showed flowers resembling carnations (figure 5.4). These decorated five plate sherds that came from different provenances at the Palais de Justice and probably belonged to several vessels.

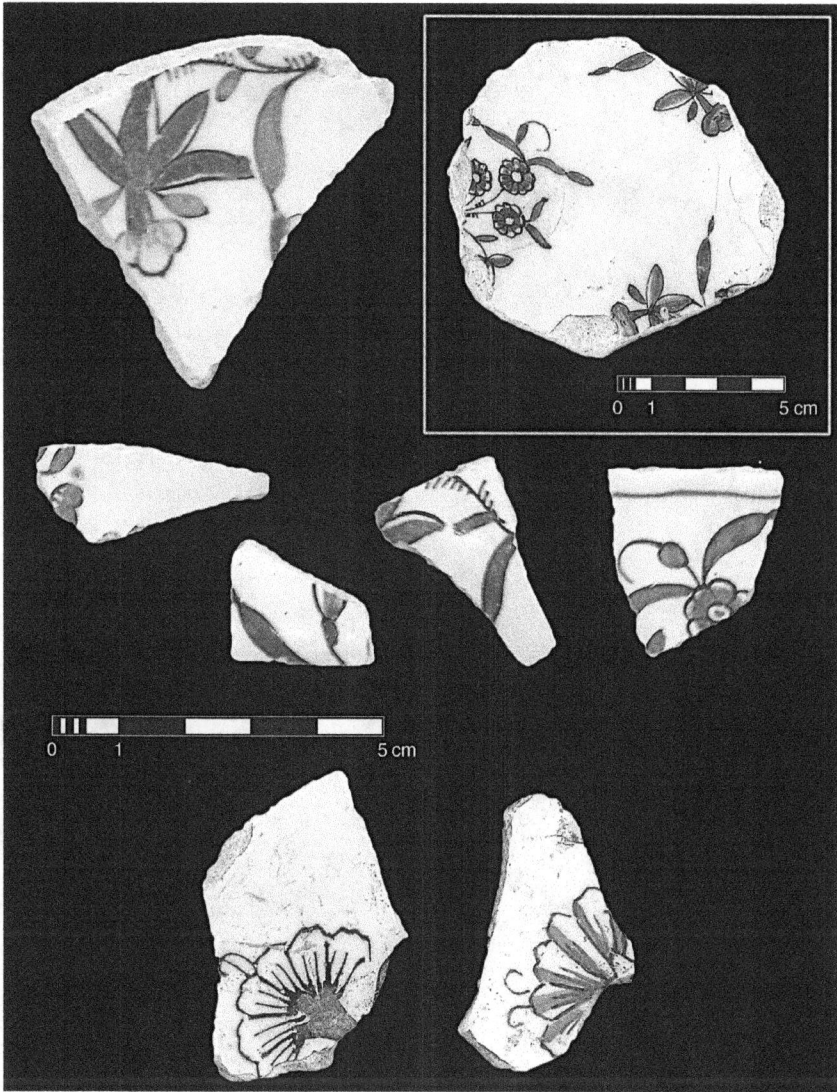

Figure 5.4. Faience tableware in floral patterns that recurred at the sites. *Top*: daffodils in camaïeu bleu (blue and dark blue) and polychrome (blue, yellow, and green) styles. *Bottom*: carnations in camaïeu bleu (blue and gray). Photograph by author.

The same Rouen-inspired pattern in camaïeu bleu with flowers, buds, ser-rated leaves, and tendrils was identified on the tableware at three of the sites (figure 5.5). A quick survey revealed that this design was quite common on eighteenth-century faiences even outside of Guadeloupe. It showed up not only on some museum pieces in France, but also at several colonial sites: on a dish and a plate from the Jesuit plantation of Saint-Ignace de Loyola in French Guiana, on a salad bowl and a dish from Place-Royale in Quebec, and

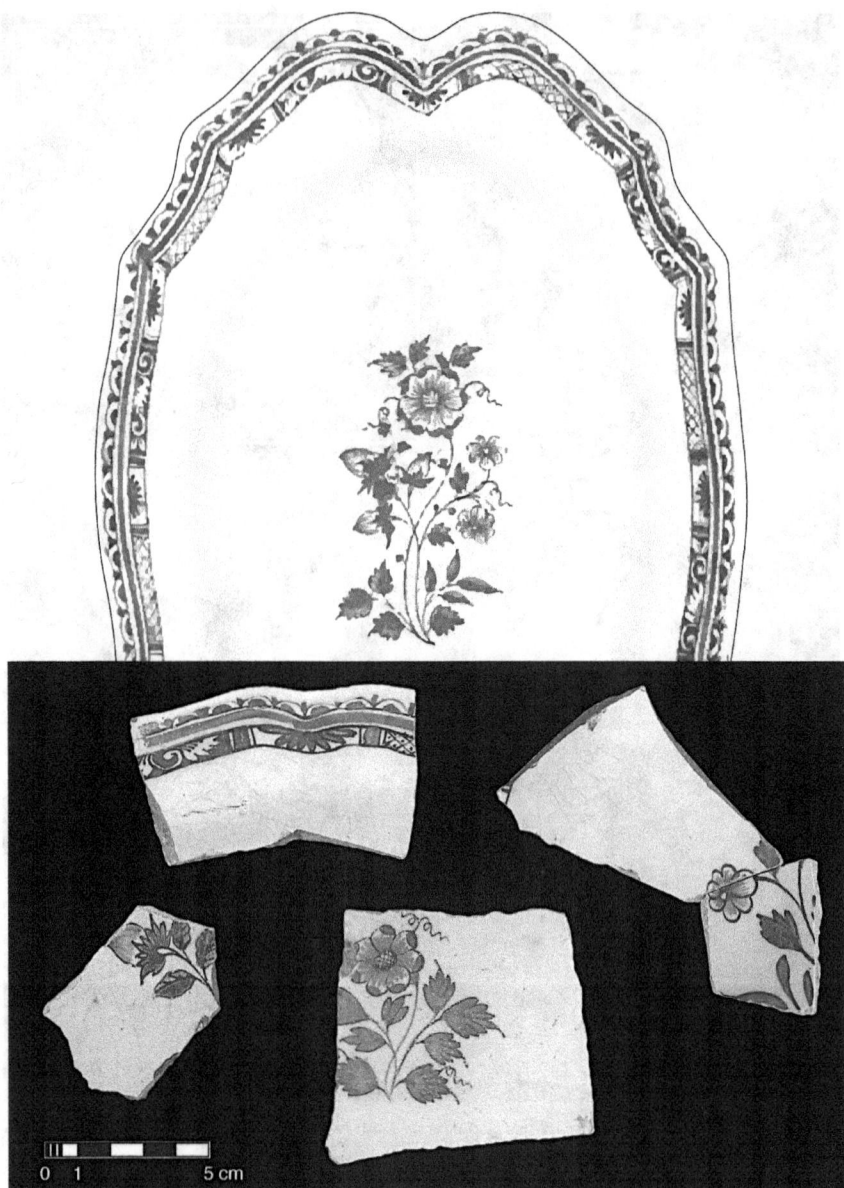

Figure 5.5. *Bottom*: common eighteenth-century faience tableware pattern of flowers, buds, tendrils, and serrated leaves in camaïeu bleu (blue and dark blue). *Top*: example of complete pattern. Photograph and illustration by author.

on a faience brune dish excavated at Williamsburg, Virginia (Bernier 2002: 17, plates 14, 39, 40; Genêt 1980: plate 23b; Noël Hume 1960: 561).

Another flower arrangement pattern common outside of Guadeloupe—one that often comes to mind when one thinks of eighteenth-century faiences from Rouen—appeared on a dish from the Palais de Justice (figure

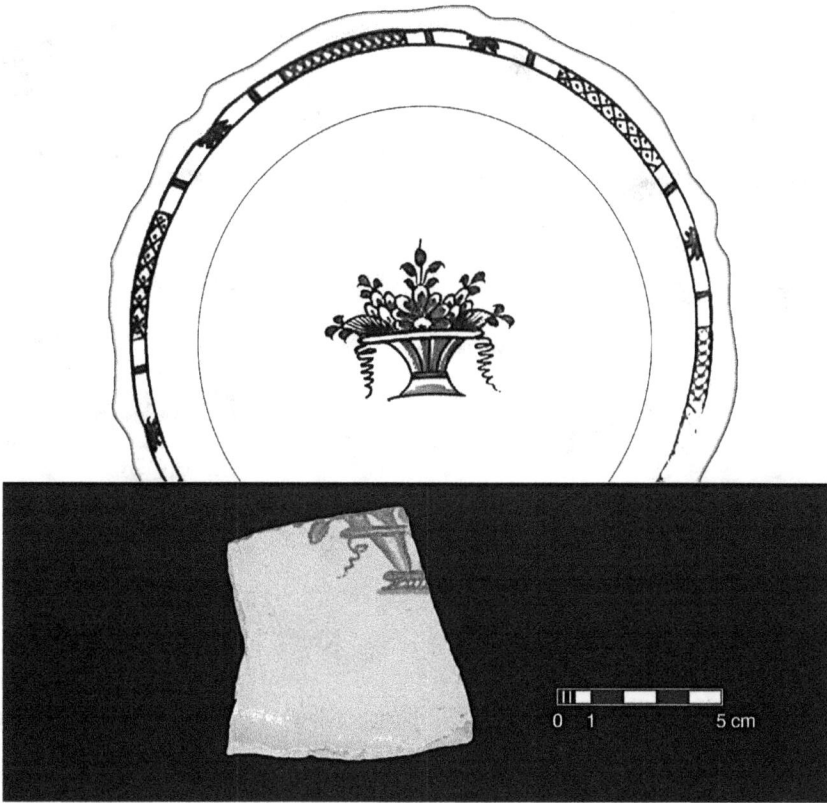

Figure 5.6. *Bottom*: common eighteenth-century faience tableware pattern of flower arrangement in camaïeu bleu (blue and black). *Top*: example of complete pattern. Photograph and illustration by author.

5.6). This kind of pattern adorns faiences excavated at both French and non-French colonial sites as well as in France and England.

Common colonial rim decorations, as identified by Gregory Waselkov and John Walthall (2002), were present on 44 percent of the faience vessels (figure 5.7). The designs present in Guadeloupe run the gamut of styles, excepting those labeled F and K. An additional recurring pattern (labeled Rim N) was not present in Waselkov and Walthall's sample. Rim G was by far the most popular, as it was at other colonial sites in northwest Louisiana and Illinois that postdated the mid-eighteenth century (for the data see Avery et al. 2007). A particular rendering in green and violet of a derivative of Rim C found in Basse-Terre also probably originated from the Bordeaux area and postdated the 1760s (Costes 2010).

Among the pitcher sherds, variations of the Rouen Lambrequin pattern were the most popular (figure 5.8). These vessels showed up in eighteenth-

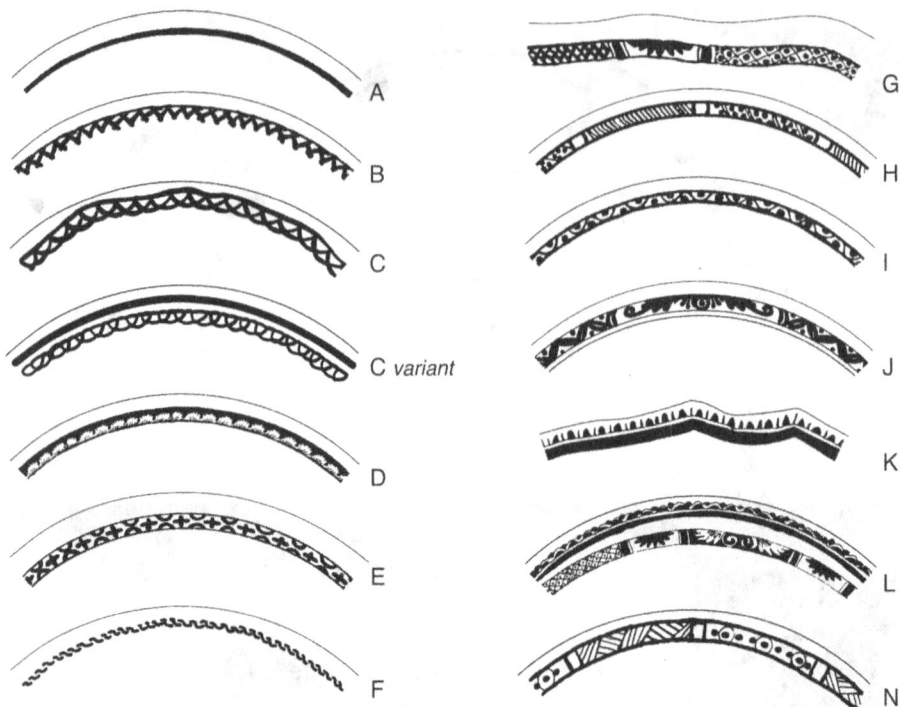

Figure 5.7. Common rim patterns on colonial French faience. Illustration by author (adapted from Waselkov and Walthall 2002: 66, fig. 3).

century contexts at three of the sites and also in the more recent context at 28 Rue Amédée Fengarol. The last was either an heirloom or a rare eighteenth-century vessel mixed with the nineteenth-century ceramics that made up the bulk of this assemblage.

As these examples illustrate, most of the French faience was decorated in hues of blue (blue appeared on at least 120 vessels) and camaïeu bleu, which included on occasion some black (69 vessels), purple (5 vessels), or brown (3 vessels). Other rarer colors, listed in descending order, were yellow (13 vessels) or orange (7 vessels), green (16 vessels), and red (12 vessels). In sum it appears the inventories were correct in listing mostly flower patterns but were biased about colors. Notaries and appraisers noted the rare colors but overlooked the more common ones.

This was less true for the porcelain entries, which would have accurately described three-quarters of the archaeological sample. There were many blue underglaze painted porcelains, several of which showed some floral compositions (figures 5.9 and 5.10). A red color appeared on most vessels that

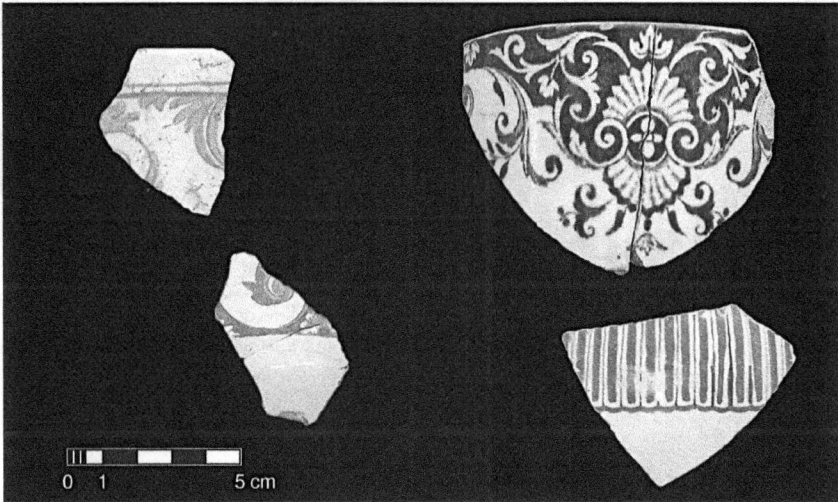

Figure 5.8. *Bottom*: faience table pitchers decorated in the Lambrequin style in blue and yellow (*left*) and blue (*right*). *Top*: example of a typical complete vessel. Illustration and photograph by author.

belonged to the so-called pink family, and actual red flowers were present on Chinese Imari and on some Batavia ware that was also decorated in the pink family style. The main difference was that gilded pieces were less prevalent in the archaeological collections than in the documents: only two such vessels were recovered.

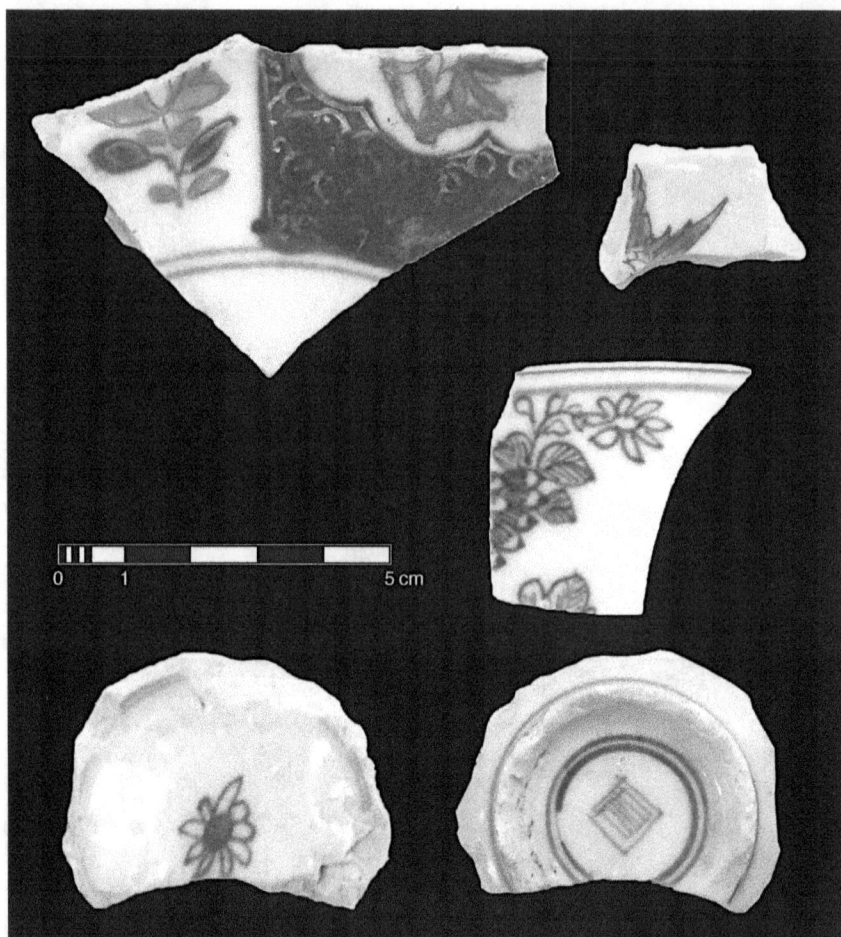

Figure 5.9. Porcelain tableware. *Top left*: Chinese Imari plate decorated in blue, red, and gold. *Top right*: bowl base with red decoration in the pink family style. *Middle and bottom*: plate rim and bowl bases with blue underglaze floral decorations. Photograph by author.

The "painted stoneware" of the inventories best corresponded to the group of hand-painted pearlwares in the collections (figure 5.10). The inventories did not specify how they were decorated, but in this group, flowery themes were not as prevalent.

Most faiences fines recovered from the sites postdated the inventories, so they illustrated what some of the major French potteries produced after about 1830—all of the marks or identified patterns were from well-known potteries. The decorative techniques ranged from hand-painting to banding, stenciling, transfer printing, and clobbering (a technique where colors are hand-painted over a printed pattern) (figures 5.11 and 5.12). Some popular

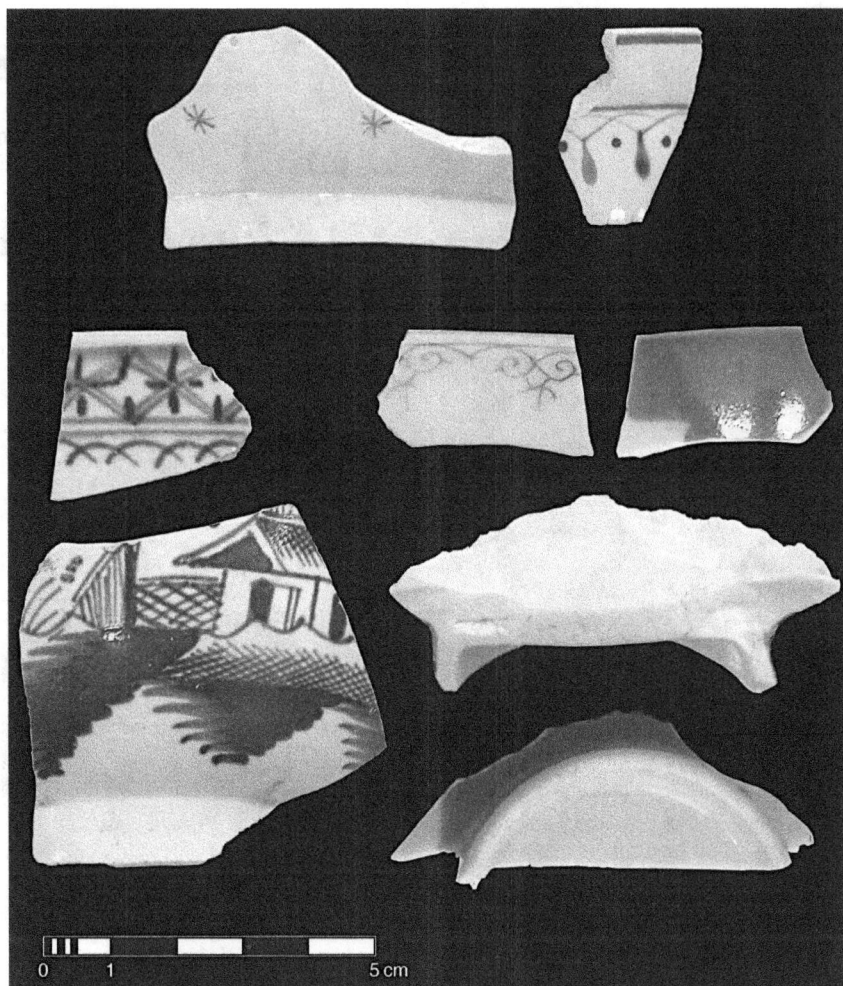

Figure 5.10. Pearlware bowls and saucers. *Top*: polychrome (yellow, brown, orange, and blue) hand-painted pearlware bowl rim and base. *Left*: hand-painted pearlware bowl rim and base with a blue Chinese house pattern. *Right*: Batavia ware bowl rim and base with red decoration in the pink family style. Photograph by author.

slip-based patterns from the first half of the nineteenth century, such as dendritic, agate, cable, and cat's-eye decorations, were absent (Guillemé Brulon 2000; Rickard and Ashworth 2006). The transfer-printed vessels did cover the range of colors used by French potteries: black, brown, blue, pink, and green (Maire 2008: 401).

Compared to faiences and porcelains, the decorations on faience fines were slightly more varied, although they still included a lot of floral designs. Geometric patterns expanded to cover entire vessels. Chinoiserie,

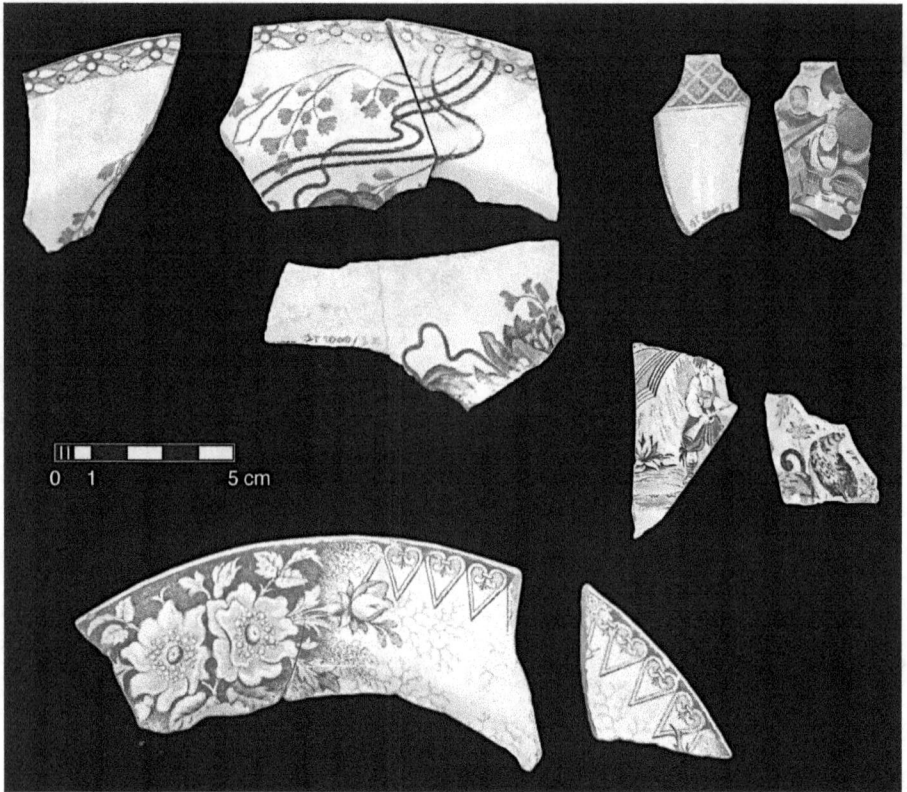

Figure 5.11. French faience fine tableware. *Top left*: dark turquoise transfer-printed plate from Sarreguemines with Royat floral pattern. *Top right*: brown transfer-printed cup with yellow and green clobbering from Sarreguemines, 1890s. *Middle right*: black transfer-printed hollowware with hunting and nature patterns. *Bottom*: blue transfer-printed plate from Lunéville with Eglantine floral pattern. Photograph by author.

or Chinese-inspired subjects, seemed popular, as were outdoor scenes or landscapes and animals. Overall, these patterns and themes appeared conventional. The range of prints in France, in particular on faiences fines, was much larger and included scenes from folk tales, political and historical topics, exotic or local landscapes, notable architecture, or social caricatures. That these themes were absent from the collections does not preclude their presence in Guadeloupe. After all, the bulk of the transfer-printed sample came from a single household living at 28 Rue Amédée Fengarol and reflected their particular taste.

One of the patterns they selected deserves a brief discussion (figure 5.13). It depicts an outdoor scene in a Chinese landscape. The background consists of several buildings, some mountains, and a ship on a lake. In the fore-

Figure 5.12. French faience fine tableware. *Top*: bowl base and teapot lid with hand-painted and stenciled geometric decorations in pink and green. *Middle*: plate with hand-painted rooster in yellow, red, and green from Moulin des Loups. *Bottom*: stenciled plate in blue and red. Photograph by author.

ground, two men in a garden under a fruit tree seem engaged in conversation. The man on the right, who appears to be the landowner, is dressed in Western clothes and a Chinese hat. Standing between them, a servant in a Chinese outfit is carrying a tray of drinks or snacks. A few feet behind them, two camels are resting on the lawn or eating grass. Interestingly, these camels are not two-humped Asian Bactrian camels, as one would expect to encounter in China, but rather single-humped African species. Their presence in a Chinese garden is whimsical and maybe also made for a good conversation

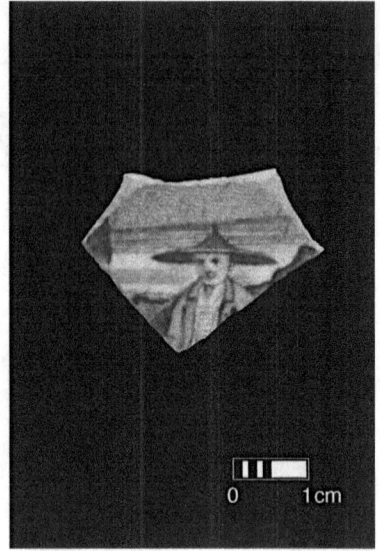

Figure 5.13. Blue transfer-printed plate from Creil et Montereau, 1830s, with a Chinese-inspired colonial theme. Illustration and photograph by author.

starter and an evocation of exotic themes such as the Silk Road. The group of men in the foreground lends this setting a colonial flavor: if the man dressed as a Westerner is in fact in charge, the scene reads as an allegory of the comfortable and desirable colonial lifestyle. In a place like Guadeloupe (which remained a French colony until 1946)—this message would have resonated with the people who ate off this plate.

Outside of the faience fines, a few sherds with figurative themes from Palais de Justice highlighted the rarity of these decorations compared to floral patterns. Human characters or animals were featured on a handful of faience or porcelain vessels.

In France, blue-on-white faiences preceded polychromy, and faiences brunes started to appear in the 1720s, partly to compete with Albisola wares. Faience production was driven by a few large potteries, like Nevers in the seventeenth century and Rouen and Moustiers in the eighteenth century. These major potteries all benefited from good transportation or nearby regional fairs that ensured their ceramics sold well and broadly (Rosen 1995: 106–7). Secondary centers copied these potteries' most popular styles, specialized in niche productions, or both, to carve out their own market share.

About 80 percent of the faiences in Basse-Terre fell under the general "Rouen" style. These faiences could have been made in Rouen itself, at nearby potteries in direct competition with Rouen (such as Paris or Lille), or at any other pottery that copied Rouen-style designs (such as La Rochelle or Bordeaux). This group also included faiences brunes, for which Rouen was certainly not the sole producer (Rosen 1995: 130–31); according to the inventories some came from Marmande, a small town not far from Bordeaux. The faiences that exhibited designs in the Nevers or Moustiers styles were far rarer, a fact corroborated in the inventories: a third of the faiences with a stated provenance or style were from Provence (the region around Moustiers) and the rest was from Normandy (the region around Rouen); there were no recorded faiences from Nevers. This ratio included a few large merchandise lots that came from shops. When only faiences in use were considered, the results matched the field data even better: 84 percent of the faience objects listed in Guadeloupean houses were from Normandy, and 16 percent from Provence.

By comparison, Rouen decorations appeared on a little less than 40 percent of all of the eighteenth-century faiences from the Jesuit plantation of Saint-Ignace de Loyola in French Guiana (Bernier 2002: 62). At Place-Royale in Quebec the Rouen style dominated, but Moustiers and Nevers examples seemed far more numerous and varied than in Guadeloupe (Genêt 1980). Since Guadeloupeans imported from Provence a lot of their water-storage ceramics and cookware (Biot jars, Vallauris cooking pots, and Huveaune Valley bowls), it would not be surprising if the bulk of their faiences came from there as well. They overwhelmingly preferred to get such items from Rouen.

The quality of the decorations on their faiences appeared to be consistently average (figure 5.14). More refined decorations, be they in the Guillibaud (figure 5.3), Lambrequin (figure 5.8), or figurative families, were rare. Guadeloupeans were on the outskirts of the French commercial empire, so they might not have had much choice about the range of ceramics they could acquire. One of the ceramic services owned by notary Pierre Debort bore his personal mark, which signaled that he, at least, had been able to place a special order (ADG: Mimerel, 2E 2/198, 7/21/1781). Yet even if Guadeloupeans were offered only a limited range of common tableware, they still managed to tailor their ceramic services to their needs and tastes. They selected the objects that were the most useful to them and complemented them with foreign ceramics as needed. They preferred Rouen-style faiences, and within that style focused on flowery patterns that were often rendered in camaïeu bleu.

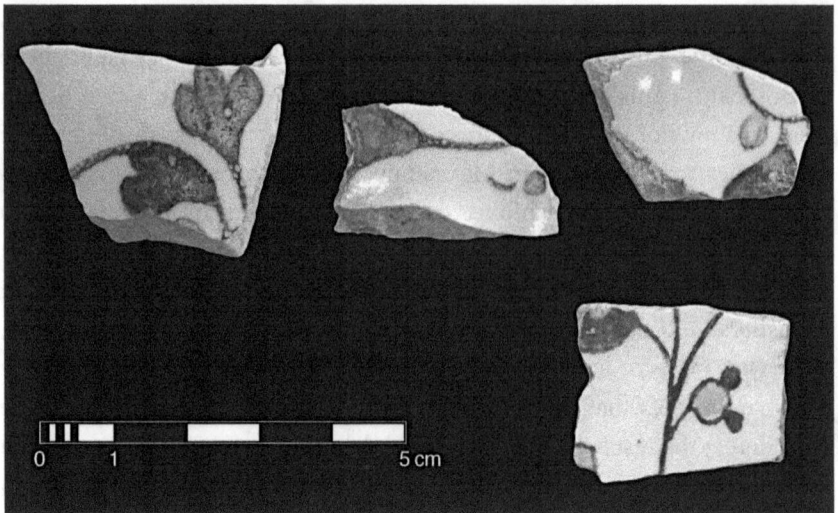

Figure 5.14. Simple floral pattern in blue, green, and yellow typical of the average quality of faience tableware made in the Rouen area. Photograph by author.

As the figures illustrate, some vessels recovered from the sites belonged to matching sets. Definite design matches were present in small quantities in all of the contexts or sites, but many more ceramics were decorated in styles that were sufficiently similar to be used together. For example, the 22 flatware faiences from Palais de Justice that had a Rim G type were coordinated, although they technically were not a set—in order to classify them as such, one would have to see their central pattern. In effect, much of the tableware in Guadeloupe was visually homogeneous due to the fact that patterns, colors, and execution were consistent. The result was that it was easy for Guadeloupeans to put together whole faience services that would create a harmonious effect on their tables (figure 5.15).

Entertaining in French Creole Homes

As Doris Garraway (2005: 129) noted, "hospitality emerge[d] as the privileged mode of colonial social contact" in the French Antilles. The tradition started based on the fact that most governors of the early colonization period kept an "open-door, open-table policy" for their constituents (Boucher 2008: 91). The first edition of Jean-Baptiste Du Tertre's (1654: 468–69) book on the French Antilles also commented on the development of this phenomenon: since neither hotels nor inns existed, travelers would stop at any house on their route and would receive free room and board. Du Tertre thought that

Figure 5.15. Re-creation of an eighteenth-century French table setting for dessert, with Rouen faiences in blue Lambrequin style. Photograph by Frédéric Bisson (used by permission from http://www.flickr.com/photos/zigazou76/4955147699/).

this was a "laudable" practice. Decades later, Médéric-Louis-Élie Moreau de Saint-Méry (1797–98: I.16–17) described the same phenomenon, deeming it a typical Creole "virtue." He attributed it both to the lack of inns and to the boredom of planters, who welcomed visitors as bearers of fresh news and a welcome change of pace. Moreover, extending munificent generosity to guests was also a matter of prestige and honor for the hosts. Some planters spent fortunes on hosting and unscrupulous individuals took advantage of them (Moreau de Saint-Méry 1797–98: I.17).

Pierre Dessalles's diary further documented this practice. While he was living on his Martiniquais plantation, Dessalles entertained guests or dined out at his neighbors' and friends' homes several nights a week. He was very much engaged in "a constant round of socialization," similar to what Trevor Burnard (2004: 81) observed for the Jamaican planter Thomas Thistlewood. From studying Thistlewood's diary, Burnard (2004: 79) perceived a "cult of hospitality" in Creole Jamaican society as well, which he interpreted as a means of manifesting racial solidarity.

Since table settings epitomized the famous Creole hospitality, it is no wonder that planters spent a great deal on them. In Saint-Domingue, Gabriel Debien (1956: 87; 1974: 90), remarked on several occasions that houses seemed lightly furnished and were decorated with few knickknacks, but that tableware was abundant by comparison. Some contemporary observers of the Antilles concurred that the table was the locus of luxurious expenditures by French Creole households (Chanvalon 1763: 78; Montlezun 1818: II.113). One such chronicler was the Baron de Montlezun, who was used to European interiors and was less than impressed by Creole houses. If Creole houses were regarded as subpar compared French ones though, Creole tables made a better impression. The "luxury of the table" to which he referred might have included the food, the service, and the quality of the table setting.

From the inventories and other sources like Baron de Montlezun's travelogue, it appears clear that dinners and other social events took place in the reception areas of Creole houses; namely, in a parlor called the salle and in the gallery. The latter was a typically Creole architectural feature. Christophe Charlery (2005) thinks that it might have emerged from the Spanish colonies in Saint-Domingue first, then spread to the Caribbean and Louisiana during the second quarter of the eighteenth century. Creole galleries often ended in two small enclosed spaces that were called cabinets, bedrooms, or offices (that is, pantries). When a house had two floors, it sometimes also had two galleries. The lower one was used for dining, and the upstairs one was an annex of bedrooms or pantries.

Indoor entertaining rooms analogous to the Creole salles did exist in eighteenth-century France, but much less frequently than in Guadeloupe. They were present in about one-third of Parisian houses, versus 60 percent for the Guadeloupean sample (Pardailhé-Galabrun 1988: 259). A remarkable 64 percent of Guadeloupean households had at least one space that was generally deemed suitable for entertaining, whether it was a gallery or other room. Salles also had a long history in the colonies. During the settlement era, they served as the main living space, along with a bedroom and a storeroom (Charlery 2005). In the Antilles and Louisiana, they have become part of the vernacular domestic architecture and can be found in most two- and three-room historical floor plans (Denise 2005; Maygarden 2006: 229–30; Pérotin-Dumon 2000: 438).

The homes that had neither a salle nor a gallery typically belonged to poor or middling households and only rarely to the wealthy ones (4 percent). This shows that if people could afford it, they would choose to devote a space in their house to entertaining guests. The inventories of the gens de couleur were particularly instructive: those that were classified in the middling group usually listed a salle, whereas the ones in the poor group rarely did. It seemed that hommes and femmes de couleur made a special effort to have a salle as soon as their net worth and social position made this feasible.

The dining function of the salle and gallery was made apparent by the presence of large tables and much seating, such as chairs, armchairs, and sofas. An example of a small entertaining ensemble was described in the inventory of the merchant Jean Blanchet: his gallery was furnished with a table, a sofa, an armchair, and four chairs. At the other end of the spectrum, the salle of Pierre Jean-Baptiste Avril had 32 chairs, two armchairs, one sofa, and two tables that could seat a total of 24 people. That of planter Jacques Brun Beaupein Miresse was furnished with 36 chairs, two armchairs, one sofa, and a table with a luxurious marble top (ADG: Mollenthiel, 2E 3/80, 1/27/1780). Notaries did not always record the sizes of the tables, but those that were documented could generally seat between 10 and 12 people.

This furniture was a mix of locally made items and imports from several areas. Some of the French chairs were straw-seated models from Normandy, and others came from coastal ports such as Bordeaux or Dunkirk. Dutch chairs were present in 5 percent of households and "English" ones in 3 percent. Sofas and armchairs could also be "English," and some were described as made of wood painted in green. Danielle Bégot (1994) found mentions of armchairs and table knives in that style, dating from 1792 and 1782, respectively. Given these descriptions, most of these "English" pieces of furniture must have come from North America, as Pérotin-Dumon (2000: 591–92) observed. A lot of painted wooden pieces, like the famous Windsor chairs, were exported from New England to the French Antilles in the 1780s and 1790s.

In eighteenth-century salles and galleries, other types of furniture like desks, guéridons,[5] or low chests of drawers (commodes) were found rarely. The spaces were, however, decorated with care: 21 percent of households had wall mirrors, some of which were of English or Dutch manufacture. There were also paintings; decorative crystal and glass globes; carpets, which were usually green and not for floor coverings but for protecting and decorating tables; candleholders; drapes; crystal lamps; and some ill-described crystal or glass cylinders in 17 percent of households. Objects related to scientific pursuits were also located there, such as spyglasses (owned by 8 percent of households), English clocks (6 percent), hourglasses with a one- or two-hour capacity (5 percent), and geographical maps and calendars; along with game tables for playing trictrac and checkers (Desmoulins 2006: 226; Pardailhé-Galabrun 1988: 422).

The inventories from the 1830s revealed an increase in the variety of furniture placed in entertaining areas. In addition to traditional tables and seats, sideboards became popular, as did small French tables with curved feet called *consoles*. Storage furniture like armoires, dressers, or desks became much more common, along with wall decorations such as gravures. If this furniture was identified as imported, the source was unequivocally American and no longer "English" or Dutch.

More importantly, the trend also affected ceramics. In the eighteenth century, the only vessels that were stored in salles or galleries were water jars and wall fountains. Tableware, in contrast, was most often kept in the office or a bedroom. Only seven poor to middling houses (5 percent of the entire sample), stored some of their tableware in the salle. By the 1830s, however, objects made of fine ceramics were considered suitable ornaments for these spaces. Porcelain sets for hot drinks like tea, coffee, or chocolate turned up in three houses, and porcelain decorative objects were mentioned in two cases. In Paris, ceramics such as pots, vases, urns, or cups were used as elements of decor starting much earlier, commonly adorning Parisian mantelpieces by the eighteenth century (Pardailhé-Galabrun 1988: 393–95). Other types of decoration also appeared more frequently in Paris than in Guadeloupe at the beginning of the century: clocks showed up in 40 percent of Parisian houses after 1750, paintings and other wall art in 71.5 percent, and mirrors in 70 percent (Pardailhé-Galabrun 1988: 377, 390, 396). Emphasizing mirrors and a few tapestries or curtains, Guadeloupean decor was in line with French fashion, but was still sparse by comparison. An interesting counterexample was the larger number of spyglasses in Guadeloupe. Pardailhé-Galabrun (1988: 427) listed four Parisian households that owned telescopes and one that had a spyglass, which together amounted to less than 0.1 percent of her sample. Spyglasses were much more frequent in Guadeloupe and were probably not used for stargazing. They were a natural part of the maritime culture of the colonies, and in a port like Basse-Terre or even in coastal towns around the island, they could be used to observe seaside activities as well as to watch the comings and goings of ships (Pardailhé-Galabrun 1988: 603–5).

In addition to their architecture, the organization of Guadeloupean houses was a testament to the importance of entertaining in the Creole world. In Paris tables and chairs were present in great quantities as well—there were on average three to four tables and a dozen seats per household—but they were not systematically located in a separate room devoted to entertaining, analogous to the Creole salle (Pardailhé-Galabrun 1988: 302–5). Instead, they often appeared in rooms that had other functions, such as kitchens and bedrooms. Nothing like the Guadeloupean office existed for storing Parisian tableware, which was originally kept in the kitchen but started to be moved to the dining room or bedrooms in the 1770s (Pardailhé-Galabrun 1988: 343). Similarly, most portable lighting in Paris was found in kitchens, whereas in Guadeloupe this was kept in the office with the tableware. Consequently, these objects were apparently used mostly during social events in Creole houses. Compared to Parisian residences, Guadeloupean houses appeared to have been more purposefully designed to accommodate frequent organized dining events.

Behaviors and Manners

According to Pierre Dessalles's diary, both dinner and lunch parties were held, though the evening variety was much more common (Dessalles and Frémont 1980). Lunch parties occurred anytime between 10 a.m. and 1:30 p.m. (Flandrin 1999: 369–70; Montlezun 1818: II.101). Whether the invitation was for lunch or dinner, showing up at least a couple of hours in advance was considered polite in the Antilles. For a lunch served at 1:30 in the afternoon, Dessalles thus arrived—as his hosts expected—at 8:30 in the morning. Although the prelude was lengthy, the meal itself probably did not stretch on beyond the time necessary to serve its various courses. Dessalles complained that an unusually fancy dinner in the capital of Martinique, which would have started in the late afternoon or early evening, had finished at 9:30 p.m.

Fortunately, Dessalles liked to comment on the parties he threw or attended, and some of his remarks reveal general norms and customs for such events, at least within his circle of wealthy Creole planters. Dessalles was rarely specific about dishes but did emphasize that the food ought to taste good and be served warm, when applicable (Dessalles and Frémont 1980: entries for February 1837, June 29, 1838, and January 8, 1840). Its presentation also had to be aesthetically pleasing, which a beautiful ceramic service would enhance. Profusion was desirable, as Montlezun (1818: II.112) also noted. The goal was to present a cornucopia of dishes at each course. Given this ideal, it makes sense that many flatware objects and bowls were necessary to serve the food, on top of the individual place settings for guests. Finally, if a dinner or lunch party was given on a Friday, fish would be served instead of meat, as required by Catholic custom. In Dessalles's view it was harder to serve good food on Fridays, probably because if fresh fish were not available, vegetables, legumes, and grains were the only alternatives.

Regarding table manners, children would sit at a smaller table, separate from the adults. Washing one's hands with water just before the meal, a practice in the metropole since the Middle Ages, seemed to be a habit shared by at least the Creole elite. This gesture, which was as much ritualistic as hygienic (Marenco 1992: 33), explained the presence of wall fountains in salles and galleries.

As in France, lunches were generally of shorter duration and less formal than dinners (Marenco 1992: 108). When invited to luncheons, Dessalles generally departed immediately after eating. Dinners, though, often stretched into the night and good hosts provided entertainment such as music, singing, and dancing, as well as gambling and popular card games such as écarté or whist, Boston, piquet, and reversis. Occasionally, guests would compete at target shooting or bet on cockfights. Some of these activities took place outside, in courtyards illuminated with torchlight.

Courtyards allowed for another form of entertainment: watching slaves dance, sing, and play drums, as Dessalles and his fellow guests did on several occasions. Dessalles periodically organized "balls" for his slaves, as he did for the wedding of his servant Césaire, during the holidays, and at the request of his wife and daughters for their entertainment. Free gens de couleur could come and mix with the slaves, but decency forbade Dessalles or his friends, as members of the planters' class, from mingling with this crowd. In one instance, Dessalles even resorted to hiding himself in order to be able to enjoy the show: "Hidden in a corner, I saw everything without being visible: Nothing was more pleasant" (Dessalles and Frémont 1980: entry from January 29, 1837). In contrast, during a visit to the metropole he described a wedding where guests and servants ended up dancing together at the end of the night.

Dinner parties were expected to be entertaining, but Dessalles was even more concerned about the quality of the company. If certain guests at the table did not have the correct "manners," "education," and "tone," nothing could save the event in his view. Needless to say, social status was not his only criterion for quality company; race was an even greater preoccupation. Dessalles strongly resisted the idea of eating with gens de couleur, although he was forced to do so at least once, onboard a boat headed for the metropole. During the year when slavery was abolished, in 1848, he also participated in several political banquets organized by colonial officials to which both whites and gens de couleur were invited. Dessalles commented at length on each of these events, and his ramblings about social and racial differences made clear that he found them deeply uncomfortable. Dessalles was not an isolated case. The abolitionist Victor Schoelcher (1842: 191–92) complained that white planters in general were more willing to eat with white people of lower status, such as retired government workers, soldiers, or immigrant farmers, than with the gens de couleur who were their social peers.

Masters did not dance with their slaves, nor did they eat with them, even on the special occasions when both attended the same party. At Césaire's wedding, for example, the enslaved guests danced in the salon while Dessalles and the 21 other white guests ate their meal. After the whites were finished, a separate meal was served to the enslaved guests.

If slaves were present during a meal, it was simply for serving the food. Unfortunately, most historical sources remain silent about who these servers were and how they handled the task. Dessalles himself never bothered to record a single pertinent detail, and he used the generic pronoun "one" on the only occasion he referred to these servers. Since a majority of domestics in Guadeloupe were female servants, they likely shouldered this responsibility. The fact that servers were completely overlooked in the written accounts of dinners might also reflect what was ideally expected of them. During a meal, they had to be actively helpful—for example, when they brought out dishes or filled glasses—but had to do their work unobtrusively, as attentive, well-behaved, and silent witnesses. In her novel about white Creole Guadeloupeans at the beginning of the twentieth century, Arlette Blandin-Pauvert (1986: 106) seemed to imply as much in her writing of a scene with an old male server during a meal where the family had a guest: "The old Bolo was moving silently, avoiding making the smallest noise with the crockery, since Madame de la Coste had a strong aversion to defective service."

Naturally, servants had to know how to set the table in preparation for a meal. Victor Schoelcher (1842: 194) mentioned that during a visit to a Creole house, he was left alone for several minutes in a downstairs room where the table was fully set, silverware included. Dessalles also complained that members of his household lived on different schedules and that as a result his table was constantly set (Dessalles and Frémont 1980: entry for July 23, 1839). This meant that even if someone checked their work, enslaved servants had to acquire some basic knowledge about the art of setting a table. If Creole tables were set the way they were in the metropole, this meant the tablecloth had to be draped appropriately, the silverware had to be arranged around each plate, glasses had to be placed on a dish or in a cooler, napkins had to be folded in a decorative way, and perhaps centerpieces created with fruits or colored sugar powder (Marenco 1992: 41–48). They might also have carefully arranged the dishes for the first course in advance, as was done in France (Marenco 1992: 61).

Hot drinks could be served at the end of a meal or at breakfast and as a daytime snack. Making tea required boiling water and ensuring there was enough cream, sugar, and tea leaves in the service but did not need much more advance preparation. This was not the case for coffee and chocolate. Coffee beans had to be roasted and crushed, then mixed with boiling water in a pitcher or pot over the fire. If the same decoction method that was originally popular in France was used, the mixture was brought to a boil several times (Desmet-Grégoire 1994: 167). For hot chocolate the process was similar but involved the addition of spices like cinnamon and, at the end of the eighteenth century, a beaten egg white (Huyghues-Belrose 2006: 210–12). Once these drinks had been prepared in the kitchen, they were probably poured into pots or cups and carefully carried to the masters or guests.

Men could socialize around these drinks outside of the domestic sphere. Places like Bernier's inn, La Grande Auberge, with its billiard table and dining room, catered as much to the local male bourgeoisie as to travelers (Pérotin-Dumon 2000: 602–6). There, Creole men could meet, play cards and gamble, watch activities at the harbor, have a meal, and of course, drink hot and cold beverages. The inventories suggested the existence of other similar places in town: the male customers of the wigmaker Jean-Bernard Poudensan de la Grange could shop for bulk tea or coffee cups while they ordered wigs and bought grooming items such as soaps, pomade, lavender-scented water, or barber's bowls (ADG: Mimerel, 2E 2/196, 4/5/1777).

Creole women seemingly had different opportunities to meet and socialize around hot drinks. A painting by Le Masurier, probably done in Martinique in the 1770s, immortalized such an occasion (figure 5.16). It shows a group of three women de couleur sitting around a table in a large room,

Figure 5.16. *Une famille métisse* by Le Masurier, oil on canvas, 1775. Courtesy of the Ministère des Outre-Mer.

probably in the home of the woman who is located to the far right and has no shoes on. They all wear fashionable clothing for women of their social caste at the time (Réache and Gargar 2009). These elegant women de couleur are using a matching ensemble of faience cups, saucers, and a sugar bowl but are pouring their drink from a pewter pitcher. This scene closely matches the data in the inventories and accurately renders the kind of tea or coffee items that a middling household de couleur likely owned in the 1770s: they would use faience cups, silver spoons, and possibly a sugar bowl, but not a faience pot. Also on the table are a glass bottle, perhaps holding some kind of alcohol or flavoring syrup, and a basket of what could be flat manioc cakes. The inclusion of a butter dish in some of the inventoried coffee or tea sets suggests that breads or pastries were sometimes served with hot drinks.

Creole women of all races and various statuses might have taken part in this kind of social activity. Dessalles mentioned in his diary that elite ladies in Martinique had tea together at night in the spa where he was staying. Commenting on the women de couleur in Saint-Domingue, Médéric-Louis-Élie Moreau de Saint-Méry (1797–98: I.93) noted that they loved luxury and that one of their common expenditures was to buy a beautiful tea or coffee set made of porcelain. Moreover, several observers noted that white Creole women ate very little during meals. Moreau de Saint-Méry (1797–98: I.20) commented that they lived on coffee with milk and hot chocolate. Both this author and Boyer-Peyreleau (1823) attributed women's lack of appetite at the table to the fact that they consumed such drinks all day long, together with fruits and sweets. Such practices could explain why, when the population of women in Basse-Terre increased, tea and coffee services became more widespread in the inventories.

Creole commensal events, such as dinners, lunches, and teas, had several functions. First, they were entertaining and helped break up the monotony of plantation life. Pierre Dessalles, for example, complained about having to eat alone when his family or friends were not available. Dinner or luncheon parties also helped celebrate holidays or mark the major milestones in the lives of Creole families, such as baptisms, weddings, and funerals. They helped to develop relationships, sustain social networks, and nurture alliances.

As in the metropole, reciprocity was implicit, and inviting someone to a social gathering ensured that they would have to return the courtesy (Marenco 1992: 57). In the Antilles, however, it seemed acceptable for members of the same social circle to call on someone directly without an advance invitation and with little advance notice. Thus the Sanois family informed Dessalles that they intended to dine with him the next day (Dessalles and Frémont 1980: entry for March 12, 1844). On learning the news, Dessalles was annoyed at the expense that this spontaneous entertainment would entail, but not at their having invited themselves. About two months later, he returned the courtesy and invited himself to their home in the same fashion. The reciprocity rule was so strong in the Antilles that people could take advantage of it, stretch its boundaries, and use it to transgress racial boundaries. When gens de couleur showed up at his home after having attended the same party as he the day before in honor of the mixed-race children of one of his acquaintances, Dessalles was annoyed but could not turn them away (Dessalles and Frémont 1980: entry for August 28, 1843). Individuals who refused to participate in these rounds of invitations lost some of their clout. Dessalles cited the example of a mayor who wanted to leave his position and stopped inviting people to his home (Dessalles and Frémont 1980: entry for November 7, 1842). As a result, he lost all social "respect." In the final analysis, Creole dinners were social performances that, among other things, were opportunities for self-fashioning. Dessalles revealed the Sanois family's motives for wanting him to come to their house: M. de Sanois was always seeking to impress, and his wife and daughters were constantly putting themselves forward.

In early modern France, table seating arrangements and invitations to dine reinforced sharp social distinctions (Figeac 2007:433; Marenco 1992). Even when the hierarchy among upper-class guests started to soften in the eighteenth century, people who had to work for a living, including wealthy bourgeois, were still excluded (Flandrin 1999:370). Unlike in Poland or Germany for example, the French elite never ate with their servants (Marenco 1992:38, 57). As soon as colonial commensality appeared, however, it transgressed the rigid social hierarchy that existed in France, and in Doris Garraway's (2005: 128) words, provoked a "reinvention of social life." Both nobles and commoners could eat at the same table, and people of low birth had the opportunity to refashion themselves. That performance and display trumped social origin made observers such as Jean-Baptiste Du Tertre very nervous (Garraway 2005:129). A century and a half later, table manners were still crucial to sustaining one's position in the Antilles, as shown by Dessalles's aforementioned remarks and also noted by the traveler Granier de Cassagnac (1842–44:115). Cassagnac commented that all of the planters displayed a high level of dining etiquette, comparable only to what he witnessed among European elite.

In the Antilles, however, commensal hospitality could reinforce caste segregation between white and free gens de couleur, and particularly between masters and slaves. Creole tables represented important loci of social performances, making these commensal events akin to feasting rituals. Archaeologists such as Michael Dietler (2001) have explored how feasting practices relate to politics and the marking of social boundaries. Dietler's classic typology includes three nonexclusive forms of feasting events. Applying his typology to the evidence collected for the Antilles, many Creole dinners and luncheons were "empowering feasts," since they aimed at increasing one's social capital among one's peers and they implied reciprocity between hosts and guests. Perhaps in some instances these events also acted more as "patron feasts" that helped superior households secure the labor and allegiance of inferior ones. In that case, no reciprocity would be expected, just as when the planter Dessalles attended political banquets organized by high-ranking colonial officials. Yet any Creole commensal gathering could also have acted as a "diacretical feast," in the sense that it reinforced existing social boundaries and manifestations of social control. Diacretical feasts typically perpetuate class endogamy, most often among the elite, but they are also sometimes emulated by non-elites. They reify social status and confirm elite membership through the use of special foods, material culture, and particular knowledge or behaviors. In Guadeloupe, dinners, lunches, or refreshments were by definition divisive and exclusive along caste lines, even among non-elites or second-rate citizens such as free gens de couleur. The labor of enslaved servants could be harnessed for these events, but slaves could never participate. Thus, slave-based societies such as Guadeloupe's show that diacretical feasts can materialize in a culture by defining not only who will attend (that is, which guests can be present), but also who among the persons involved in the feast can be considered to be a participant. Whatever their functions, these Creole feasts required an abundance of foods, perhaps some special dishes, but more certainly a particular type of material culture that included faience tableware and beverage services.

Conclusion

These few observations could explain why the decoration of faience tableware mattered. Faiences from the village of La Mahaudière showed a remarkably high amount of undecorated vessels: 67.8 percent of the faience blanche and 83.4 percent of the faience brune were plain. By comparison, undecorated faiences in Basse-Terre represented 48 percent of the sherds but a mere 23 percent of the vessels. As this analysis has demonstrated, a lot of the decorated tableware was coordinated visually if not matched. Upon entering a salle, guests would gaze on a table laden with food and subtly harmonized ceramics.

Mimi Hellman's (2007) study of seriality in elite interiors offers an astute look at the role of sets in early modern France. As she discovered, ceramics were an important tool for enhancing seriality in the decor. They either were purchased as matching sets or could be assembled and arranged in a way that highlighted a common visual quality, such as a shared color or pattern.

Hellman's clever contribution was to recontextualize serial design and recognize that seriality had more connotations of luxury then than nowadays. Compared to their European counterparts, elite French households were particularly fond of serialization, and amplified it by adding symmetry and regularity in both architecture and room decor.

Hellman's interpretation is multifold. First, sets were associated with formality and gave visual cues about what kind of social interactions were expected. For example, a room decorated with a cluster of different types of chairs was more intimate than one where all of the chairs matched and were arranged symmetrically. Second, using elements of the same sets reinforced the coherence of a group or, in Hellman's view, transformed the people themselves into a set. Yet individuality and hierarchy shone through in the way each person handled these objects. Third, sets were repetitive, but self-fashioning was permitted through making slightly different choices. Each household could select a unique design, color, or pattern. The fact that sets demonstrated social mastery—in that they were more expensive to acquire and maintain—but also allowed for the expression of status or taste made them uniquely qualified for elite performances. Finally, the effect of sets was reinforced by excess and accumulation that Hellman (2007: 147) dubbed an "aesthetics of surplus." Hosts displayed more chairs than were necessary for sitting, more vases than they had flowers to decorate, and so on. Noting that "repetition is a form of insistence in the face of tenuous control" (149), Hellman suggested that sets represented a "struggle for psychological control" (148). Like Rococo design, they might have manifested the anxiety felt by the traditional elite toward the up-and-coming bourgeois class.

In Guadeloupe, tableware could have had many of the same powers. Wealthy households, in particular, frequently used coordinated ceramics when sharing foods and drinks together. Perhaps the extent of the service was proportional to the formality of the occasion. Matching services probably also reinforced self-fashioning and the displays of manners that were so crucial to performing one's identity in Creole society. Handling similar objects might have allowed the participants to feel more integrated as a group, especially when enslaved servers and other excluded bystanders were watching these events or simply were aware of them. In most cases, these gatherings seemed to be a display of both social solidarity and racial mastery as well as a symbolic reenactment of the colonial caste system. A table covered with plates and dishes and an abundance of food and drink might have accentuated the effect of sets and introduced the "aesthetics of surplus" that Hellman recognized. Because of their frequency, these gatherings were already by definition repetitive rituals, and they might have helped alleviate some deeper social anxiety. In Guadeloupe, this angst could have been provoked not only by other members of one's social group—for example, powerful colonial officials for elite planters—but also by other castes. Perhaps the tight control that masters exerted over their faiences, porcelains, and other refined ceramics was another manifestation of this angst. They kept them close to their living spaces and strictly reserved them for their own use, appearing not to trust their slaves with them.

These observations may help explain some of the tableware choices that Guadeloupeans made. At the very least, Creole families matched their services functionally with the foods they ate and aesthetically with their preferred faience style. In doing so, they developed a distinctly Creole art of the table as part of their ceramic culture.

CHAPTER SIX

For Healthy Bodies and Clean Houses

One day I had been taking a long walk in the sun, and returned so thirsty that all of the old stories about travelers suffering in waterless deserts returned to memory with new significance;—visions of simoons arose before me. What a delight to see and grasp the heavy, red, thick-lipped dobanne, the water-jar, dewy and cool with the exudation of the Eau-de-Gouyave which filled it to the brim,—toutt vivant, as Cyrillia says, "all alive"! There was a sudden scream,—the water-pitcher was snatched from my hands by Cyrillia with the question: "Ess ou lé tchoué cò-ou?—Saint Joseph!" (Did I want to kill my body?) . . . Then Cyrillia made me a little punch with sugar and rum, and told me I must never drink fresh-water after a walk unless I wanted to kill my body. In this matter her advice was good.

LAFCADIO HEARN, *TWO YEARS IN THE FRENCH WEST INDIES*

If the behavior of Lafcadio Hearn's servant Cyrillia in this story appears strange, her motives will become clear once Creole hygiene, health, and medicinal practices are explained. These themes help recontextualize the use of chamber pots, bidets, barber's bowls, soap dishes, drug pots, and foot-baths in Guadeloupe. The information gathered on these vessels reveals that Guadeloupeans developed different hygienic practices than their contemporaries in the metropole. Personal appearance mattered in the colonies, because social rank was not necessarily dictated by birth, as it was in France, and could be established instead through clothing and manners (Boucher 2008: 138). The local beliefs about medicine and health also help explain why Guadeloupeans developed different standards of cleanliness. Exploring the principles of Guadeloupe's folk medicine requires briefly revisiting the use of some ceramics presented earlier, such as terrines, as well as previous themes, like use of water and eating and drinking habits.

Chamber Pots (*Pots de chambre, Vases de nuit*)

The 2,113 chamber pots listed in the inventories were present in 10 percent of the poorest households, 14 percent of the middling ones, and 38 percent of the wealthier houses (figure 1.1). These numbers are somewhat misleading because they do not account for the reality of the utilization of these objects. One of the pots was an expensive porcelain piece that was not in active use and was kept with the tableware. Five others were appraised as part of a piece of wooden furniture that cost a great deal more than the pots themselves. Two examples were stored in an attic and reserved for the treatment of illnesses. Last but not least, 2,047 additional pots were salable merchandise kept in merchants' houses. The vessels that were inventoried as individual objects and were possibly in active use represented less than 3 percent of the total sample.

On the other hand, chamber pots were not rare at the sites. The collections included 35 sherds and 19 different vessels distributed among most of the contexts. Many were made of glazed coarse earthenware, a few of faience and a couple of whiteware or faience fine (figure 6.1). This corroborated the information in the inventory documents: out of the 273 vessels described by material, 90 percent were in coarse earthenware and 8 percent in faience.

In general then, the inventories yielded reliable data on material composition but not the quantity of chamber pots. The inventory of Bernier's inn is an instructive example: the four chamber pots listed were part of a set of ceramics that Bernier had sold to someone and was temporarily storing in the office. Meanwhile, there were no recorded chamber pots in his seven guest rooms, even in the ones that were being actively rented. Yet the excavation of the Auberge du Sauvage Inn in France yielded 43 chamber pots and demonstrated that each guest room was equipped with its own vessel, even though there were also outdoor privies (Goy 1995). At Bernier's, it seems that the guests' chamber pots were either overlooked or ignored during the inventory process.

The inventories recorded brand-new pots or pots that were not in use at the time of the notary's visit. The vessels that were part of large pieces of furniture were also difficult to ignore. Mentions of single pots in use, however,

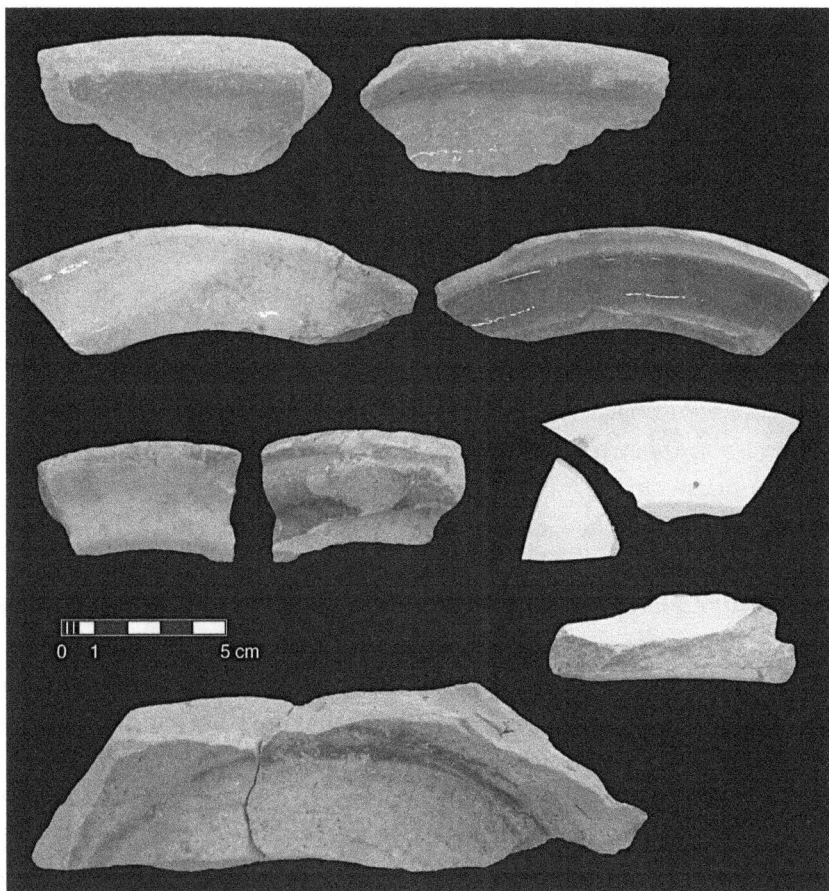

Figure 6.1. Chamber pots. *Top*: coarse earthenware rims with orange, white, and red slip. *Middle left*: coarse earthenware rim with white slip, green lead glaze, and a mark where the handle broke off. *Middle right*: faience fine or whiteware rim. *Bottom left*: coarse earthenware base with red-on-white slip. *Bottom right*: faience base. Photograph by author.

are scarce. Perhaps these pots were not to be inventoried, so notaries and appraisers turned a blind eye to their presence. Alternatively, they might have been taken out of rooms or hidden from view before the inventory started. The proclivity to ignore chamber pots was not confined to Guadeloupe. At Place-Royale in Quebec a similar discrepancy was evident between the documentary and archaeological evidence. Nicole Genêt (1980: 25) stated that the faience models were rare in the inventories: her footnote cited only two examples for the entire eighteenth century. Yet her analysis of the archaeological collections identified at least 11 faience and 12 English delftware vessels that were almost complete. For the coarse earthenware, the 77 inventories consulted by Camille Lapointe and Richard Lueger (1997: 214) yielded a single chamber pot, which represented 0.1 percent of their entire object sample. Meanwhile, Paul-Gaston L'Anglais (1994: 311) synthesized the results of the archaeology conducted at Place-Royale and concluded that ceramic chamber pots in general seemed "very popular" in both the seventeenth and eighteenth centuries.

This cultural blindness probably affected French inventories in much the same way. In Toulouse, chamber pots were nearly absent from the documentary evidence before the eighteenth century, even though coarse earthenware types existed by the mid-sixteenth century, as evidenced in archaeological collections (Arcangeli 2000: 41, 158). In Paris and in Guadeloupe the identical percentage of inventories listed chamber pots—16.5 percent of the sample in both cases—suggesting that the same phenomenon was probably at play there as well (Pardailhé-Galabrun 1988: 363).[1] It seems that historical sources do not reveal the frequency of use of these objects and that archaeological data are more accurate.

In Guadeloupe the inventory documents were useful in ascribing a provenance to the coarse earthenware models: 100 percent of the 250 vessels for which such information was recorded came from Provence. This corresponded to the tentative attribution of a vessel in the assemblages (figure 6.1, middle left, with green lead-glazed rim).

In the eighteenth century, the coarse earthenware models were appraised at 13 sols on average, and those of faience at 50 sols. The porcelain chamber pot stored with tableware was a luxurious oddity and was worth much more, at 480 sols. Although faience models were more valuable, they appeared in as many poor and middling households as the coarse earthenware versions did. Some coarse earthenware models also belonged to wealthy households. Perhaps material selection was a matter of personal choice.

Chamber pots constituted the most affordable solution for toileting needs out of all the options listed in the inventories. Ceramics had little competition from other materials, given that there was only one pewter pot in the entire sample—it came with a mahogany commode that was fabricated either in England or one of its colonies. Some chamber pots had a "support made of oak," a lid, or an accompanying commode called a chaise de commodité. The last cost around 15 livres if it was made of local wood and twice as much if it was of mahogany. A few households owned less fancy commodes called *chaises percées,* which would in theory be used in combination with a chamber pot and which were worth a lot less, between 2 and 5 livres. Most of these commodes belonged to wealthy families. The total percentage of houses so equipped was quite low in Guadeloupe, at 5 percent of the sample versus close to 30 percent in Paris (Pardailhé-Galabrun 1988: 363).

The individuals who found these objects useful often bought more than one. In some cases, each commode was obviously reserved for a particular member of the household. For example, one was used by the couple who owned the house and the other either by the man's father or by a female relative who lived in the home. A widower kept the simplest model for himself and placed two fancier ones—one of which might have belonged to his deceased wife—in an upstairs room that acted as the library and a parlor for receiving guests. Finally, in the household of Jacques Charousset, a mixed-race trader in Basse-Terre, and his partner Marie Rose, apparently a free woman de couleur, the commode was shared but each individual had a separate chamber pot.

Though chamber pots were present until the 1830s, the use of commodes was confined to the 1770s and 1780s. Starting in the early nineteenth century, households with sufficient means probably built indoor or outdoor privies instead.

Usually, chamber pots were stored in bedrooms or in nearby galleries, but a few appeared in more unexpected places. In particular, an inventory listed a faience pot in a small room next to the office that was furnished only with a small bed and two clothes irons. Given the location and sparse furnishing, this room was likely occupied by one of the house slaves. Was the faience chamber pot for the slave's own use, or was it merely kept there until one of the masters asked for it? Two other chamber pots were found in a space where slaves worked; namely, in a coffee-drying shed amongst some tools. Storing them there would be impractical if someone in the house still needed them, so either they were being recycled for coffee-related tasks or they had been given to the slaves for their own use. Finally, in two houses, chamber pots that were described as being for "sick people" were stored in attics, indicating that their use was specialized and sporadic.

Chamber pots in use had to be emptied and rinsed on a regular basis, which must usually have been one of the repetitive and thankless chores left to female house slaves. In her novel about early twentieth-century Guadeloupe, Arlette Blandin-Pauvert (1986: 88) described "a procession" of women going to the seashore in the evenings to empty and clean their "Thomases."[2] Women dumping chamber pots in the sea, rivers, or canals early in the morning or late at night is an established trope of modern French Caribbean literature.[3]

Seven wealthy households each owned a bidet (see figure 1.1), which corresponded to 5 percent of the inventory sample compared to an estimated rate of ownership of 7.5 percent in Paris (Pardailhé-Galabrun 1988: 357). In both places, these objects belonged to the elite. In Guadeloupe, some of the wealthiest individuals represented in the inventories owned bidets, including the merchant-surgeon Antoine Belost, two traders, and three sugar planters. Compared to chamber pots and commodes, bidets were relatively new innovations. They arrived in France from Italy during the sixteenth century but only gained popularity in the early eighteenth century when they became a source of modern comfort and refinement for French aristocrats (Ashenburg 2007: 151). The most prestigious cabinetmakers started making very elaborate models with mechanical hiding systems and expensive materials (Figeac 2007: 231).

A bidet consisted of a wooden seat that held, and might help hide, a kidney-shaped or oblong basin. The basin was usually made of faience but was sometimes fashioned from pewter or silver. Basins could be ordered directly from potteries as part of faience services, as demonstrated by the wedding order of the duc de Richelieu in 1734 (Peyre 2001). His purchase included plates, dishes, coolers, a sauceboat, a *surtout* (decorative centerpiece), and a bidet. Both men and women used bidets for cleaning their genitals and for giving douches and enemas. Some bidets contained a small drawer or a box where one could store associated accessories, such as flasks and syringes.

The information recorded in Guadeloupean inventories tells a similar story. Bidets were found in the bedrooms of ladies, in rooms used by men, and in bedrooms shared by couples. Some households had several and kept an additional one in a small closet or a guest bedroom. Three entries specifically noted the presence of faience basins. Bidets were appraised at a wide range of values—between 8 livres 5 sols and 66 livres—depending on their condition and degree of refinement. The two examples that came with a syringe were the most expensive. In most instances, the bidet was in proximity to a commode or other piece of furniture used for toiletries, like a dressing table.

A total of 34 barber's bowls (*plats à barbe*) appeared in 20 houses (figure 1.1). They were more numerous in affluent households, showing up in 6 percent of poor houses, 10 percent of middling ones, and 24 percent of wealthy ones. In total, 14 percent of households were so equipped, which was slightly higher than the 10 percent figure reported for Paris (Pardailhé-Galabrun

1988: 360). A lot of these households also had a razor, which was recorded in 7 percent of the total sample. In Guadeloupe, when razors and their accessories, such as cases and sharpening stones, were taken into account on top of the bowls, the share of houses so equipped was still higher, jumping to 21 percent.

Guadeloupean men who shaved likely had similar options to their counterparts in Paris: they could shave at home, using these tools with the help of a servant; go to a professional barber, such as the wigmaker Jean-Bernard Poudensan de la Grange in Basse-Terre; or have someone with shaving equipment come to their house (Pardailhé-Galabrun 1988: 360). The Martiniquais planter Pierre Dessalles, for example, usually shaved at home but also asked a barber to come to him when he needed a hairpiece (Dessalles and Frémont 1980: entry for August 21, 1844). Using a barber's bowl was a two-man job. When no barber was present, Dessalles would need the help of a servant to shave him or hold the basin while he shaved himself.

Comparing the percentage of homes with shaving objects in Guadeloupe and in Paris revealed that more Guadeloupean men had the option to shave at home and that Creole men were meticulous in their grooming practices. Their shaving equipment was fairly refined. One of the most complete shaving kits included not only a barber's bowl but also a pot of unidentified material that the inventory referred to as a *coquemar*.[4] Another set had a small boxed soap and sponge, some little flasks, and some undetermined cases. A third was accompanied by four boxes, a large sharpening stone, and a locking razor case that was missing its leather, its sharpening stone, and its scissors. Another locking razor case was used in tandem with a barber's bowl and a soap box.

With regard to barber's bowls, an important difference with Paris was that there they also came in copper alloy, whereas the entire sample in Guadeloupe was ceramic. All were in faience, except for a single porcelain example. The average appraisal of these faiences was 38 sols, which was slightly less than for the faience chamber pots. As expected, the porcelain object was worth twice as much as the most expensive faience, 180 sols versus 90, and plain faiences tended to be cheaper—they were appraised at 20 and 30 sols.

Even though they were not particularly expensive compared to other hygiene-related ceramics, barber's bowls occupied a niche: they represented the accessory of choice for well-groomed eighteenth-century white men. First, unlike razors, bowls fell out of favor in the nineteenth century and were most concentrated in the inventories of the 1770s. As a rule, there was one vessel per household and it was kept with the man's clothes and other personal items, usually in his bedroom. Analyzing the marital status of these individuals, about 16 percent of single men and 18 percent of men who were or had been married owned a barber's bowl. These percentages are nearly equal, yet single men tended to be much less well off than married ones—16 percent of inventories of single men were classified in the wealthy group, compared to 39 percent for married men. In fact, some single men stretched their finances to buy a barber's bowl, even though they did not have many other material possessions. Furthermore, in 8 instances, or 40 percent of the inventories that listed a bowl, the same individuals who used a barber's bowl also owned other stylish male accessories, such as tobacco boxes or watches, and thus exhibited a concern with being fashionable. Finally, although this sample was minuscule, neither of the two hommes de couleur whose possessions were inventoried in the eighteenth century used a bowl.

The only identifiable barber's bowl in the archaeological collections was a Dutch delftware decorated in the Wan-Li style (figure 6.2), which is usually dated from the second quarter of the seventeenth century (Ray 2000:

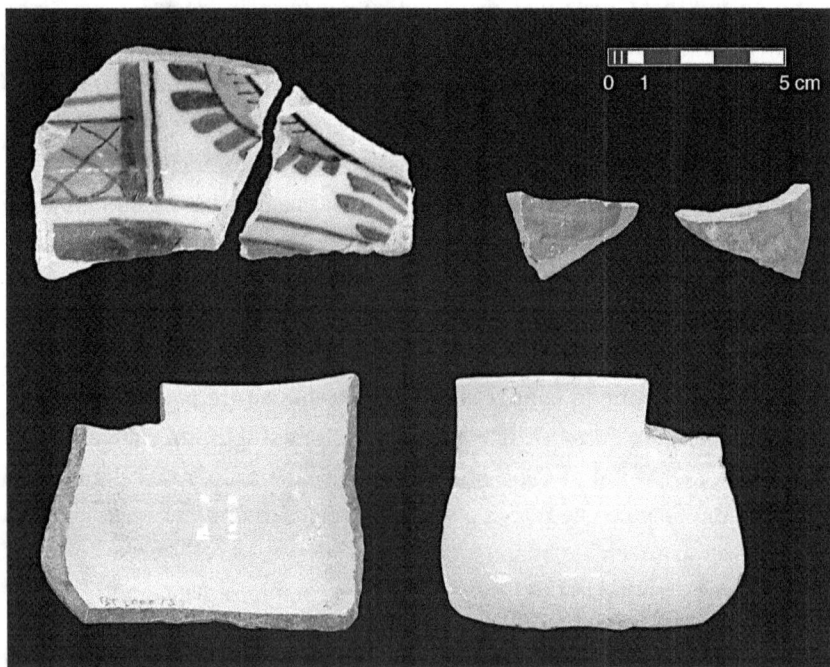

Figure 6.2. *Top left*: rim of a Dutch tin-glazed earthenware barber's bowl decorated in the Wan-Li style (blue and black). *Top right*: seventeenth-century coarse earthenware *albarelle* (drug pot) with green lead glaze on white paste. *Bottom*: faience fine pillbox. Photograph by author.

8). Given that this vessel came from Fort Houël, it could have belonged to one of the island's early officials, even Charles Houël himself. This would fit with the habits of the island elite in the frontier era, as described by Philip Boucher (2008: 138). Their wealth and military rank, more than their birth, determined their social position. As a result, they took great care with their appearance and wore fashionable clothing, such as Dutch shirts, cravats, serge breeches embroidered with gold and silver, plumed hats, ribbons, and Genoese lace, while their wives wore taffeta and satin dresses. The archaeological evidence from Fort Houël also demonstrates that they liked to use imported and nicely decorated barber's bowls to shave themselves. In doing so, they might have started a tradition that fashionable Guadeloupean men would still be following a century and a half later.

Shaving seemed to have been a common practice in the colonies. Outside of Guadeloupe, faience barber's bowls have been found at both the Perthuis and Estèbe houses at Place-Royale and at the Habitation de Champlain in Quebec (Genêt 1980: 118–21). The bowls that could be identified were faiences decorated in the Nevers style, but the others also seemed to be French made. Paul-Gaston L'Anglais (1994: 311) stated that a professional barber worked in Quebec City as early as 1660. He also quoted a visitor to Canada in the mid-eighteenth century who commented that every man shaved there, "men of quality" as well as commoners.[5]

The inventories sometimes recorded soap being packed in small boxes, but there was no ceramic object associated with it. Soap dishes, however, were present in the most recent assemblages at 28 Rue Amédée Fengarol (figure 1.1). The site yielded two different faience fine models decorated with blue transfer-printed floral patterns (figure 6.3). Several prominent faience fine potteries in France, such as Sarreguemines and Lunéville, produced oblong soap dishes.

The documents record bar soap in 12 percent of the sample, including 67 percent of the merchant shops, starting in the 1770s. There are no readily available data that would allow for comparison with other places, yet the rate of possession seems quite high, especially since bar soaps in use were considered perishable goods "in consumption" and were therefore rarely inventoried. Soap was indeed among the first commodities imported to the Antilles in large quantities: as much as 50 cases of it, worth 30,000 livres, arrived between 1666 and 1670 (Satineau 1928: 204). In 1775, the merchant Pierre Mottel alone kept a stock of 2,290 pounds of soaps packed in 47 cases.

When bar soap appeared in domestic contexts, it was often part of a shav-

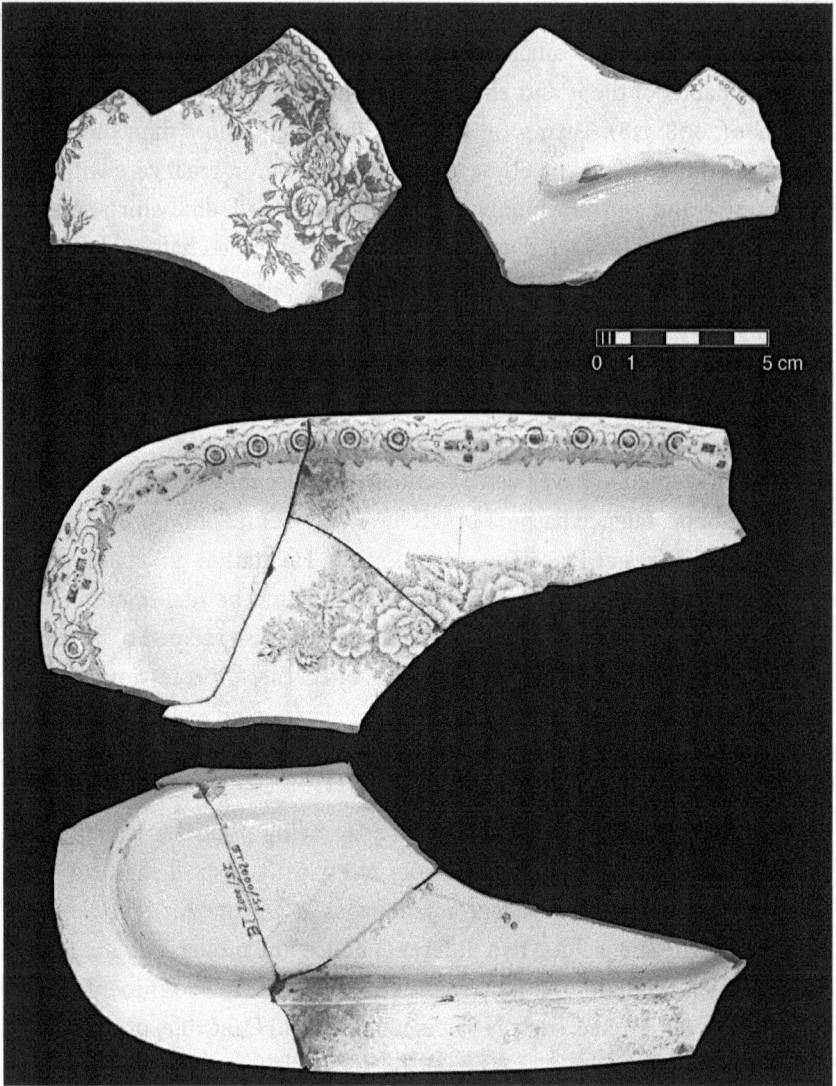

Figure 6.3. Blue transfer-printed faience fine soap dishes. Photograph by author.

ing kit, which confirmed that some soap was used for grooming. Moreover, the innkeeper Bernier possessed five bars that he kept next to his clothes and other personal items rather than with a shaving set. These data were significant because bath soap was very rare before the end of the nineteenth century and in general served as a cosmetic item for noble ladies (Ashenburg 2007: 225). In Guadeloupe, another piece of soap was located in an office among the tableware, food reserves, and some domestic equipment such as clothing irons. This case demonstrated that soap was used in housecleaning chores as well, which was less unusual. Most soap produced before the end of the nineteenth century was used to wash clothes and floors (Ashenburg 2007: 32, 223).

The soap dishes found at 28 Rue Amédée Fengarol were designed for holding bath soap. Even if they dated from the late nineteenth or early twentieth centuries—as some of the faiences fines from the same context did—the fact that they were found in a middling household reaffirmed the importance of soap to Guadeloupeans.

Creole Cleanliness

Hygiene-related objects played an important role in Guadeloupe, although they were less abundant than other categories of ceramics. Guadeloupeans owned chamber pots and bidets in similar percentages as their peers in the metropole, and used even more barber's bowls. Soap was imported in quantity, and soap dishes showed up in nineteenth-century middling households.

These data are confirmed by an analysis of other hygienic practices that did not involve ceramics. In particular, the frequency of bathtubs in probate inventories was notable. Annick Pardailhé-Galabrun (1988: 357) reported that only 3 percent of Parisian households after 1750 owned one. In Guadeloupe, bathtubs (*baignoires*) appeared in 16 houses (11 percent). They were closely associated with another object identified as a canot, originally meaning a dugout canoe but extended to refer to an elongated tub. Thirty-two inventories (22 percent) listed a canot, but only eight of these objects were actually for bathing. Others were dugout tree trunks utilized for processing coffee (7 cases) or sugar (4 cases). In addition, some canots located in kitchens were used to prepare manioc flour (5 cases) or wash laundry (3 cases). A few entries used *bathtub* and *canot* interchangeably, describing a canot as "shaped like a bathtub," referring to "bathtubs" for processing manioc or doing the laundry, or identifying bathtubs in homes as canots. In total, 14 houses had either a bathtub or canot reserved exclusively for human bathing, which still amounted to 10 percent of the sample, a rate three times higher than in Paris.

This suggests that Creole men and women took more baths than their contemporaries in the metropole. Because she married a world-famous historical figure, one Martiniquais woman had her personal hygiene habits recorded by historiographers and can corroborate these findings. Marie-Josèphe Rose Tascher de la Pagerie—who would come to be known as Joséphine, the wife of Napoleon Bonaparte—was born in Martinique and was reared there from 1763 to 1779. Both she and Napoleon were known to have an especial fondness for hot and fragrant baths, which manifested in the lavish bathrooms that graced all of their houses (Ashenburg 2007: 154; Stamelman 2006: 55–57). Joséphine even supported the French soap industry (Stamelman 2006: 57). Napoleon had a skin condition that was relieved by taking long baths, but it is unclear whether or not Joséphine first suggested he do so. In any case, based on the analysis of Guadeloupean inventories, the fact that Joséphine was Creole and was particular about her hygiene does not appear to be a coincidence.

Another indication that bathtubs were important to Guadeloupeans was that several examples in the sample were manufactured locally. These models were simple, based on the local dugout canoes, and made from the same tree, a large local species called *gommier blanc* (*Dacryodes excelsa*). As would be expected, these wooden bathtubs tended to be less valuable than imported ones, being appraised at between 3 and 41 livres versus up to 200 livres for imported copper models. Bathtubs were more frequent in wealthy houses, but became more common in poor and middling households during the nineteenth century.

People who either could not afford a local canot or had no space for it in their house could still bathe in rivers and in Guadeloupe's hot and cold springs. Hot springs were so numerous than no fewer than 10 spas existed on the island by the early twentieth century (Jennings 2002: 251). Perhaps the custom of bathing and washing outdoors explained in part why so few Guadeloupeans kept washbasins and pitchers in their bedrooms. In modern Guadeloupe, Catherine Benoît (2000: 175) remarked that elderly people in particular continued washing themselves in their backyards, even after their homes were equipped with an indoor bathroom.

Some travelers to the Antilles wrote that bathing was a regular pastime among their hosts (Montlezun 1818: II.100). In late-eighteenth-century Saint-Domingue, Baron Alexandre-Stanislas Wimpffen's (1993: 113) routine was to bathe at noon, just before lunch. The planter Pierre Dessalles started taking regular sea and river baths in 1842 to improve his health. He also claimed that these swims were a welcome distraction, especially when followed by a picnic (Dessalles and Frémont 1980: entry for July 12, 1842). Almost a century later, Anne Querillac (1931: 104–5) reported that bathing outings were ideal occasions for eating a calalou soup prepared on-site by servant cooks. At the Bains Jaunes hot springs near Basse-Terre, planks were laid across the basin so that bathers could eat while they floated in the water. Eugène Edouard Boyer-Peyreleau (1823: 1.122) further explained that the climate of the Antilles demanded a greater standard of cleanliness and that Creoles of all classes behaved accordingly. In contrast to the poor in Europe (Ashenburg 2007: 229–61; Vigarello 1985: 159), slaves were praised for their remarkable hygienic habits. In Saint-Domingue, Médéric-Louis-Élie Moreau de Saint-Méry (1797–98: I.43) noted that female slaves, in particular, took frequent baths in rivers or in water that they collected from rain or from wells. In addition, workers always washed their hands and faces after they ate, and female slaves used pieces of "soapy vine" to keep their teeth "healthy and white."

Nineteenth-century Creole households had access to the latest bathroom technologies. While he was visiting one of his daughters at her plantation in Martinique, Pierre Dessalles recorded that the bathtub had taps and received running water from the nearby canal (Dessalles and Frémont 1980: entry for November 17, 1840). In the inventory sample from 1833, one house was also equipped with a modern washstand called a lavabo. Yet whereas bathrooms started to appear in Paris after 1750, such rooms did not exist until much later in Guadeloupe (Pardailhé-Galabrun 1988: 356–58). In Paris, when an elite household invested in a fancy copper bathtub, they usually set it up in a separate space that they decorated with care. In Guadeloupe, bathtubs were kept in various parts of the house—including in galleries—but were never in a dedicated space. Bathrooms started to appear only much later, in smaller numbers, and in a particular Creole vernacular form as an outbuilding near the water-storage shed or the kitchen, rather than as an indoor room (Desmoulins 2006: 206).

The absence of indoor bathrooms in colonial Guadeloupe could be interpreted as an outcome of its social organization and reliance on slavery. The historian Elizabeth M. Collingham (2001: 174–77) observed that in nineteenth-century Europe the trend was toward having more personal and bodily privacy in homes. Within bourgeois households, bathing became a very private activity that excluded the presence of others and was confined to the bathroom. This evolution was made possible by the spread of indoor plumbing. Following Georges Vigarello (1985), Collingham characterized these new places as "self-sufficient spheres." Meanwhile, in colonial India the exact opposite was true—and not because colonists in India were less clean than their British counterparts. Yet bathing spaces remained "backwards" and open to the gaze of others. Collingham attributed this difference to the fact that servants were still needed to fill and empty the bathtub, and to empty and clean the "thunderbox."[6] One of Collingham's (2001: 175) British historical sources even remarked that in India "servants . . . stand for what is represented by water pipes and by sanitary systems at home." Having servants to help one dress and undress, to pour water, to scrub one's back, or to give a massages was the norm for the British in India. This meant that bathrooms could not become private spaces.

The circumstances were similar in the Antilles. Wealthy planters like Pierre Dessalles could rely on the constant help of personal servants, and others simply depended on their house slaves. Slaves could empty and clean chamber pots, heat water in the kitchen, and assist with every part of the toilet, including washing, shaving, and dressing. Their constant presence precluded the development of bodily privacy for their masters, which made private bathroom spaces quite irrelevant as long as slavery existed. Today, in contrast, luxurious indoor bathrooms are popular in Creole houses and can be found even in modest houses (Benoît 2000: 175).

Principles of Creole Health and Folk Medicine

The anthropologist Alice Peeters (1982: 23–25) sees Antillean cleanliness as a tradition inherited from the colonial period, and as one that stemmed from medical and spiritual beliefs as well as hygienic concerns. Since some Creole therapies were linked to the use of ceramic objects, these points warrant a quick review.

In early modern France, cleanliness was attained not by washing oneself with soap and water but by changing clothes and by exhibiting perfectly white undergarments (Vigarello 1985). Putting on an immaculate shirt was cleansing because it helped remove sweat, grease, and dirt from the body without endangering it through exposure to water, which was considered a health risk. Personal care was also achieved through an array of dry practices, such as brushing or changing one's clothes, wiping one's face and arms with a dry cloth, spraying powders in place of using soaps and shampoos, and applying perfume or cosmetics.

People shied away from water because of its perceived power to penetrate the skin and the belief that it could have dire consequences on health (Vigarello 1985: 15–29). Human skin was not thought of as a protective envelope but as a porous sieve that water could percolate through and enter the body. Doctors believed that when people were submerged, they absorbed all manner of contagious elements and their organs became dangerously bloated. A bath was thought not only to alter the state of the body but also to leave it "open" to the surrounding air and to airborne diseases. Bathing was reserved as a rare therapeutic practice to be done in a controlled setting, and it was never a benign activity. People who had just bathed were to take extreme precautions and were advised to remain indoors afterwards.

During the first half of the eighteenth century, metropolitan attitudes toward water and bathing evolved, and competing social models coexisted. At the time they started building cabinets and bathrooms, aristocrats also discovered the sensual pleasure of taking warm baths, which they believed would help balance humoral fluxes (Vigarello 1985: 105–24). After 1750 some hygienists also began to praise the invigorating effect of a cold bath (Vigarello 1985: 125–43). Cold water was supposed to be a tonic that shocked the body, reinforced its fibers, and stimulated its vital defense. Across the English Channel, the British heartily embraced this philosophy and launched the new fashion of sea bathing (Ashenburg 2007: 125–39).

As the century ended, progress was made in using water for bodily hygiene, starting with the elite. Fancy public baths opened in Paris in the 1780s, and early-nineteenth-century hygienic treatises promoted the use of water and soap (Vigarello 1985: 169–84). Among the popular classes change was generally slower, although Nicole Pellegrin (2005: 143) pointed out the existence of widespread and perhaps little reported separate hygienic practices, such as river bathing. This activity apparently remained popular among the lower class in France. Taking a daily bath indoors, however, was still unimaginable for most people in the 1880s (Vigarello 1985: 239).

Compared to their European contemporaries, Guadeloupeans had a very different relationship with water. As early as the second half of the eighteenth century, the wealthiest Guadeloupeans were taking baths at home. Bathing in rivers, springs, or even the sea was a ubiquitous activity. In addition, city dwellers of the late eighteenth century might have been able to visit bathhouses—there is evidence that one such place was open in Basse-Terre at least from the 1780s to 1860 (Desmoulins 2006: 75; Pérotin-Dumon 2000: 776). In addition, hydrotherapies were part of the alternative medical practices used in the Antilles very early on. Springs and highlands were seen as healthy refuges against the tropical climate and its possible bad effects on the body (Jennings 2002). Both Jean-Baptiste Labat and Jean-Baptiste Du Tertre raved about the water cures offered in Guadeloupe (Eymeri 1992: 200–201; Jennings 2002: 232). In Saint-Domingue, thermal or mineral waters were often used to treat sick slaves: local surgeons would open an office near a spring and receive ailing slaves in residence (Debien 1974: 325).

Modern Creole folk medicine confirms that Guadeloupeans embraced the curative properties of water. Scholars who have studied the question state that Antillean folk medicine was born during the colonial period; Christiane Bougerol (1983: 91–98) traced its presence in the French Antilles back to the seventeenth-century writings of Jean-Baptiste Du Tertre. Folk cures hinge on the notions of hot and cold being opposite and having opposing effects on the body (Benoît 2000; Bougerol 1983; Eymeri 1992; Peeters 1979). In this view, good health results from balancing the influence of extremes and keeping oneself at the correct symbolic "temperature." This temperature is thought to be influenced by a variety of factors, from the foods people eat—some foods provide a heating effect, others a cooling one—to the time of day—the body is usually warmer at night. Sudden transitions are judged to be dangerous, especially going abruptly from a hot state to a cold one. The reverse, a change from cold to hot, is felt to be less harmful because cold can provoke sudden ruptures in the body whereas heat acts more gradually. Heat only becomes detrimental in excess when it brings on an "inflammation" (Benoît 2000: 70; Bougerol 1983: 22–26). People are therefore thought to be extremely vulnerable when in a heated state, because they are most susceptible to rapid cooling. Actions that take one abruptly from a hot state to a cold one are called "imprudences" (Benoît 2000: 68–69; Bougerol 1983: 16–22; Peeters 1979: 131). Prevention is the most common strategy for remaining healthy, and the main prophylaxis is to avoid all imprudences. A specific imprudence called the "pleurisy" is believed to be especially deadly because it penetrates deep inside the body, causing swelling and turning the blood into water or ice (Benoît 2000: 68–69; Bougerol 1983: 161).

This belief system shares some similarities with other folk medicines that developed throughout the Americas (Benoît 2000: 72–78; Bougerol 1983: 69). Many systems have integrated the cold/hot dualism, but Christiane Bougerol (1983: 70) thinks that the extreme imbalance between the perceived potency of hot and cold, in favor of the latter, is typical of the French Antilles. Most of these traditions are based on local variations of the humoral theory of Hippocrates (Benoît 2000: 72–78; Bougerol 1983: 69; Peeters 1979: 130). In the French Antilles phlegm has disappeared from the current belief system, and the two humors left are bile and blood, the latter being by far the most important one. The state of one's blood is felt to have a direct impact on one's health. Blood that is heated can become thick and dirty, requiring purification, whereas cold blood is thought to be so thin and watery that it no longer supplies the body adequately (Benoît 2000: 53–55). A blow or a fall is believed to cause blood to stagnate at the wound site, and strong negative emotions, such as anger, depression, or sadness, cause it to rise to the head and no longer circulate through the body.

As is often the case in folk medicine, religion and magic have key roles. Creole diseases are exogenous, but some are natural (for example, the ones brought about by a humoral imbalance) whereas others are "sent" by witchcraft (Benoît 2000: 65). Remedies are thus based on both practical and magical therapies (Leti 2000; Lirus 1979: 44–46). A lot of preventative and curative treatments aim at "refreshing" the body and a few at heating it, with the common goal of restoring its balance (Benoît 2000: 71; Peeters 1979: 132). The "refreshing" precept applies outside of the body and extends to the immediate environment, in particular to houses and gardens. The home must be purified and kept very clean so that dirtiness, which is equated with evil influences, will not be able to harm its occupants (Benoît 2000: 78–79). A second ensemble of therapies focuses on closing off the body and reinforcing its envelope, which includes but is not limited to the skin (Benoît 2000: 79–80). In particular, traditional gold jewelry makes an excellent protective barrier (Benoît 2000: 82–83).

During the colonial period these folk medicine beliefs evidently coexisted with European medical practices (Bougerol 1983: 100–110; Debien 1974: 321–27). Surgeons outnumbered physicians in the colonies and were in charge of providing care for most of the population and their slaves (Weaver 2006: 33–37). Despite having a reputation for careerism, greed, and even ignorance surgeons did well for themselves, because planters needed them to keep the workforce healthy (Debien 1974: 326). At the end of the eighteenth century in Saint-Domingue, plantation account ledgers showed that health care trumped any other category of spending on slaves, including food. Surgeons could be hired to reside on the premises or to visit on a regular basis. In Guadeloupe sick slaves could also be sent to recover at a surgeon's office or hospital (Vanony-Frisch 1985: 130).

Surgeons were expensive, so planters looked for alternatives. Many tried to treat their slaves themselves. They bought medical guides, imported drugs from the metropole, or even consulted doctors abroad by mail. These practices helped promote a flurry of publications on slave diseases and treatments after the 1770s (Debien 1974: 480). They are also possibly illustrated in the inventory sample. Planter Étienne Guilloton did not belong to the medical profession yet owned a 20-volume dictionary of medical sciences along with several instruments for amputations and tooth extractions (ADG: Nesty, 2E 2/79, 8/4/1830). Furthermore, the planter Hurault de Gondrecourt converted one of the sheds on his sugar plantation into a "pharmacy" where he kept around 40 pots of different substances and drugs (ADG: Jaille, 2E 3/7, 6/14/1793).

Planters also did not hesitate to consult enslaved healers for their own and their workers' health needs (Debien 1974: 323). Karol Weaver (2006: 61–75) discovered that in Saint-Domingue these healers specialized in caring for wounds, reducing fevers, or dealing with scurvy. Her research also revealed that they were herbalists who fused their African medical knowledge with use of local plants as well as some therapies learned from the indigenous population. In addition, planters often put an elderly female slave in charge of the infirmary or of delivering basic care to the workers. Nicole Vanony-Frisch (1985: 94–95) described the profile of these women in Guadeloupe: they tended to be black Creole slaves (as opposed to mixed-race Creole or African-born slaves), to be in their fifties, and to be mothers. These female paramedics mostly acted as nurses, midwives, or *hospitalières* (Moitt 2001: 62–68; Weaver 2006: 41–43). Hospitalières, in particular, had some knowledge of both European and folk medicine. They received the instructions of plantation surgeons and were capable of assisting them (Weaver 2006: 46–48). Yet they could also administer "refreshing" teas while they waited for the surgeon to arrive (Moitt 2001: 66). Both these plantation paramedics and other enslaved healers drew on herbal remedies that might have been well known among the wider slave population (Weaver 2006: 65).

Apothecaries and Imported Drugs

Surgeons and doctors in the early modern era used therapies such as bloodletting, enemas, and drugs to purge the body. In principle, drugs were prepared and sold by apothecaries, who ranked below doctors and surgeons in the hierarchy of medical professions. In the colonies, however, surgeons often took on the role of apothecaries as well. This seemingly was the case in Guadeloupe, at least until real pharmacies opened toward the end of the eighteenth century (Pérotin-Dumon 2000: 594). In 1775, the office of surgeon Antoine Belost held 15 containers identified as *paubeaux,* as well as some smaller pots and flasks filled with drugs. Given that they were not inventoried in detail and that his widow declared all of the drugs were reserved for household use, it appears that Antoine Belost was not legally allowed to sell drugs to his customers. Nevertheless, their quantities and the fact that they were stored in the room where he received his patients suggested that he used them in his practice.

The pharmacy of surgeon André Campan (ADG: Chuche, 2E 3/75, 6/27/1780), inventoried in 1780, was run as a legal business and its stock compared favorably to the main pharmacy of the city about 25 years later (Pérotin-Dumon 2000: 861–62 published a complete list of the products it sold in 1804). The first impression was that Campan sold a hodgepodge of ingredients that came from all over the world. There were drugs such as opium; chemicals such as vitriol (sulfuric acid); *pierre infernale* (lunar caustic), a cauterizing agent made of fused nitrate silver; and a plethora of "salts," such as absinthe salts or martial (iron) salts. Also present were processed or dried plant parts, such as the flowers of violets and red poppies; hyacinth powder; a dye of gentian; a "tessitura" of rhubarb; cinchona (a source of quinine to combat malaria); ipecacuanha, a South American plant whose root was used as an emetic; and *terre du Japon* (catechu), a tonic and astringent agent obtained from the Asian tree *Acacia catechu*. Among animal or insect extracts were dried cochineal, which had many uses in Western medicine (Greenfield 2005: 83–84); a spirit of "deer antlers" that was supposed to be restorative; red coral; "eyes of crayfish," which probably referred to the "crayfish stones" that in Sweden were recommended for heartburn and for removing foreign bodies from under the eyelid (Swahn 2004). The list of ingredients also included such preparations as a scented "Commander's balm" and a balm called *baume de copahou* that was made with copaiba (an oleoresin from the *Copaifera* genus of Amazonian trees).[7]

Some of these elements must have had a mainly symbolic value rather than true medicinal powers. Several of them—the red poppies, red coral, catechu, cochineal, a "red precipitate," and even cinchona to a certain extent—have in common the color red, a color imbued with many meanings throughout human history (Greenfield 2005). Red substances must have been considered beneficial in the Antilles, resonating with the preeminence of blood in folk beliefs about health. Other substances, such as cinchona or ipecacuanha, have active ingredients that could have a measurable effect on diseases. In total, André Campan had access to an impressive list of 68 processed ingredients known to early modern medicine. In addition, an inventory from 1831 mentioned a preparation called *rob Giraudeau de*

Saint-Gervais (syrup from Giraudeau de Saint-Gervais). This was a treatment for syphilis marketed by a French doctor called Jean Giraudeau, from the town of Saint-Gervais, sometime after 1818. Apparently, medical professionals in Guadeloupe were able to stay abreast of the latest trends in the metropole.

The inventories did not describe the containers in which these ingredients or preparations were stored. Fortunately, the archaeological collections yielded some complementary data. A few sherds corresponded to an early type of drug pot called *albarelle* or *albarello* by French archaeologists (figure 1.1). A possible plain faience example was found at the Palais de Justice, and a green glazed coarse earthenware one at Fort Houël (figure 6.2). Since these items were made for holding drugs, the coarse earthenware models were usually glazed on both sides. At French urban sites, these vessels typically date to the sixteenth and seventeenth centuries (see Arcangeli 2000: 159 for Toulouse; Guilhot and Richard 1995: 214–15 for Lyon; and Henigfeld 2005: 228–29 for Strasbourg). Based on the measurements made in Paris by Fabienne Ravoire (2006: 156–58), the coarse earthenware albarelle found at Fort Houël would have been between 5 and 8 cm high, a relatively small model. Given that it was found together with a contemporaneous delftware barber's bowl, there is also a chance that this particular vessel contained an imported substance used for male grooming, such as a perfume.

The albarelle was replaced by a squatter form of drug pot that French archaeologists often call *pillulier* (pillbox) (figure 1.1). The base of a possible small pillulier made of faience was found at the Cathédrale. Another slightly bigger and almost complete example in faience fine came from 28 Rue Amédée Fengarol (figure 6.2). Both were plain. In sum, drug pots were not rare in Guadeloupe, given that there are hints of their presence at all four sites. Their typological evolution indicates that their use spanned a long period, from the seventeenth century to the late nineteenth century, which agrees with written sources.

Guadeloupean apothecaries were able to import many substances that belonged to the Western pharmacopeia, so it was significant that they did not sell a lot of local remedies. Very few ingredients at Campan's pharmacy seemed to have a local origin. According to an 1804 inventory of Basse-Terre's main pharmacy, spices were more prevalent there, and some (such as cinnamon), could have been produced locally. There was also some "Gayac," which was an indigenous tree. Nonetheless, most of the products seem to have been imported, just like at Campan's. In Saint-Domingue one of the common complaints against apothecaries was that they did not use the local plants and minerals, relying instead on imported remedies (Weaver 2006: 38).

Access to imported drugs was theoretically regulated and, in particular, denied to slaves after 1738 because of the fear of poisoning (Moitt 2001: 66; Weaver 2006: 38). In practice, rules like these were not convenient and not always enforced—as the case of Belost might have illustrated (Weaver 2006: 38). Yet they gave enslaved healers and other preparers of homemade remedies one more reason to turn to the local resources.

Folk Therapies and Ceramics

Some of these colonial drugs still appear in modern folk remedies: for instance, deer antlers and mercury enter into the composition of a protective potion called the *plombage* (Benoît 2000: 80) and of *beaume du commandeur* which is a recipe for a protective bath (182n148). Yet many more folk therapies make use of local ingredients, starting with an essential one, water.

In the Antilles water in general is seen as a protective element, whereas air is thought to be dangerous and transport diseases (Benoît 2000: 80; Boghen and Boghen 1972: 238). Antilleans place so much trust in water that this attitude at one point hampered progress in combatting schistosomiasis, an endemic disease caused by parasitic flukes that live in freshwater (Peeters 1982: 27–29). As long as water looks crystal clear, Antilleans are certain that it is pure and cleansing, even though it might be infected.

Water is used as a base and ingredient for preparing baths and teas, which along with massages are the most common forms of remedies in folk medicine (Benoît 2000; Boghen and Boghen 1972; Bougerol 1983, 1985; Leti 2000). Several types of water are recognized, each with its own properties. Holy water is a good defense against evil, as well as an ingredient for therapeutic baths to treat elephantiasis (Leti 2000: 25, 62–63). As early as the seventeenth century, Jean-Baptiste Labat (1722: II.458–59) noted its popularity amongst slaves. They would collect it in a gourd after mass and drink a few drops every morning for protection. Today, drinking holy water on New Year's Day is thought to give one yearlong health (Leti 2000: 62). Rainwater collected on Good Friday is said never to evaporate and to be a cure-all (169). Seawater is used in protective talismans and sea baths that help to "close" the body (38, 115). The sea and any standing water are considered "hot," whereas rain and rivers are classified as "cold" (Benoît 2000: 81; Leti 2000: 15). Some of the most effective baths combined three kinds of water: rainwater, seawater, and freshwater from a river (Benoît 2000: 81).

Water that has been in contact with the body or has been used to wash a house can be reused for harm and has to be disposed of with great care. Until recent times, water infused with soursop leaves was used to wash the dead then afterwards kept in a terrine and thrown behind the cortège during the funeral (Leti 2000: 118). If this water were poured around a house instead, the spirit of the deceased could return and haunt its occupants. Similarly, the liquid of the powerful baths called *bains démarrés* (water left over from housecleaning) should be thrown into a river or at a crossroads, so that diseases and evil are dispersed (Benoît 2000: 79; Leti 2000: 28). In some cases, such leftover water has to be reused to complete rituals (Leti 2000: 106). The water of some baths is transformed into teas or serves to rinse and protect the house. According to oral history, enslaved servants also kept the water used to wash their masters' pillows to gain some influence over them (Leti 2000: 61). They bottled it and buried it under the floor of their house or underneath a large stone outside.

Baths are taken to defend the house, not just the body, from bad influences (Benoît 2000: 182). Protective baths like the bains démarrés generally involve plants, soap, and spoken prayers (Benoît 2000: 81). In her compendium of magic beliefs, Geneviève Leti (2000: 25–29) also indicated that a host of other possible ingredients—such as vinegar, milk, medallions of Catholic saints, nails, or chalk—can be added, depending on the specific purpose of the bath.

Teas are both curative and prophylactic, and can help protect the body from bad influences by "purifying" and "cleaning" it from the inside (Benoît 2000: 72). Numerous plants used in making these remedies grow in the wild or in Creole gardens (Benoît 2000). In her study of Creole diseases and remedies, Christiane Bougerol (1983) listed 34 different species used for baths and no less than 107 used for therapeutic decoctions.

In short, Guadeloupean folk medicine uses many herbal and water-based therapies, and some common Creole prophylactic behaviors, such as cleaning the house or taking a bath, are also hygienic practices. Under these conditions, it may be unnecessary to distinguish between the two. For instance, were the daily baths that sitters gave to slave children on the plantation of Poyen de Sainte-Marie in Guadeloupe only for washing, or were they believed to provide the children with some magical protection as well (Gautier 1985: 206)? In terms of ceramics, this meant that some objects that had other primary purposes also had roles in therapeutic or magical practices.

Finally, a small category of objects that was entirely reserved for medical treatments also needs to be considered. Like baths, footbaths (*bains de jambes*) are common in Creole folk medicine (figure 1.1); for example, soaking one's feet in salted water and the grass called *pied à poule* (goosegrass, *Eleusine indica* (L.) Gaertn) "reheats" the body (Bougerol 1983: 162). Another footbath made with two bottles of spring water provides good protection against spells (Leti 2000). The ceramic containers in which such footbaths were taken occasionally appeared in the inventories. A "large coarse earthenware vase" stored in the office of the planter Pierre Guys in 1789 was used for "leg baths" (ADG: Dupuch, 2E 2/22, 11/10/1789). In 1830, the planter Pierre Guilloton also kept a "leg bath" in his bedroom right next to a terrine, a pitcher, and two chamber pots (ADG: Nesty, 2E 2/79, 8/4/1830). Given this unusual ceramic assemblage, it is possible that Guilloton was bedridden before he died and was treated with leg baths, among other things.

In addition, the planter Pierre Dessalles mentioned footbaths in his diary. In April 1841 he acquired one, along with a bathtub, for his house. A year later, leg baths were part of the regimen prescribed by the enslaved cook whom he consulted about his leg sores. His acquaintances were also familiar with this therapy: in February 1842 he paid a visit to a neighbor, Mrs. Bence, and found her sitting in the dark in her bedroom, soaking in a leg bath. Dessalles deduced that she was ill but could not determine the nature of her ailment. That he could not make a guess confirmed that leg baths had broader applications and were not used just as a topical treatment for wounds.

Footbaths do not seem to have been very expensive. The large coarse earthenware model recorded in the inventory sample cost only 3 livres in 1789, and Dessalles paid 110 francs in 1842 for both his footbath and bathtub. Footbaths were not entirely necessary, as any large container with a wide opening would do. Terrines or buckets could have been used as well. Perhaps only people who had frequent health problems bothered to buy a true leg bath, which would explain why they were not more abundant in the sample.

In a number of instances terrines, which are often associated with cooking, served in the domain of personal care. In three instances at least they were stored in the master's bedroom and were directly associated with other hygienic or therapeutic objects such as chamber pots and bathtubs. Moreover, modern publications describe terrines as objects that are mostly used for washing oneself (Beuze 1990: 42; De Roo Lemos 1979: 31). In 12 other instances, terrines were stored near the water reserve, which made them handy for doing household chores such as housecleaning or laundry. The washerwoman of merchant Jean Blanchet worked out of a small laundry in the courtyard that was very well equipped: among other things it had a table, a laundry tub, a barrel of charcoal, a water jar, three clothes irons, two pewter dishes, two large laundry baskets, another small basket, and five imported coarse earthenware terrines. In her study Nicole Vanony-Frisch (1985: 92–93) identified 24 washerwomen, two-thirds of whom belonged to merchant households in the cities, just like in the aforementioned case. Anne Pérotin-Dumon (2000: 554–55) also counted a total of 110 washerwomen in Basse-Terre, who mainly worked out of two rivers, the Rivière aux Herbes and the Rivière du Galion. Creole washerwomen were generally thought to be particularly skilled. Oral history (Debien 1974: 91) and historical sources (for example, Médéric-Louis-Élie Moreau de Saint-Méry cited in Peeters 1982: 25) reported that traders in French ports sent baskets of laundry to the Antilles because of the washerwomen's reputation. True or not, this anecdote was a compliment to the quality of their work. The historian Gabriel Debien (1974: 91) remarked that if Creole washerwomen had any particular knowledge, it mostly related to reserving the soap that they received for their work in order to resell it for a profit. They would replace it with cheaper local resources such as "soap vines," ashes, oranges, and lemons, which would lend a pleasant fragrance to the laundry. Similarly, when servants were getting ready to clean something in the house, they might have grabbed a terrine and prepared their own detergent mixture.

Modern Antillean folk medicine includes specific conceptions about which foods or drinks have a "heating" or "cooling" effect. Since individuals have more or less "heat" depending on their age, sex, and general health, they should eat different kinds of food to achieve balance, but the anthropologist Alice Peeters (1979) observed that there is not always consensus on exactly which foods are warm, cold, or refreshing. Disagreement arises in part because this quality is a cultural construct that does not depend on physical characteristics: for example, young coconut water is "refreshing," which fits with its actual hydrating qualities, but the substance considered most refreshing of all is manioc flour, a colonial-era staple. In Martinique at least, spices, rum, coconut, and salt are classified as hot foods (Peeters 1979). In general, cold items should be avoided at night, and some foods, like milk and green fruits, can also be dangerous because they carry "worms."

In Guadeloupe, a glass of rum is consumed ritually on many occasions; for example, during some types of agricultural work, throughout the day when friends meet, or during a wake (Rey-Hulman 1983). It is also traditionally chased down with a glass of cold water, probably to counterbalance its effect, since rum is "hot." The motto of agricultural workers and fishermen is "a little bit and often" (*peu et souvent*), a phrase they sometimes even say out loud after each drink. The gendarme Bonnemaison witnessed this practice in 1900: in all of the Guadeloupean homes he visited, he was welcomed with a glass of rum that was to be drunk at once and chased with a glass of cold water (Martin 2001: 90). In eighteenth-century Saint-Domingue, Médéric-Louis-Élie Moreau de Saint-Méry (1797–98: I.43) stated that slaves always finished their meal with a large glass of water. The visitor Alexandre-Stanislas Wimpffen (1993: 148) was led to believe that in the colonies it was healthier to drink water instead of pure or diluted wine. As it turned out, his host mostly wanted to save money on expensive imported wine, but the anecdote also implied that drinking water was less unusual in the Antilles than in Europe at the time.

The enslaved cooks and servants who prepared the foods and drinks for their masters could have incorporated these health precepts into their work. Perhaps they paid special attention to the way they cleaned and prepared foods, just as Guadeloupeans do today (Peeters 1982: 25): the bad parts are carefully cut out, fruits and vegetables are washed very well, and fish and meat are marinated with lime juice and garlic before they are fully cooked. If servants had any say, they might have tried to organize their workday around these principles, just as today household chores may be scheduled according to how much they heat the body. Cold chores, like washing the dishes or cleaning the house, are done in the morning, when the body is at its coldest state. Chores that have a heating effect, such as cooking and ironing, are done later, when the body is getting warmer. One must be careful to avoid the "imprudence" of doing a cold chore immediately after a warming chore.

Since body odor is thought to make one vulnerable to evil spirits (Peeters 1982: 27), slaves who were aware of these health principles might have washed themselves very regularly to protect themselves from evil influences as well as for reasons of hygiene. Alice Peeters (1982: 24) even suggested that the slave population tried to take one or two daily baths but did not cite her sources. Regardless, slaves could have bathed in the rivers, in vessels like terrines that they could temporarily appropriate and, in some instances, in the canots they used for agricultural or household chores and present in 13 percent of households.

House slaves who had any knowledge of local plants and folk medicine could also help prepare teas and baths for their masters. Given that they worked with local foods and plants, it is no surprise that some cooks were among the enslaved healers whom planters liked to consult. Although Karol K. Weaver (2006), who studied the population of enslaved healers in Saint-Domingue, did not expressly identify cooks' contributions, Dessalles's diary revealed one such case. The unnamed cook of his planter friend Louis Littée was also an "empiric" who treated Dessalles for leg sores in the winter and spring of 1840 and in the spring of 1842. As remedies, he prescribed leg baths, teas, and poultices of manioc flour, apparently with some success (Dessalles and Frémont 1980: entries for April 1, 1840 and March 12, 1842).

Unfortunately, historical sources tend to focus on cases when these kinds of behaviors led to suspicious deaths rather than healing. The waves of poisoning recorded in Saint-Domingue after 1750, as well as the many individual cases chronicled across the French Caribbean, confirm that slaves could secure drugs and poisons, even illegally (Moitt 2001: 143–45; Pluchon 1987). The juice extracted from bitter manioc was readily accessible and very potent if it was ingested quickly before it lost its power, as the suicide of a slave recorded by the doctor Jean-Baptiste Leblond (1813: 203) in Saint-Vincent demonstrated. The *brinvilier* (West Indian pinkroot, *Spigelia anthelmia* L.) and the *mancenillier* tree (manchineel, *Hippomane mancinella*) are two lethal local poisons (see, for example, Leti 2000: 135). In Guadeloupe and Martinique, the giant granadilla vine (*Passiflora quadrangularis* L.) is known for yielding a strong narcotic that can be deadly if just a fingertip's worth is spread on the rim of a drinking glass (Eymeri 1992: 196). Londa Schiebinger's (2004) detailed study of wild cassava and other abortifacients in the West Indies also showed that slaves knew to control their fertility with the help of local plants.

These drugs could be administered surreptitiously, especially in drinks. In most recorded cases, poison was delivered in herbal teas, coffee, chocolate drinks, or tafia (Moitt 2001: 143–45). When multiple individuals were targeted, water jars or wells could also be tainted (Debien 1974: 408). When he lived in Guadeloupe, the gendarme Bonnemaison was told that people who knew how to handle drugs could give small, repeated doses that would act more slowly but were also harder to detect (Martin 2001: 127).

In Guadeloupe, black nurses were accused of poisoning French soldiers in 1802 in support of slave revolts (Moitt 2001: 143). Plantation workers also apparently resorted to poison after slavery was reinstated and planters who had fled the island were thinking of returning (Dubois 2004: 357). Poison was used to signal to some of these men that they were not welcome. An important detail is that in most cases of fatal poisoning recorded throughout the French Caribbean, the targets were animals or other slaves (Moitt 2001: 141–42). As far as poisoning was concerned, then, it was advisable for everyone, not just the masters, to take some basic precautions. Some protective baths, teas, and other health-related behaviors like washing regularly must have helped alleviate these concerns.

It is possible that some protective or harmful rituals entailed marking pottery. In the archaeological collections, incisions appeared mostly on local coarse earthenware from three of the sites (figures 3.4 and 6.4). The marks were located on the outside, often on the base of the object. Whereas some could have been made before firing, others appear to have been incised after the ceramics were finished, which suggests that the users of the vessels made the marks. The most complete ones show a cross, three lines that joined to form a K-like figure, and an upside-down V. At 28 Rue Amédée Fengarol four out of a set of identical pitchers showed different marks at the base (figure 3.4).

Crosses, Xs, and other signs have been found in a number of archaeological contexts in South Carolina, and their meaning has been debated since the 1990s. In particular, they appear on stoneware vessels made by Dave, an enslaved African American potter who worked for the Landrum family in Edgefield, South Carolina, from the 1830s onward. J. W. Joseph (2011) analyzed the marks identified on Edgefield stoneware: they include Xs, crosses, and a cross-in-circle pattern called a Landrum cross. The marks are usually incised or stamped and are placed on highly visible parts of the vessels, such as the shoulder or the handle. More recently, a variety of incised, punctuated, rouletted, and drab-and-jab marks, as well as stamped Landrum crosses and a waffle-iron pattern have also been discovered on colonoware excavated at the slave settlement of Dean Hall, inside what appears to be a ceremonial area (Agha and Isenbarger 2011). This context predated the Edgefield pottery by about 20 years.

Studying marked colonoware bowls from several sites in South Carolina,

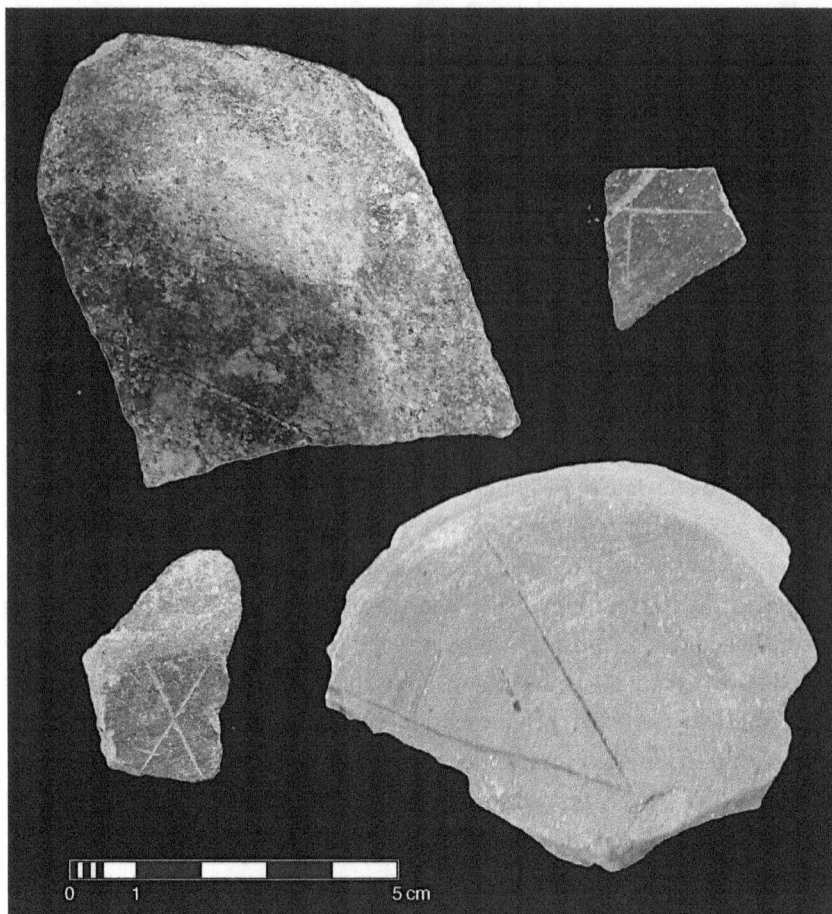

Figure 6.4. Incised marks on the bottoms of local coarse earthenware cookware and pitcher. Photograph by author.

Leland Ferguson (1999) interpreted the cross-in-circle pattern and its variations as Bakongo cosmograms (*dikenga*). Other authors have either agreed with his hypothesis and explored possible meanings (Fennell 2011; Gundaker 2011; Joseph 2011) or expressed doubts about it (Steen 2011).

Ferguson's original hypothesis also proposed that the vessels could have been used in therapeutic rituals such as African *minkisi*, which involved packing various materials in containers. This interpretation is congruent with the fact that these vessels were intact and often recovered from rivers. J. W. Joseph (2007) argued that ritualistic behaviors were not the only explanation for finding whole vessels in rivers: they could also have fallen from canoes that capsized on their way to market or simply been tossed in or near the water. Since then, therapeutic rituals have not been further debated, but the latest findings at Dean Hall might challenge this situation.

The marks in Guadeloupe do not closely resemble the dikenga discussed in South Carolina, but Laurie Wilkie (2000) has found a very similar version of the Bakongo cosmogram on Clifton plantation in the Bahamas. Unlike the Landrum crosses, the incisions found in Guadeloupe are never stamped and appear in inconspicuous places instead of highly visible ones. They are also not necessarily centered and do not appear on footed vessels like the bowls discussed by Ferguson. The marked ceramics in Guadeloupe do however share some similarities with his sample: they are locally made vessels, and the existing evidence points to the users of these vessels as the authors of the marks.

These could be owners' marks that helped differentiate between similar objects because, for instance, they were used by several different people or for different purposes. They could also have had a ritual function, although none of the modern behaviors recorded in studies of Antillean folk medicine and magic beliefs involved marking ceramics. As a group, however, the marked objects included bowls used for cleaning and cooking, pitchers for storing and reheating water, and a possible cooking pot. Those who handled these objects the most were enslaved servants. Barbara J. Mills and T. J. Ferguson (2008) observed that animate objects used in ceremonial practices tend to exist in networks—much like the marked coarse earthenware found at various Guadeloupean colonial sites—and have different depositional histories due to their particular biographies. The set of five similar pitchers from 28 Rue Amédée Fengarol, at least four of which were marked, suggest that these objects might have been discarded in a single, perhaps meaningful or even ritualistic, event. The fact that pitchers were also generally used for water could also be cited in support of their possible ritualistic function.

Conclusion

Together, hygiene- and health-related objects reveal that Guadeloupeans paid special attention to cleanliness and grooming. Compared to their eighteenth-century contemporaries in Paris, they appear to have used at least as many chamber pots, slightly fewer bidets and commodes, but notably more barber's bowls and bathtubs. Further evidence of the importance of cleanliness in Creole culture is provided by the fact that commodes and bathtubs were made locally and that sherds of soap dishes were found in middling nineteenth-century households.

Such grooming practices might have been introduced early on by Guadeloupe's colonial and military elite. They must also have been fostered by the fact that Creole men and women of all castes had a more trusting attitude toward water than their French counterparts did. The lack of indoor bathrooms and wash sets in the inventories resonated with the greater frequency of outdoor washing and bathing.

Modern folk medical principles further imply that water was seen as a protective element and reminds us that although Guadeloupeans had access to European drugs they probably also engaged in herbal and water-based therapies, such as baths and teas, which were mostly developed and transmitted by the slave population. While servants went about their daily chores, like washing the laundry, cleaning the house, preparing and cooking food, or simply fetching and heating water, they might have been aware of and have followed many of the customs that persist in Antillean folk medicine.

The ceramics related to health and hygiene formed a relatively small group, yet their role in understanding Creole culture is crucial. Other classes of artifacts used to study these topics—such as pharmaceutical bottles, glass vials, bell metals, mortars and pestles, and so on—are more rarely found in excavations. Ceramics also represent a large part of the evidence about health and hygiene in probate inventories as well. A study of Creole ceramic culture would be incomplete without them.

CHAPTER SEVEN

Conclusion

Water storage in homes was a consistent feature of early modern life. Information gleaned from the study of ceramics can contribute significantly to our understanding of how early modern households managed this vital resource. Large coarse earthenware jars, in particular, made excellent containers: they held large quantities of water, yielded a cleaner supply through decantation, and were known to keep stored water fresh-tasting.

There is evidence that they were common throughout the Caribbean. Both Martinique and St. Lucia produced local jars into the twentieth century at least (De Roo Lemos 1979; Vérin 1967). Unfortunately, by the time anthropological surveys occurred in Martinique, these jars had gone out of style and nothing had been recorded about their use. In St. Lucia however, the *jè* were used just as they were in Guadeloupe: for storing freshwater at home and for collecting rainwater from the roof or from the carved trunk of a coconut tree (Vérin 1967: 476). In eighteenth-century Barbados, so-called Spanish olive jars, which had a capacity of about 91 liters, were used in conjunction with stone water filters (Coleman and Porter 2007). Like Biot jars, these ceramics were designed to ship olive oil. The oil was produced in Lucca, Tuscany, and exported to England, whence it was shipped to its overseas colonies. These Montelupo jars tended to be reused for water in Nevis as well (Morris et al. 1999). Barbara Heath (1999) found jar sherds on St. Eustatius and cited sources indicating that these objects existed in Jamaica, Antigua, and Montserrat. In 1838, Isaac Belisario illustrated some examples from Jamaica and discussed their role there as water-storage ceramics (Hauser 2008: 137–38). The French scientist and explorer Jean-Baptiste Leblond (1813: 361) described a scene in early nineteenth-century Grenada where a mulatto who had been poisoned stumbled across his room and drew water out of a water jar using a small pot. Jars seemingly were the container of choice for water reserves throughout the Caribbean.

Biot jars were disseminated as shipping containers all over the French colonial world and could have been reused as water containers in numerous places. A few jars were thus listed in the inventories from Place-Royale in Quebec City (Lapointe and Lueger 1997: 220–21). The 1785 inventory of Marianne Lelièvre showed that water jars were present at Ile Bourbon, too— unlike in Guadeloupe, these vessels were made of both stoneware and ceramic (Jauze 2006). In eighteenth-century New Orleans, data published by Jill-Karen Yakubik (1990: 376–92) indicate that water jars were listed in both French and Spanish households. Their inventories mentioned, respectively, "jars from Provence" (*jarres de Provence*) and "jars for water" (*jarros para agua*).

How did households manage water elsewhere? Naturally, it is not always easy to distinguish ceramics for water from other types of storage vessels. Nonetheless, Guadeloupe's colonial ceramic culture suggests that a jar or large jug found in a domestic context was likely to have been recycled for that purpose. In addition, as this book has shown, water-storage ceramics can yield unique insights into past practices and norms. For instance, in Guadeloupe people preferred to keep ceramics holding water outside of their bedrooms, probably to avoid attracting or breeding mosquitoes near their beds. Meanwhile in the Quebecois inventories, out of the 9 jars whose positions were precisely recorded, 4 were kept in bedrooms and 5 in parlor rooms (Lapointe and Lueger 1997: 224).

More generally, the Guadeloupean water-storage repertoire made up of ceramic jars, drip jars, pitchers, and wall fountains seemed to be the result of local choices. Certainly, it did not include French water jugs such as the cruche or its regional variants. Water ceramics also represented a large portion of the local domestic pottery production. Since these water-storage ceramics exhibit such notable cultural variations, it would be interesting to study them on a larger scale. Interestingly, as Steven J. Mithen (2012) recently noted, the adoption of ceramic technology in the Neolithic Levant was accompanied by an intensification of water management strategies. Perhaps ceramics and water have shared a common history all along.

The management of the domestic water reserve was probably a chore typically assigned to women. In the French Caribbean it should be added (just like cooking) to the list of tasks that were typically relegated to female slaves (Debien 1974: 87). Fetching water, sometimes over long distances; lugging it around the house; filling large and heavy containers; and scrubbing pots and stone filters were seemingly menial duties but ones that had to be performed often and required a great deal of stamina. They were also not much different than the type of work done by low-income women in France. In eighteenth-century visual representations of French crafts, manufacture, and commerce, women were shown to be responsible for some of the most exhausting work, including transporting heavy loads (Sheridan 2009). Yet women's responsibility for managing the domestic water reserve has left only tenuous traces in Guadeloupean sources, surely because enslaved women were among the most subordinate elements of Creole society. Consequently, this topic has been largely neglected in historical research and in the literature on slavery (Moitt 2001: 70). Archaeology can help to fill this void.

The ceramic culture approach confirmed that the foundations of Antillean cuisine were laid during the colonial period by an army of anonymous servants, many of whom were women. Women cooks used more ceramics than male chefs when they prepared food for their masters, and they might have relied on ceramics even more heavily when they cooked for their families. At La Mahaudière plantation the cooking pot fragments excavated in the slave village were 95 percent ceramic versus 5 percent metallic (Brunache 2011; Gibson 2007, 226). Perhaps slaves lacked access to metal cookware, or perhaps women preferred ceramics, in part because they were lighter and therefore easier to handle than metal pots.

At any rate, using ceramics would have enabled them to cook foods more slowly. Their inventiveness is already impressive, because they developed an array of recipes using a limited, unsophisticated, and well-worn body of cookware. Another recognized characteristic of soup- and stew-based dishes, however, is that they require little labor (Voss 2008: 249–50). Slow-cooked foods such as stews, soups, and rice and bean recipes demand less effort than, for example, grilled foods or, for Guadeloupe, fried appetizers or manioc-based preparations. House slaves may have been better able to manage their labor if they could find ways to save time in preparing most of what constituted their masters' common diet.

Guadeloupean tableware showed that many of the customs and norms of Creole entertaining centered on the table. In most houses the salle was the space devoted to these activities. Households of sufficient means configured theirs with a mix of local and imported pieces of furniture. The latter were sourced not only from France, but also from China, the Netherlands, England, and even North America. The furniture found in French ports involved in the Atlantic trade, such as Bordeaux, Nantes, La Rochelle, or Rouen, shared some of the same stylistic characteristics, such as the use of exotic hardwoods like mahogany and Oriental lacquerware (Dobie 2007). Overall, the furnishing of salles seemed to reflect Guadeloupe's participation in the culture of the broader Atlantic world. Anne Pérotin-Dumon (2000) reaches a similar conclusion in her work on Guadeloupean cities.

Given the marginal position of the colony on French trading routes, it was however significant that the bulk of the eighteenth-century Guadeloupean tableware was French faience. The repertoire consisted of many examples decorated in a Rouen style with relatively simple, common flowery designs that had common visual qualities, which facilitated assembling matching services. More importantly, this tableware was also well adapted to Creole foods and made heavy use of tureens and bols well suited for serving and eating soups and stews. These findings show that it is possible to study foodways through tableware by focusing on the function of each vessel. Compared to contemporaneous French cities, in Guadeloupe tableware was widely distributed among middling and poor households, and wealthy households owned comparable quantities to well-off households in the metropole.

In Guadeloupe Creole norms of hospitality and commensality helped both bind people together and separate them by class, as feasting practices often do (Dietler 2001). Such events could both reenact the racial segregations and caste divisions that constituted Guadeloupean society and offer ways to challenge them (for instance, if a white planter invited his family de couleur to eat at his table). Because the help of enslaved domestics must have been enlisted before, during, and after these events, racial and caste differences manifested not in who was present at the event but in who was allowed to partake of it.

Creole elite feasts required an abundance of foods and tableware, the latter being preferably French. Even though the ideal was to serve exotic and unusual foods—perhaps imported from France or from elsewhere in the Atlantic world—in most cases a rich selection of common, familiar foods probably sufficed. In the context of Andean society, Christine A. Hastorf (2003) has already demonstrated that feasts could involve not just rare, luxury fare, but also large quantities of local foods. At any rate, given who the cooks were and what kind of cookware they used, most of these ingredients would have been prepared in a Creole style. If people of all social ranks largely ate the same local foods and Creole dishes, perhaps the quantity of food and type of tableware used to present and consume it became significant markers of social status. When food sources are limited in feasting practices, ceramic choices might become more salient.

Creole health and hygiene practices were harder to explore using ceramic evidence alone, but the effort proved fruitful. Health- and hygiene-related ceramics are more rarely the focus of archaeological studies, for a variety of reasons. In Guadeloupe hindering factors were small sample sizes for certain objects, the absence of some object types in either documentary or archaeological sources, and the frequent use of multipurpose vessels such as coarse earthenware bowls. Nonetheless, this group of ceramics demonstrated that Creole men and women had a different view of hygiene than their French counterparts did. By the end of the eighteenth century, they appear more modern because they feared neither using water nor bathing. Their practices must also have been influenced by local medical and religious beliefs that placed a premium on bodily and domestic cleanliness. As remains true today, colonial-era Antillean folk medicine appears to have successfully meshed the principles and pharmacopeia of early modern Western medicine with the herbal- and water-based therapies of enslaved healers.

Exploring these topics revealed that in many instances ceramics were more essential to the domestic material culture of the colonies than of France. Several objects that existed in metal versions in Paris were mostly if not exclusively made of ceramic in Guadeloupe. Parisian inventories yielded troves of pewter chamber pots, copper-alloy barber's bowls, metal water fountains or beverage services, and pewter flatware in low-income households or silver services in elite ones. In contrast wealthy Guadeloupeans—those who probably could best afford metallic objects—apparently preferred ceramic alternatives. For example, metallic and ceramic coffee pots showed up in almost equal frequency across the inventories as a whole: 40 percent of Guadeloupean households so equipped had a metal pot, whereas 60 percent owned a ceramic one. Yet three-quarters of wealthy households chose to own a stoneware, faience, or porcelain model rather than a metal one. Ceramics seemed to be the material of choice even when other options were available, which explains why despite their bulkiness and fragility, they were still shipped across oceans. There could have been a variety of reasons for this phenomenon, including the high price and rarity of metal in the colonies, market forces that pushed French potteries and ceramic merchants to market goods abroad, or simply a demand factor that modern ceramic materials such as faiences, faiences fines, and English china were more sought after in the colonies. Whatever the reason, the greater prevalence of such objects makes archaeological ceramic studies even more relevant in the colonial world.

Because the ceramic culture of Guadeloupe was so extensive, its examination yielded an analysis of a large swath of Creole society. It provided information about free married or cohabiting couples de couleur, craftsmen, widows living alone, and other types of poor to middling households. Given that most of the documentary sources from the colonial period concentrate on the planter elite, this information offers a valuable complement. Yet the most important strength of the concept of ceramic culture is its focus on the handlers of ceramics—who are not always the same people who acquire or use them. This feature enables research to shed light on some of the most disenfranchised elements of Creole society.

In particular, ceramics shed light on the lives of serving women and other enslaved domestics. Their daily management of domestic chores and handling of certain objects might explain some patterns of ceramic choices. In the domains of water management and cooking at least, the selection of only a few plain shapes, the importance of locally made ceramics, and the glaring absence of some obvious French options—such as cruches and chafing dishes—appear to be direct outcomes of domestics' managing roles. Like ghosts, they make their presence and involvement felt through subdued evidence and small interstices in colonial material culture.

Among all their domestic tasks, cooking is the one that has received the most attention from scholars. Studies such as Theresa W. Devasahayam's (2005) are informative because they explore the relationship between power and cooking. Using the work of Judith P. Butler (1993) and Lisa M. Heldke (1992) among others, Devasahayam demonstrates that cooking is a creative, "thoughtful" practice through which women may perform their identity. Even when they cook for others, women derive power from the multifold decision making this activity requires: What kinds of foods should I get? Which ones should be prepared quickly before they spoil? Which ones can wait? How should each be prepared? Which foods complement each other? How should they be served? Devasahayam notes that the middle-class Hindu women she interviewed find greatest fulfillment in being the ultimate provider or decision maker, even when they enlist the help of maids, kitchen appliances, or convenience foods. Yet their discourses also make clear that much power resides in the execution of cooking itself, since no dish can ever be exactly replicated even when the same recipe is followed. In consequence, these women also tend to restrict their maids' roles to the preparatory work (such as washing and cutting) as opposed to the actual cooking.

In Guadeloupe, the material environment indicates that most enslaved servants had a lot of leeway in their cooking practices. Even when they did not decide what kinds of foods would be served on their masters' tables, they apparently were entirely responsible for the execution of dishes. Similarly, they might not have had to contend with a lot of oversight with regard to their role in ensuring that the household water reserves were well maintained. In managing these daily, ordinary tasks they might have found some basic measures of freedom and fulfillment, or they might have reveled in small acts of defiance—such as not filling the water jar completely or not salting a dish. Similarly, they might also have carved out some "actual power" through providing all of the last-minute labor that Creole feasts required, as well as the gestures of assistance, comfort, and relief that their masters expected in the realm of health and hygiene.

The concept of ceramic culture has guided this exploration of Creole domestic life and of the most common uses of ceramics in Guadeloupe. It has outlined large trends in colonial society but has also revealed a myriad of small unknown facts about ceramics, without coming close to depleting the possible themes of study. For example, when Lafcadio Hearn asked his servant Cyrillia if she wanted to use his telescope to gaze at the moon, she refused but told him this story: "I saw the Sun and the Moon once fighting together: that was what people call an eclipse,—is not that the word? . . . They fought together a long time: I was looking at them. We put a terrine full of water on the ground, and looked into the water to see them" (Hearn 1903: 336). And as I myself learned during a visit to the Némausat house in downtown Basse-Terre, water jars also made excellent hiding places for small valuables. As these anecdotes signal, even in Guadeloupe ceramics have yet to tell us all of their stories.

Notes

Chapter 1. A Ceramic Culture

1. Faience is a French tin-glazed earthenware that comes in two varieties: a base type that has a uniform white tin glaze (blanche) all over the vessel and a type that has a brown lead glaze on the outside. The latter is named *faience brune* (brown faience).

Chapter 2. From Kakukera to Guadeloupe

1. Anne Pérotin-Dumon calculated that Basse-Terre, the largest city at the time, had around 4,500 residents.

2. Du Tertre started writing about the Antilles in 1654, and published his main history in 1664–65.

3. Throughout the text, I reference probate inventories located in the Archives Départementales de la Guadeloupe (ADG). These records are part of the notarial record of the Basse-Terre area (*notariat Basse-Terre*) and are filed under the surname of the man who was in charge of each notary office at the time (Mimerel, Nesty, Fontaine, etc.). The ADG also assigns a unique combination of numbers and letters to each book produced by each office (e.g., 2E 2/198), and inside the book the inventories are arranged by the date the inventory started. See table 1.1, p. 10, for the list of inventories analyzed for this study.

4. The rest of the sample was undetermined.

Chapter 3. Just Add Water

1. This document is the best source of information about the state of Basse-Terre's water supply at the end of the eighteenth century. It is partially reproduced in Pérotin-Dumon 2000: 775–76.

2. In my sample, water rights appeared in the inventory of a house in Capes-terre that had two small sources of freshwater. These water sources were worth only 80 francs, a modest sum in 1830, but this house was located in a village, not in the city where the value presumably would have been higher.

3. The muid was a capacity unit used for dry goods such as cereals, and for wine and alcohol. Its value varied, but in Paris one muid equaled about 268 liters.

4. Jean-Baptiste Labat lived in Martinique and Guadeloupe from 1694 to 1705.

Chapter 4. A Canari in the Kitchen

1. *Journal politique et commercial de la Pointe-à-Pitre*, sale ad, April 16, 1820.

2. Ibid., sale ad from April 1, 1819.

3. Ibid., sale ad from August 12, 1819.

4. A distilled liquor made from sugarcane juice.

5. The bark of the tree *Richeria grandis*.

6. A large fruit-eating rodent with long hind legs and a short tail.

7. This role fits with the derivation of the word. In the patois of Normandy, *cannes* designated jugs or pots that were used to store and transport milk.

8. In Quebec, the collections from Place-Royale confirmed that faience brune casseroles existed but were extremely rare (Genêt 1980).

9. Two dozen "rosettes à fleur de lis pour la pâtisserie" (ADG: Fontaine, 2E 3/5, 11/23/1778).

10. Chafing dishes were called *réchauds* in French, from *réchauffer* (reheat). They not only kept dishes warm during a meal but could also be used for any preparation that required slow and gentle cooking.

Chapter 5. The Creole Art of the Table

1. Spoons were present in 72 percent of households, knives in 49 percent, and forks in 42 percent. Spoons were the most specialized and there were different types for general use, for soups and stews, or for coffee. Table silverware also might include big serving ladles called *salsepannes* (11 percent of houses). Other metallic objects were a lot less common: for example, *écuelles* (shallow bowls with two flat handles and often a lid and dish) appeared in three instances, pitchers or pots in three others.

2. *Entremets* were traditionally served after the meats and before the dessert.

3. For dishes, the highest appraisal was only 13 times greater than the lowest.

4. Used by Pardailhé-Galabrun (1988), the quotation marks around India in-dicate that it is not the actual place of porcelain production. When ceramics of

the period "come from India," they actually originate from somewhere else, such as China or Japan.

5. A guéridon was a high round table on which candlesticks or lamps were originally placed for lighting an area.

Chapter 6. For Healthy Bodies and Clean Houses

1. Furthermore, there were commodes—which generally were used with chamber pots—in about 30 percent of households.

2. A chamber pot is sometimes called a "Thomas" in Guadeloupe.

3. See, for example, the 1997 thriller *Le meurtre du Samedi-Gloria* by the famous Martiniquais writer Raphaël Confiant and the 1989 novel *Mélody des faubourgs* by the Guadeloupean writer Lucie Julia.

4. In France, *coquemars* were one-handled cooking pots.

5. The source was Pehr Kalm, 1977, *Voyage de Pehr Kalm au Canada en 1749*, Pierre Tisseyre, Montreal.

6. The local equivalent of a commode.

7. This oleoresin is a stimulant and is supposed to have a variety of curative properties as an astringent, diuretic, disinfectant, and so on.

Bibliography

Abel, Véronique, and Henri Amouric

1995   Les ateliers du l'Huveaune à l'époque moderne. In *Actes du Ve Colloque sur la Céramique Médiévale en Méditerranée Occidentale, Rabat 1991*, pp. 84–94. Insap, Rabat.

Adélaïde-Merlande, Jacques

1985   Problématique d'une histoire de l'esclavage urbain, Guadeloupe–Guyane– Martinique (vers 1815–1848). *Bulletin de la société d'histoire de la Guadeloupe* 65–66: 3–23.

Agha, Andrew, and Nicole M. Isenbarger

2011   Recently Discovered Marked Colonoware from Dean Hall Plantation, Berkeley County, South Carolina. *Historical Archaeology* 45(2): 184–87.

Alexandre-Bidon, Danièle

2005   *Une archéologie du goût: Céramique et consommation*. Espaces Médiévaux. A. & J. Picard, Paris.

Amouric, Henri, Laurence Argueyrolles, and Lucy Vallauri

2006   *Biot: Jarres, terrailles et fontaines, XVIème–XXème siècles*. Association Arezzo, Biot.

Amy, Joseph

1759   *Tableau des acheteurs des nouvelles fontaines filtrantes, domestiques, militaires & marines, nouvellement perfectionnées*. Antoine-Chrétien Boudet, Rotterdam, Paris.

Arcangeli, Myriam

2000   Approche de la culture matérielle moderne à Toulouse: les céramiques, par les textes et l'archéologie. Unpublished master's thesis, Department of History, Art History, and Archaeology, Université de Toulouse-le-Mirail, Toulouse, France.

2014   Water Supply and Storage. In *The Archaeology of Food: An Encyclopedia*, edited by Mary C. Beaudry and Karen B. Metheny. Altamira Press, Lanham, MD.

Armstrong, Douglas V., and Mark W. Hauser

2009   A Sea of Diversity: Historical Archaeology in the Caribbean. In *International Handbook of Historical Archaeology*, edited by Teresita Majewski and David Gaimster, pp. 583–612. Springer, New York.

Ashenburg, Katherine

2007   *The Dirt on Clean: An Unsanitized History*. North Point Press, New York.

Avery, George

2007   *French Colonial Pottery: An International Conference*. Northwestern State University Press, Natchitoches, LA.

Avery, George, H. F. Gregory, Jason Emery, and Jeffrey Girard

2007   French Faience in Northwest Louisiana. In *French Colonial Pottery: An International Conference*, edited by George Avery, pp. 411–67. Northwestern State University Press, Natchitoches, LA.

Baker, Moses N.

1981   *The Quest for Pure Water*. Vol. I. 2nd ed. American Water Works Association, Denver, CO.

Beaudry, Mary C.

1988   Words for Things: Linguistic Analysis of Probate Inventories. In *Documentary Archaeology in the New World*, edited by Mary C. Beaudry, pp. 43–50. Cambridge University Press, New York.

2006   *Findings: The Material Culture of Needlework and Sewing*. Yale University Press, New Haven, CT.

Beaudry, Mary C., and James Symonds

2011   Introduction: Transatlantic Dialogues and Convergence. In *Interpreting the Early Modern World: Transatlantic Perspectives*, edited by Mary C. Beaudry and James Symonds, pp. xi–xxii. Springer, New York.

Bégot, Danielle

1994   À la recherche du paradis perdu: Les colons des Antilles françaises et le monde anglo-saxon de 1815 à 1848. In *Guadeloupe, Martinique et Guyane dans le monde américain. Réalités d'hier, mutations d'aujourd'hui, perspectives 2000*, edited by Maurice Burac, pp. 127–46. Karthala, Paris.

Benoît, Catherine

2000   *Corps, jardins, mémoires: Anthropologie du corps et de l'espace à la Guadeloupe*. CNRS; Maison des sciences de l'homme, Paris.

Bernier, Maggy

2002   *Caractérisation typologique, microscopique et chimique des faïences du XVIIIe siècle du site Saint-Ignace de Loyola en Guyane française*. Cahiers d'archéologie du CELAT 14. CELAT, Université Laval, Quebec City.

Beuze, Lyne-Rose

1990   La poterie en Martinique. *Les Cahiers du Patrimoine* 7–8: 39–46.

Blandin-Pauvert, Arlette

1986   *Au temps des Mabos: les Blancs créoles de la Guadeloupe au début du siècle.* Éditions Desormeaux, Fort-de-France.

Bigot, Franck

2005   *Le matériel céramique du site de l'Embouchure de la Rivière de Baillif. Document Final de Synthèse.* Service Régional de l'Archéologie de Guadeloupe.

Boghen, Dan, and Miriam Boghen

1972   Notes sur la médecine populaire à la Martinique. In *L'archipel inachevé; culture et société aux Antilles françaises*, edited by Jean Benoist, pp. 233–48. Presses de l'Université de Montréal, Montreal.

Bonnissent, Dominique

1995   *Fort Houël (Basse-Terre, Guadeloupe), 971-05-001. Document Final de Synthèse.* Service Régional de l'Archéologie de Guadeloupe.

Bonnissent, Dominique, and Thomas Romon

2004   *Fouilles de la Cathédrale de Basse-Terre, commune de Basse-Terre. Document Final de Synthèse.* Service Régional de l'Archéologie de Guadeloupe.

Boucher, Philip P.

2008   *France and the American Tropics to 1700: Tropics of Discontent?* Johns Hopkins University Press, Baltimore, MD.

Bougerol, Christiane

1983   *La médecine populaire à la Guadeloupe.* Karthala, Paris.

1985   Logique de l'excès, logique de la rupture: Le chaud et le froid dans la médecine populaire de la Guadeloupe. *L'Ethnographie* 81(96–97): 159–67.

Boyer-Peyreleau, Eugène Édouard

1823   *Les Antilles françaises, particulièrement la Guadeloupe, depuis leur découverte jusqu'au 1er janvier 1823.* 3 vols. Brissot-Thivars, Paris.

Brassard, Michel, and Myriam Leclerc

2001   *Identifier la céramique et le verre anciens au Québec: Guide à l'usage des amateurs et des professionnels.* Cahiers d'archéologie du CELAT 12. CELAT, Université Laval, Quebec City.

Bray, Tamara L.

2003   To Dine Splendidly: Imperial Pottery, Commensal Politics, and the Inca State. In *The Archaeology and Politics of Food and Feasting in Early States and Empires*, edited by Tamara L. Bray, pp. 93–142. Kluwer Academic/Plenum, New York.

Bresc-Bautier, Geneviève (editor)

2001 *Archéologie du Grand Louvre. Le quartier du Louvre au XVIIe siècle.* Éditions de la Réunion des Musées Nationaux, Paris.

Breton, Raymond

1999 *Dictionnaire caraïbe-français.* IRD-Karthala, Paris.

Brongniart, Alexandre, and Désiré Riocreux

1845 *Description méthodique du Musée Céramique de la Manufacture Royale de Porcelaine de Sèvres* 1. 2 vols. A. Leleux, Paris.

Brunache, Peggy L.

2011 Enslaved Women, Foodways, and Identity Formation: The Archaeology of Habitation La Mahaudière, Guadeloupe, circa Late 18th Century to Mid-19th Century. Unpublished PhD dissertation, Department of Anthropology, University of Texas at Austin.

Buffon, Alain

1979 *Monnaie et crédit en économie coloniale: Contribution à l'histoire économique de la Guadeloupe, 1635–1919.* Société d'Histoire de la Guadeloupe, Basse-Terre.

Burnard, Trevor G.

2004 *Mastery, Tyranny, and Desire: Thomas Thistlewood and His Slaves in the Anglo-Jamaican World.* University of North Carolina Press, Chapel Hill.

Butel, Paul

2002 *Histoire des Antilles françaises: XVIIe–XXe siècle.* Perrin, Paris.

Butler, Judith P.

1993 *Bodies That Matter: On the Discursive Limits of "Sex."* Routledge, New York.

Cailly, Claude

1998 Structure sociale et consommation dans le monde proto-industriel rural textile: Le cas du Perche ornais au XVIIIe siècle. *Revue d'histoire moderne et contemporaine* 45(4): 746–74.

Carney, Judith A., and Richard N. Rosomoff

2009 *In the Shadow of Slavery: Africa's Botanical Legacy in the Atlantic World.* University of California Press, Berkeley.

Chanvalon, Jean-Baptiste T. d.

1763 *Voyage à la Martinique: Contenant diverses observations sur la physique, l'histoire naturelle, l'agriculture, les mœurs et les usages de cette île, faites en 1751 et dans les années suivantes, lu à l'Académie royale des sciences de Paris en 1761.* C.-J.-B. Bauche, Paris.

Charlery, Christophe

2005 Maisons de maître et habitations coloniales dans les territoires français de l'Amérique tropicale. *In Situ, revue des patrimoines* [online] 5:

[10/17/2010], http://www.insitu.culture.fr/article.xsp?numero=2015&id_article=d2014-1023.

Cochran, Matthew D., and Mary C. Beaudry

2006 Material Culture Studies and Historical Archaeology. In *The Cambridge Companion to Historical Archaeology*, edited by Dan Hicks and Mary C. Beaudry, pp. 191–204. Cambridge University Press, Cambridge.

Coleman, Ronald A.

2001 Dripstones: Rudimentary Water Filters on Ship and Shore in the 18th Century. *Bulletin of the Australian Institute for Maritime Archaeology* 25: 113–20.

Coleman, Ronald A., and Anthony R. D. Porter

2007 The So-Called "Spanish Jars" of Jamaica and Their Italian Connection. *Jamaica Journal* 30(3): 50–61.

Collingham, Elizabeth M.

2001 *Imperial Bodies: The Physical Experiment of the Raj, c. 1800–1947*. Polity, Cambridge.

Costes, Alain

2010 Faïenceries, faïenciers et faïences du Sud-Ouest au XVIIIe siècle. *La Grésale* 12: 19–74.

Debien, Gabriel

1951 La société coloniale aux XVIIe et XVIIIe siècle: Les engagés pour les Antilles (1634–1715). *Revue d'histoire des colonies* 38: 141.

1956 *Études antillaises (XVIIIe siècle)*. Armand Colin, Paris.

1964 La nourriture des esclaves sur les plantations des Antilles françaises aux XVIIe et XVIIIe siècles. *Caribbean Studies* 4(2): 3–27.

1974 *Les esclaves aux Antilles françaises (XVIIe–XVIIIe siècles)*. Société d'histoire de la Guadeloupe, Société d'histoire de la Martinique, Basse-Terre, & Fort-de-France.

Décarie, Louise

1999 *Les grès français de Place-Royale*. Gouvernement du Québec, Ministère de la culture et des communications, Direction des communications, Collection Patrimoines, Dossier 46.

Denise, Christophe

2005 Une histoire évolutive de l'habitat martiniquais. *In Situ, revue des patrimoines* [online] 5: [10/17/2010], http://www.insitu.culture.fr/article.xsp?numero=2015&id_article=d2015-2528.

De Roo Lemos, Noëlle

1979 *Les dernières potières de Sainte-Anne, Martinique*. Centre de Recherches Caraïbes, Montréal.

Desmet-Grégoire, Hélène

1994   L'introduction du café en France au XVIIe siècle. *Confluences* 10: 165–74.

Desmoulins, Marie-Emmanuelle (editor)

2006   *Basse-Terre, patrimoine d'une ville antillaise.* Jasor, Pointe-à-Pitre.

Dessalles, Pierre, and Henri de Frémont

1980   *La vie d'un colon à la Martinique au XIXe siècle.* 3 vols.: Correspondence 1808–1834; journals 1837–1841, 1842–1847, and 1848–1856. H. de Frémont, ed. Courbevoie.

Dessalles, Pierre-François-Régis

[1786] 1995   *Les annales du Conseil souverain de la Martinique. Introduction, sources, bibliographie et notes de Bernard Vonglis.* L'Harmattan, Paris. Originally published by J. B. Puynesge.

Devasahayam, Theresa W.

2005   Power and Pleasure Around the Stove: The Construction of Gendered Identity in Middle-Class South Indian Hindu Households in Urban Malaysia. *Women's Studies International Forum* 28: 1–20.

Diderot, Denis, and Jean le Rond D'Alembert (editors)

1751–72   *Encyclopédie, ou dictionnaire raisonné des sciences, des arts et des métiers.* 17 vols. Briasson, David, Le Breton, Durand, Paris.

Dietler, Michael

2001   Theorizing the Feast: Rituals of Consumption, Commensal Politics, and Power in African Contexts. In *Feasts: Archaeological and Ethnographic Perspectives on Food, Politics, and Power,* edited by Michael Dietler and Brian Hayden, pp. 65–114. Smithsonian Institution Press, Washington, DC.

Dobie, Madeleine

2007   Orientalism, Colonialism, and Furniture in Eighteenth-Century France. In *Furnishing the Eighteenth Century: What Furniture Can Tell Us about the European and American Past,* edited by Dena Goodman and Kathryn Norberg, pp. 13–36. Routledge, New York.

Dousset, Christine

2003   Entre tradition et modernité: Les intérieurs toulousains au XVIIIe siècle. *Annales du Midi* 115: 31–50.

Dubois, Laurent

2004   *A Colony of Citizens: Revolution and Slave Emancipation in the French Caribbean, 1787–1804.* Published for the Omohundro Institute of Early American History and Culture, Williamsburg, VA, by the University of North Carolina Press, Chapel Hill.

Duhamel du Monceau, Henri-Louis

1777   Art du potier de terre. In *Descriptions des arts et métiers* vol. 8, edited by Académie des sciences (France) and J.-E. Bertrand, pp. 265–358. De l'imprimerie de la Société typographique, Neuchâtel.

Du Tertre, Jean-Baptiste

1667–71 *L'Histoire générale des Antilles habitées par les Français.* 3 vols. T. Jolly, Paris.

1654 *L'histoire générale des îles Saint-Christophe, de la Guadeloupe, de la Martinique et autres dans l'Amérique.* Jacques Langlois, Paris.

Ebroïn, Ary

n.d. *La cuisine créole. L'utile.* Émile Désormeaux, Martinique.

Edwards, Jay

2006 Creole Architecture: A Comparative Analysis of Upper and Lower Louisiana and Saint Domingue. *International Journal of Historical Archaeology* 10(3): 237–67.

Ekberg, Carl J.

1985 *Colonial Ste. Genevieve: An Adventure on the Mississippi Frontier.* Patrice Press, Gerald, MI.

Eymeri, Jean-Claude

1992 *Histoire de la médecine aux Antilles et en Guyane.* L'Harmattan, Paris.

Fallope, Josette

1983 Les esclaves africains à la Guadeloupe en 1848 d'après les registres d'état civil des nouveaux citoyens conservés aux Archives de la Guadeloupe. *Bulletin de la société d'histoire de la Guadeloupe* 57–58(3–4): 3–25.

1987 Les occupations d'esclaves à la Guadeloupe dans la première moitié du XIXe siècle. *Revue Française d'Histoire d'Outre-mer* 74(275): 189–205.

Fennell, Christopher C.

2011 Literate Inversions and Cultural Metaphors in Edgefield Stoneware. *Historical Archaeology* 45(2): 156–62.

Ferguson, Leland G.

1999 "The Cross Is a Magic Sign": Marks on Eighteenth-Century Bowls from South Carolina. In *I, Too, Am America*, edited by Theresa A. Singleton, pp. 83–115. University Press of Virginia, Charlottesville.

Figeac, Michel (editor)

2007 *L'ancienne France au quotidien: Vie et choses de la vie sous l'Ancien Régime.* Armand Colin, Paris.

Flandrin, Jean-Louis

1999 Dietary Choices and Culinary Technique, 1500–1800. In *Food: A Culinary History from Antiquity to the Present*, edited by Jean-Louis Flandrin, Massimo Montanari, and Albert Sonnenfeld, pp. 403–17. Columbia University Press, New York.

Forest, Dominique, Louis Franchet, Béatrice Pannequin, and Sandrine Poggi

1996 *Pignates et poêlons. Poteries culinaires de Vallauris.* Réunion des Musées Nationaux, Paris.

Fourniols, Marc-Alexandre

2000 *L'esclavage à Basse-Terre et dans sa région en 1844 vu par le procureur Fourniols.* Société d'Histoire de la Guadeloupe, Gourbeyre.

Foy, Dominique, Florence Richez, and Lucy Vallauri

1986 La céramique en usage dans l'atelier de verrier de Roquefeuille (Pourrières, Var): Exemple d'un dépotoir domestique de la première moitié du XVIIIe siècle. *Archéologie du Midi Médiéval* 4: 135–49.

Gabriel, Isabelle

2004 *Rapport de la première campagne de fouilles programmée à l'habitation-poterie Fidelin à Terre de Bas.* Direction Régionale des Affaires Culturelles, Service Régional de l'Archéologie, Basse-Terre, Guadeloupe.

Gaimster, David

1997 *German Stoneware 1200–1900. Archaeology and Cultural History.* British Museum Press, London.

Garraway, Doris L.

2005 *The Libertine Colony: Creolization in the Early French Caribbean.* Duke University Press, Durham, NC.

Gautier, Arlette

1984 Les esclaves de l'habitation Bisdary, 1763–1817. *Bulletin de la Société d'Histoire de la Guadeloupe* 60(2): 13–50.

1985 *Les sœurs de Solitude. La condition féminine dans l'esclave aux Antilles du XVIIe au XIXe siècle.* Éditions Caribéennes, Paris.

Genêt, Nicole

1980 *La faïence de Place-Royale.* Gouvernement du Québec, Ministère de la Culture et des Communications, Direction des Communications, Collection Patrimoines, Dossier 45.

Gibson, Heather R.

2007 Daily Practice and Domestic Economies in Guadeloupe: An Archaeological and Historical Study. Unpublished PhD dissertation, Department of Anthropology, Syracuse University, New York.

Glissant, Edouard

1997 *Poetics of Relation.* University of Michigan Press, Ann Arbor.

Goubert, Pierre

1989 *The Conquest of Water: The Advent of Health in the Industrial Age.* Princeton University Press, Princeton, NJ.

Goy, Corinne

1995 Besançon (Doubs). Mobilier de la poubelle d'un vigneron, second moitié du XVIe s. In *Ex pots . . . Céramiques médiévales et modernes en Franche-Comté. Catalogue de l'exposition*, edited by Jean-Olivier Guilhot and Annick Richard, pp. 123–25. Musée des ducs de Wurtemberg, Montbéliard, France.

Goy, Corinne, and Henri Brossault de Rambay

1995 Tourtières, cafetières et pochon: Vente au château de Beaufort (Jura), an premier de la République française. In *Ex pots . . . céramiques médiévales et modernes en Franche-Comté. Catalogue de l'exposition*, edited by Jean-Olivier Guilhot and Annick Richard, pp. 161–62. Musée des ducs de Wurtemberg, Montbéliard, France.

Granier de Cassagnac, Adolphe

1842–44 *Voyage aux Antilles françaises, anglaises, danoises, espagnoles, à St-Domingue et aux Etats-Unis d'Amérique.* Dauvin et Fontaine, Paris.

Greenfield, Amy B.

2005 *A Perfect Red: Empire, Espionage, and the Quest for the Color of Desire.* HarperCollins, New York.

Guilhot, Jean-Olivier, and Annick Richard (editors)

1995 *Ex pots . . . Céramiques médiévales et modernes en Franche-Comté. Catalogue de l'exposition.* Musée des ducs de Wurtemberg, Montbéliard, France.

Guillemé Brulon, Dorothée

1997a *Lyon & Nevers: Sources et rayonnement.* Histoire de la faïence française. Charles Massin, Paris.

1997b *Moustiers & Marseille: Sources et rayonnement.* Histoire de la faïence française. Charles Massin, Paris.

1998a *Bordeaux & La Rochelle: Sources et rayonnement.* Histoire de la faïence française. Charles Massin, Paris.

1998b *Paris & Rouen: Sources et rayonnement.* Histoire de la faïence française. Charles Massin, Paris.

2000 *La faïence fine française: 1750–1867.* Charles Massin, Paris.

Gundaker, Grey

2011 The Kongo Cosmogram in Historical Archaeology and the Moral Compass of Dave the Potter. *Historical Archaeology* 45(2): 176–83.

Gur-Arieh, Shira, Aren M. Maeir, and Ruth Shahack-Gross

2011 Soot Patterns on Cooking Vessels: A Short Note. In *On Cooking Pots, Drinking Cups, Loomweights and Ethnicity in Bronze Age Cyprus and Neighbouring Regions. An International Archaeological Symposium Held in*

Nicosia, November 6th–7th 2010, edited by Vassos Karageorghis and Oura-
nia Kouka, pp. 340–55. A. G. Leventis Foundation, Nicosia.

Hamlin, Christopher

2000 Water. In *The Cambridge World History of Food*, edited by Kenneth F. Kiple
and Kriemhild C. Ornelas, pp. 720–30. Cambridge University Press, New
York.

Hastorf, Christine A.

2003 Andean Luxury Foods: Special Food for the Ancestors, Deities, and the
Élite. *Antiquity* 77: 545–54.

Hatzenberger, Françoise

1996 Paysage de la Guadeloupe à la fin du XVIIIe siècle d'après le poète créole
Léonard. *Revue Française d'Histoire d'Outre-mer* 83(310): 61–82.

Hauser, Mark W.

2008 *An Archaeology of Black Markets: Local Ceramics and Economies in Eighteenth-Century Jamaica.* University Press of Florida, Gainesville.

Haviser, Jay B. (editor)

1999 *African Sites Archaeology in the Caribbean.* Markus Weiner; Ian Randle,
Princeton, NJ.

Hearn, Lafcadio

1903 *Two Years in the French West Indies.* Harper & Brothers, New York.

Heath, Barbara J.

1999 Yabbas, Monkeys, Jugs, and Jars: An Historical Context for African-Ca-
ribbean Pottery on St. Eustatius. In *African Sites Archaeology in the Caribbean*, edited by Jay B. Haviser, pp. 196–220. Markus Weiner; Ian Randle,
Princeton, NJ.

Heldke, Lisa M.

1992 Foodmaking as a Thoughtful Process. In *Cooking, Eating, Thinking: Trans-
formative Philosophies of Food*, edited by Deane W. Curtin and Lisa M.
Heldke, pp. 203–29. Indiana University Press, Bloomington.

Hellman, Mimi

2007 The Joy of Sets: The Uses of Seriality in the French Interior. In *Furnishing
the Eighteenth Century: What Furniture Can Tell Us about the European
and American Past*, edited by Dena Goodman and Kathryn Norberg, pp.
129–53. Routledge, New York.

Henigfeld, Yves

2005 *La céramique à Strasbourg de la fin du Xe au début du XVIIe siècle.* Publications du CRAHM, Caen, France.

Hicks, Dan, and Mary C. Beaudry

2010 Introduction. Material Culture Studies: A Reactionary View. In *The Oxford*

Handbook of Material Culture Studies, edited by Dan Hicks and Mary C. Beaudry, pp. 1–21. Oxford University Press, Oxford.

Huyghues-Belrose, Vincent

2006 Avant le fruit à pain: la cuisine martiniquaise au XVIIIe siècle. In *Sur les chemins de l'histoire antillaise. Mélanges offerts à Lucien Abénon*, edited by Jean Bernabé and Serge Mam Lam Fouk, pp. 201–14. Ibis Rouge, Matoury, France.

Isert, Paul E.

1972 *Voyages en Guinée et dans les îles Caraïbes en Amérique*. Reprod. de l'éd. de Paris: Maradan, 1793. Hachette, Paris.

Jauze, Albert

2000 Esclaves et patrimoine dans le sud de Bourbon de 1730 à la Révolution. *Revue des Mascareignes* 2: 63–81.

2006 La succession de Marianne Lelièvre: Les aspects de la vie quotidienne à Bourbon à la fin du XVIIIe siècle. *Outre-Mers* 94(352–53): 107–45.

Jennings, Eric T.

2002 Curing the Colonizers: Highland Hydrotherapy in Guadeloupe. *Social History of Medicine* 15(2): 229–61.

Joseph, Joe W.

2007 One More Look into the Water—Colonoware in South Carolina Rivers and Charleston's Market Economy. *African Diaspora Archaeology Newsletter*, June. http://www.diaspora.illinois.edu/news0607/news0607-2.pdf.

2011 " . . . All of Cross"—African Potters, Marks, and Meanings in the Folk Pottery of the Edgefield District, South Carolina. *Historical Archaeology* 45(2): 134–55.

Kalm, Pehr

1977 *Voyage de Pehr Kalm ou Canada en 1749*. P. Tisseyre, Montreal.

Kelly, Kenneth G.

2011 *La Vie Quotidienne*: Historical Archaeological Approaches to the Plantation Era in Guadeloupe, French West Indies. In *French Colonial Archaeology in the Southeast and Caribbean*, edited by Kenneth G. Kelly and Meredith D. Hardy, pp. 189–205. University Press of Florida, Gainesville.

Kelly, Kenneth G., and Meredith D. Hardy (editors)

2011 *French Colonial Archaeology in the Southeast and Caribbean*. University Press of Florida, Gainesville.

Kelly, Kenneth G., Mark W. Hauser, Christophe Descantes, and Michael D. Glascock

2008 Compositional Analysis of French Colonial Ceramics: Implications for Understanding Trade and Exchange. *Journal of Caribbean Archaeology* Special Publication 2: 85–107.

Labat, Jean-Baptiste

1722 *Nouveau voyage aux isles de l'Amérique.* 6 vols. Guillaume Cavelier, Paris.

L'Anglais, Paul-Gaston

1994 *Les modes de vie à Québec et à Louisbourg au milieu du XVIIIe siècle à partir de collections archéologiques.* Gouvernement du Québec, Ministère de la Culture et des Communications, Direction des Communications, Collection Patrimoines, Dossier 86.

Lapointe, Camille, and Richard Lueger

1997 *Le verre et les terres cuites communes de la maison Perthuis à Place-Royale.* Gouvernement du Québec, Ministère de la Culture et des Communications, Direction des Communications, Collection Patrimoines, Dossier 101.

Lebey, Claude (editor)

1998 *Guadeloupe: Produits du terroir et recettes traditionnelles.* Albin Michel; Conseil National des Arts Culinaires, Paris.

Leblond, Jean-Baptiste

1813 *Voyage aux Antilles et à l'Amérique méridionale commencé en 1767 et fini en 1802.* A. Bertrand, Paris.

Leti, Geneviève

2000 *L'Univers magico-religieux antillais: abc des croyances et superstitions d'hier et d'aujourd'hui.* L'Harmattan, Montréal.

Lirus, Julie

1979 *Identité antillaise.* Éditions Caribéennes, Paris.

Loftfield, Thomas C.

2001 Creolization in Seventeenth-Century Barbados: Two Case Studies. In *Island Lives: Historical Archaeologies of the Caribbean,* edited by Paul Farnsworth, pp. 207–33. University of Alabama Press, Tuscaloosa.

Maire, Christian

2008 *Histoire de la faïence fine française, 1743–1843: Le triomphe des terres blanches.* Éditions de la Reinette, Tours.

Marenco, Claudine

1992 *Manières de table, modèles de mœurs, 17ème–20ème siècle.* Éditions de l'ENS-Cachan, Cachan, France.

Martin, René (editor)

2001 *La Guadeloupe en zigzag. Journal du gendarme à cheval Georges Bonnemaison (1900–1903).* Caret, Le Gosier, Guadeloupe.

Maygarden, Benjamin

2006 Building in Colonial Louisiana: Creolization and the Survival of French Traditions. *International Journal of Historical Archaeology* 10(3): 208–36.

Mehta, Brinda J.

2005 Culinary Diasporas: Identity and the Language of Food in Gisèle Pineau's *Un papillon dans la cité* and *L'exil selon Julia*. *International Journal of Francophone Studies* 8(1): 23–51.

Meyzie, Philippe

2003 À la table des élites bordelaises du XVIIIe siècle. *Annales du Midi* 115: 69–88.

Mills, Barbara J., and T. J. Ferguson

2008 Animate Objects: Shell Trumpets and Ritual Networks in the Greater Southwest. *Journal of Archaeological Method and Theory* 15(4): 338–61.

Mithen, Steven J.

2012 *Thirst: Water and Power in the Ancient World*. Harvard University Press, Cambridge, MA.

Moitt, Bernard

2001 *Women and Slavery in the French Antilles, 1635–1848*. Indiana University Press, Indianapolis.

Montlezun, Baron de

1818 *Souvenirs des Antilles; voyages en 1815 et 1816 aux États-Unis et dans l'archipel Caraïbe; aperçu de Philadelphie et New-Yorck, description de la Trinidad, la Grenade, Saint-Vincent, Sainte-Lucie, Martinique, Guadeloupe, Marie-Galante, Saint-Christophe, Sainte-Croix et Saint-Thomas. . . .* 2 vols. Gide Fils, Paris.

Moreau de Saint-Méry, Médéric-Louis-Élie

1797–98 *Description topographique, physique, civile, politique et historique de la partie française de l'isle Saint-Domingue.* 2 vols. Chez l'auteur, Philadelphie.

Morris, Elaine, Robert Read, S. Elizabeth James, and Tessa Machling

1999 " . . . the old stone fortt at Newcastle . . ." The Redoubt, Nevis, Eastern Caribbean. *Post-Medieval Archaeology* 33: 194–221.

Moussette, Marcel

1996 *Les terres cuites communes des maisons Estèbe et Boisseau.* Gouvernement du Québec, Ministère de la Culture et des Communications, Direction des Communications, Collection Patrimoines, Dossier 51.

Munier, Claudine

1995 De la table des ducs au réfectoire du couvent: Le service aux XVIIe et XVIIIe s. In *Ex pots . . . céramiques médiévales et modernes en Franche-Comté. Catalogue de l'exposition*, edited by Jean-Olivier Guilhot and Annick Richard, pp. 13–16. Musée des ducs de Wurtemberg, Montbéliard, France.

Noël Hume, Ivor

1960 Rouen Faïence in Eighteenth-Century America. *Antiques* 78(6): 559–61.

Ovide, Stéphanie

2002   *French Caribbean Cuisine*. Hippocrene Books, New York.

Pardailhé-Galabrun, Annick

1988   *La naissance de l'intime: 3000 foyers parisiens, XVIIe–XVIIIe siècles*. Presses Universitaires de France, Paris.

Parisis, Denise, and Henri Parisis

2010   La Guadeloupe industrielle. *Généalogie et Histoire de la Caraïbe* Special issue, September 2010.

Paya, Didier, and Thomas Romon

2001   *Le cimetière de l'Hôpital de la Charité, Palais de Justice (Basse-Terre, Guadeloupe), 971-05-002. Document Final de Synthèse*. Ministère de la Justice, Service Régional de l'Archéologie de la Guadeloupe, AFAN.

Peeters, Alice

1979   La pocaution cé manma, félicité. Alimentation et santé aux Antilles et dans la médecine des XVIIe et XVIIIe siècles. *Communications* 31: 130–44.

1982   L'hygiène et les traditions de propreté: L'exemple des Antilles françaises. *Bulletin d'Ethnomédecine* 11: 23–31.

Pellegrin, Nicole

2005   Corps du commun, usages communs du corps. In *Histoire du corps*, edited by Alain Corbin, Jean-Jacques Courtine, and Georges Vigarello, pp. 109–65. vol. 1: De la Renaissance aux Lumières. Seuil, Paris.

Pérotin-Dumon, Anne

2000   *La ville aux îles, la ville dans l'île: Basse-Terre et Pointe-à-Pitre, Guadeloupe, 1650–1820*. Karthala, Paris.

Petrucci, Jean Ferdinand

1991   Formes et usages méconnus: Les pots à raisin. In *La céramique, l'archéologue et le potier. Études de céramiques à Aubagne et en Provence du XVIe au XIXe siècle. Catalogue de l'exposition*, edited by Véronique Abel and Henri Amouric, p. 35. Ville d'Aubagne, Aubagne.

1999   Les poteries et les potiers de Vallauris, 1501–1945. Master's thesis, École des Hautes Études en Science Sociale, Paris.

Peyre, Jean-Gabriel

2001   Le service du mariage du duc de Richelieu et de la princesse de Lorraine-Harcourt. *Sèvres* 10: 22–29.

Pluchon, Pierre (editor)

1982   *Histoire des Antilles et de la Guyane*. Privat, Toulouse.

1987   *Vaudou, sorciers, empoisonneurs, de Saint-Domingue à Haïti*. Karthala, Paris.

Prosper, Ève

2000   Les esclaves de Bourbon à l'œuvre. *Revue des Mascareignes* 2: 41–62.

Querillac, Anne

1931 *Cuisine coloniale. Les bonnes recettes de Chloé Mondésir.* Société d'Éditions Géographiques, Maritimes et Coloniales, Paris.

Ravoire, Fabienne

2006 Typologie raisonnée des céramiques de la fin du Moyen Âge et du début de l'époque moderne provenant du Beauvaisis, de Paris et d'ailleurs, retrouvées sur les sites de consommation parisiens et franciliens. *Revue Archéologique de Picardie* 3–4: 105–202.

Ray, Anthony

2000 *English Delftware in the Ashmolean Museum.* Oxford, Oxford University.

Réache, Nicole and Michelle Gargar

2009 *La gazette du costume créole aux fils tissés des modes et de l'histoire.* PLB Éditions, Gosier, Guadeloupe.

Régaldo-Saint Blancard, Pierre

1986 Les céramiques de raffinage du sucre: Typologie, technologie. *Archéologie du Midi Médiéval* 4: 151–68.

1988 La céramique de la place de la Victoire. *Revue Archéologique de Bordeaux* 79: 79–88.

Régent, Frédéric

2004 *Esclavage, métissage, liberté. La Révolution française en Guadeloupe, 1789–1802.* Bernard Grasset, Paris.

Rey-Hulman, Diana

1983 Les temps du rhum en Guadeloupe. *Terrain* 13: 87–91.

Rickard, Jonathan, and Gavin Ashworth

2006 *Mocha and Related Dipped Wares, 1770–1939.* University Press of New England, East Nassau, NY.

Roche, Daniel

1984 Le temps de l'eau rare du Moyen Age à l'Époque Moderne. *Annales. Économies, Sociétés, Civilisations.* 39(2): 383–99.

1985 *The People of Paris: An Essay in Popular Culture in the 18th Century.* Berg, Dover, NH.

2000 *A History of Everyday Things: The Birth of Consumption in France, 1600–1800.* Cambridge University Press, New York.

Rosen, Jean

1995 *La faïence en France du XIVe au XIXe siècle: Histoire et technique.* Errance, Paris.

Satineau, Maurice

1928 *Histoire de la Guadeloupe sous l'Ancien Régime, 1635–1789.* Payot, Paris.

Saunier, Annie

2003   S'alimenter aux îles: De la cuisine caraïbe à la cuisine coloniale au XVIIe siècle. *Bulletin de la Société d'Histoire de la Guadeloupe* 134: 3–18.

Schiebinger, Londa L.

2004   *Plants and Empire: Colonial Bioprospecting in the Atlantic World.* Harvard University Press, Cambridge, MA.

Schoelcher, Victor

1842   *Des colonies françaises: Abolition immédiate de l'esclavage.* Pagnerre, Paris.

Sheridan, Geraldine

2009   *Louder Than Words.* Texas Tech University Press, Lubbock.

Sobsey, Mark D.

2002   *Managing Water in the Home: Accelerated Health Gains from Improved Water Supply.* World Health Organization.

Stamelman, Richard

2006   *Perfume: Joy, Obsession, Scandal, Sin: A Cultural History of Fragrance from 1750 to the Present.* Rizzoli, New York.

Steen, Carl

2011   Cosmograms, Crosses, and Xs: Context and Inference. *Historical Archaeology* 45(2): 166–75.

Stewart-Abernathy, Leslie C.

2004   Separate Kitchens and Intimate Archaeology: Constructing Urban Slavery on the Antebellum Cotton Frontier in Washington, Arkansas. In *Household Chores and Household Choices: Theorizing the Domestic Sphere*, edited by Kerri S. Barile and James C. Brandon, pp. 51–74. University of Alabama Press, Tuscaloosa.

Sullivan, Catherine

1986   *Legacy of the Machault: A Collection of 18th-Century Artifacts.* Studies in Archaeology Architecture and History. Minister of Supply and Services Canada, Ottawa.

Swahn, Jan-Öjvind

2004   The Cultural History of Crayfish. *Bulletin Français de la Pêche et de la Pisciculture* 372–73: 243–51.

Toczyski, Suzanne

2010   Jean-Baptiste Labat and the Buccaneer Barbecue in Seventeenth-Century Martinique. *Gastronomica: The Journal of Food and Culture* 10(1): 61–69.

Vanony-Frisch, Nicole

1985   Les esclaves de la Guadeloupe à la fin de l'Ancien Régime d'après les sources notariales (1770–1789). *Bulletin de la Société d'Histoire de la Guadeloupe* (63–64): 3–165.

Vérin, Pierre

1967   Quelques aspects de la culture matérielle de la région de Choiseul (Île Sainte-Lucie). *Journal de la Société des Américanistes* 2: 460–94.

Victor, Paul-Émile

1941   La poterie de Sainte-Anne (Martinique). *Bulletin Agricole de la Martinique* 10(1–2): 1–54.

Vigarello, Georges

1985   *Le propre et le sale: L'hygiène du corps depuis le moyen âge.* Seuil, Paris.

Vlach, John M.

1993   *Back of the Big House: The Architecture of Plantation Slavery.* University of North Carolina, Chapel Hill.

Voss, Barbara L.

2008   *The Archaeology of Ethnogenesis: Race and Sexuality in Colonial San Francisco.* University of California Press, Berkeley.

Walker, William H., and Michael B. Schiffer

2006   The Materiality of Social Power: The Artifact-Acquisition Perspective. *Journal of Archaeological Method and Theory* 13(2): 67–88.

Waselkov, Gregory A., and John A. Walthall

2002   Faience Styles in French Colonial North America: A Revised Classification. *Historical Archaeology* 36(1): 62–78.

Weaver, Karol K.

2006   *Medical Revolutionaries: The Enslaved Healers of Eighteenth-Century Saint Domingue.* University of Illinois Press, Urbana.

Webre, Stephen

1990   Water and Society in a Spanish American City: Santiago de Guatemala, 1555–1773. *Hispanic American Historical Review* 70(1): 57–84.

Wheaton, Barbara K.

1983   *Savoring the Past: The French Kitchen and Table from 1300 to 1789.* University of Pennsylvania Press, Philadelphia.

Widmer, Rudolf

2006   Désastres "naturels" et sécurité alimentaire. La Martinique et Santiago de Cap-Vert au XVIIIe siècle. In *Sur les chemins de l'histoire antillaise. Mélanges offerts à Lucien Abénon,* edited by Jean Bernabé and Serge Mam Lam Fouk, pp. 181–200. Ibis Rouge, Matoury, France.

Wilkie, Laurie A.

1999   Evidence of African Continuities in the Material Culture of Clifton Plantation, Bahamas. In *African Sites Archaeology in the Caribbean,* edited by Jay B. Haviser, pp. 264–75. Markus Weiner; Ian Randle, Princeton, NJ.

2000 Culture Bought: Evidence of Creolization in the Consumer Goods of an Enslaved Bahamian Family. *Historical Archaeology* 34(3): 10–26.

2006 Documentary Archaeology. In *The Cambridge Companion to Historical Archaeology*, edited by Dan Hicks and Mary C. Beaudry, pp. 13–33. Cambridge University Press, Cambridge.

2009 Interpretive Historical Archaeologies. In *International Handbook of Historical Archaeology*, edited by Teresita Majewski and David Gaimster, pp. 333–45. Springer, New York.

Wimpffen, Alexandre-Stanislas, Baron de

1993 *Haïti au XVIIIe siècle: Richesse et esclavage dans une colonie française. Édition présentée et annotée par Pierre Pluchon*. Karthala, Paris.

Yakubik, Jill-Karen

1990 Ceramic Use in Late-Eighteenth-Century and Early-Nineteenth-Century Southeastern Louisiana. Unpublished PhD dissertation, Department of Anthropology, Tulane University, New Orleans, LA.

Index

Page numbers in italics refer to illustrations.

ADG. *See* Archives Départementales de la Guadeloupe

African slaves, 65

Albarelle (drug pot), 164

Alcoholic drinks, 96

American planter kitchens, 70–71

Americas, and folk medicine, 160

Amy, Joseph, 62

Ancien Régime, 21

Antilles, 20; cooks, 64, 97–98, 177; cuisine and slave cooks, 64, 97–98, 177; domestic slaves, 33; French, 130; kitchens, 70

Antilles water, 165. *See also* Guadeloupe water

Apothecaries, and drugs, 162–65

Appraisals, Guadeloupe, 12

Arawak people, 17

Archaeological ceramic studies, 4

Archaeology, 7

Archives Départementales de la Guadeloupe (ADG), 183n3

Bakongo cosmograms (dikenga), 172, 173

Barber's bowls, 150–53, *152*

Bar soap, 153–55

Basse-Terre, 6, 183n1; kitchens, 70; overview, 17, 18, 21; reconstruction of, *9*; Vallauris cooking pots from, 83. *See also* Guadeloupe

Basse-Terre ceramic water uses, 14. *See also* Basse-Terre water-storage ceramics

Basse-Terre inventories, 183n3; demographic information in, 27–35, *28*; planters in, 28–31

Basse-Terre slaves. *See* Guadeloupe slaves

Basse-Terre study sites, 8, *9*; cemeteries, 22–24; overview, 22–27. *See also specific sites*

Basse-Terre water: distribution, 38–41, 43; health and, 40, 42; inequalities of distribution, 40–41; lack of sewage system and, 41–42; maintenance, 42; management, 56, 62–63; overview, 37–43, 62–63; public fountains, 38–40, 41; reserves, 48; rights, 41, 184n2; sources, 37–43; supply, 39–43, 59, 62, 63, 183n1; wells and cisterns, 38. *See also* Guadeloupe water

Basse-Terre water jars: Biot water jars, 43–45, *44*, 47; coarse earthenware, *44*, 46, *46*, 49; damage and longevity of, 47–48; disappearance of, 48; drip jars, *44*, 48–50; locally made, 43–47, *46*, 49; overview, 43, 45–55; 28 Rue Amédée Fengarol, 48; value of, 47

Basse-Terre water-storage ceramics: fountains, 50–52, *51*; overview, 43–55, 62; pitchers, 52–55. *See also* Basse-Terre water jars

Bathing: Creole cleanliness and, 155–59; folk therapies, 166–67, 168–69

Bathrooms, indoor, 157–58

Bathtubs, 155–57, 167

Behavior and manners: French Creole home entertaining, 135–42; hot drinks and socializing, 138–40, *139*; reciprocity in socializing, 140–41; table, 136, 141

Belost, Antoine, 50, 162–63

Benoît, Catherine, 69, 77, 156

Bernier, Jean-François, 65, 73, 90, 106, 115, 146

Bernier's inn, 73, 90, 115, 146

Beverage services ceramics, 107–11, 115–17, 143
Bidets, 150
Biot water jars, 43–45, *44, 47*, 176
Blanchet, Jean, 133, 168
Blandin-Pauvert, Arlette, 137, 149
Blood, in folk medicine, 160–61
Bols (bowls), 106–7, 112
Bonaparte, Napoleon, 155–56
Bonnemaison, Georges, 88, 169, 170
Bottles: coolers, 106; dame-jeannes, 56
Bowls: barber's, 150–53, *152*; bols, 106–7, 112; coarse earthenware, 84–85, *86*, 87; pearlware, 124, *125*; salad, 103–4, 112; terrines, 84, 167–68; tureens, 102–3, *103*, 112, 184n3
Bray, Tamara, 4
Britain. *See* England
Brothers of Charity, 23
Brunache, Peggy, 97
Buckets, wooden, 43
Burnard, Trevor, 131

Cabaret (small chest of drawers), 109
Cadenas (chains), 4–5
Campan, André, 163
Canaris (coarse earthenware cooking pots), 80, 83, 96
Cannes (ceramic food containers), 77–79, 184n7
Canots (elongated tub), 155, 156
Capuchin cemetery, 24
Capuchin Franciscans, 24
Caribbean: archaeology, 7; England and, 19; trade, 20, 21; tubers in, 77. *See also* French Caribbean
Caribbean ceramics: studies, 7. *See also* Creole hygiene ceramics; Guadeloupe ceramics
Caribbean ceramic water containers, 55, 175. *See also* Guadeloupe ceramic water containers
Caribbean history: overview, 19–22, 30; slavery in, 19, 21, 22. *See also* Guadeloupe history
Castes, 31; segregation, 141–44, 178
Cathedral of Basse-Terre site, 24
Cemeteries: Basse-Terre study sites, 22–24; Capuchin, 24
Ceramic cultures: approach, 177; overview, 1–6, 180, 181; understanding, 1; variations in, 1–2. *See also* Guadeloupe ceramic culture

Ceramic food containers: coarse earthenware, 79–80; overview, 77–79; stoneware, 78, *79. See also* Ceramic water containers
Ceramic kitchen equipment, 77–78, *79*, 80–82, *81*
Ceramics: forms, 2–3; use throughout history, 2. *See also* Caribbean ceramics
Ceramic studies: archaeological, 4; Caribbean, 7; methods, 1; overview, 1, 5. *See also* Guadeloupe study
Ceramic uses: ceramic users, 4. *See also* Guadeloupe ceramic water uses
Ceramic water containers: Martinique, 55. *See also* Caribbean ceramic water containers; Water-storage ceramics
Chafing dishes, 88–89, 184n10
Chamber pots: coarse earthenware, 146–48, *147*; commodes and, 148, 149; faience, 146–48, *147*; French, 148; women and, 149–50, 185n3. *See also* Guadeloupe chamber pots
Chefs. *See* Cooks
Chinoiserie patterns, 125–28, *128*
Chocolate, cups and saucers, 108
Cleanliness. *See* Creole cleanliness
Coarse earthenware: Basse-Terre water jars, *44*, 46, *46*, 49; bowls, 84–85, *86*, 87; ceramic food containers, 79–80; chamber pots, 146–48, *147*; cooking pots, 80–83, *81*, 96; cookware from Vallauris, 82–85, *85*, *86*, 87–90; pitchers, 52–55, *54*; saucepans, 83–84, *85*
Code Noir, 19, 74, 75
Coffee and tea ware, 110, 115, 116
Coffeepots, 108, 109, 110, 115–16
Coffee sets or services. *See* Services tableware
Cold/hot dualism, in folk medicine, 160–61
Cold drinks, tableware for, 105–6
Collingham, Elizabeth M., 157, 158
Colonial cookware: metallic, 87; usage, 93–97; Vallauris, *79*, 82–85, *85*, *86*, 87–90. *See also* Cooking pots
Colonial foods, 73–77, 184n4
Colonial study sites. *See* Basse-Terre study sites
Colonies, French. *See* French colonies
Colors, of Guadeloupe tableware, 122–23
Columbus, Christopher, 17
Commodes, 148, 149; thunderbox, 158, 185n6
Condiment ceramic vessels, 104–5

Conil, Baptiste, 83
Containers. *See* Ceramic food containers; Ceramic water containers
Cooking: French colonies and outdoor, 69; Guadeloupe essentials for, 89; power and, 180–81
Cooking pots: coarse earthenware, 80–83, *81*, 96; French, 88; from 28 Rue Amédée Fengarol site, 82, 83, 84
Cooks: Antilles, 64, 97–98, 177; Creole, 64; slave cooks and professional, 65–66, 89–90. *See also* Female cooks; Guadeloupe cooks; Male cooks; Slave cooks
Cookware. *See* Colonial cookware
Coolers, bottle, 106
Coquemar, 151, 185n4
Creole, 5–6; cooks, 64; foods, 64; galleries, 132, 133, 134; kitchens, 69–73, 88, 97; salles, 14, 132–34, 177–78; women, hot drinks and socializing, 138–40, *139*
Créole, 5–6
Creole art of table, 99, 138, 144. *See also* Guadeloupe tableware
Creole cleanliness: bathtubs and bathing, 155–57, 159; canots, 155, 156; indoor bathrooms and, 157–58; overview, 155–58, 173–74. *See also* Creole hygiene
Creole cuisine, 71, 96; Guadeloupe tableware and, 114; overview, 90–93
Creole folk medicine: overview, 160–61; principles of health and, 158–62, 174. *See also* Folk therapies
Creole health: overview, 15–16, 173–74, 178–79; principles of folk medicine and, 158–62. *See also* Creole hygiene; Creole medicinal practices
Creole homes: galleries, 14, 132, 133, 134; salles, 14, 132–34, 177–78. *See also* French Creole home entertaining
Creole hygiene: bar soap, 153–55; overview, 15–16, 173–74, 178–79; practices compared to Paris, 155, 157; slaves and, 157, 158. *See also* Creole cleanliness
Creole hygiene ceramics: barber's bowls, 150–53, *152*; bidets, 150; commodes, 148–49; overview, 145, 146, 155, 174, 178–79; Paris compared to, 148–51; soap dishes, 153, *154*, 155. *See also* Chamber pots
Creole medicinal practices: overview, 15–16; slaves and, 161–62. *See also* Creole folk medicine

Creole slaves: African slaves and, 65; hygiene and, 157, 158. *See also* Guadeloupe slaves
Creole society and culture: cadenas, 4, 5; Guadeloupe ceramics and, 5–6; hospitality and commensality, 14–15, 178
CRM. *See* Cultural resource management
Cruche (water jug), 55–56
Cuisine: Antillean, 64, 97–98, 177; Creole, 71, 90–93, 96, 114; French, 96; French Caribbean, 90
Cultural resource management (CRM), 7
Culture. *See* Ceramic cultures; Creole society and culture
Cups, and saucers, 108, 109, 110, 115
Currency: French, 12; *livre coloniale*, 12; *livre tournois*, 12
Cyrillia, 145, 181

D'Alembert, Jean Le Rond, 58
Dame-jeannes (glass bottles), 56
Debien, Gabriel, 131–32
Decorations: faiences fines decorative patterns, 124–28, *128*; Paris, 134; rim, 121, *122*. *See also* Tableware, style and decoration
Déjeuners (services tableware), 107–10. *See also* Services tableware
Delftware barber's bowl, Dutch, 152, 152–53
Desmoulins, Marie-Emmanuelle, 38, 41
Dessalles, Pierre, 66, 68, 70, 97, 131, 135–38, 140–41; hygiene and, 151, 156, 157, 158, 167, 170
Devasahayam, Theresa W., 180
Diacretical feasts, 142
Diderot, Denis, 58
Dietler, Michael, 141
Dikenga (Bakongo cosmograms), 172, 173
Dinner: as feasting ritual, 141–42; parties, 136–37. *See also* Meals
Dishes: chafing, 88–89, 184n10; plates and, 100–102, 111; soap, 153, *154*, 155. *See also* Flatware
Domestic slaves: Antilles, 33; ceramics and, 180; Guadeloupe, 33–34
Drinks: alcoholic, 96; socializing around hot, 138–40, *139*; tableware for water, wine, and cold, 105–6
Drip jars, *44*, 48–50, 55
Dripstones, 57, 59. *See also* Stone water filters
Drugs: apothecaries and, 162–65; drug pots, 164; slaves and, 165

Duhamel du Moncaeu, Henri-Louis, 61–62
Dutch: delftware barber's bowl, 152, *152*; merchants and traders, 18–19

Earthenware. *See* Coarse earthenware; Faiences
Écuelles, 107
Embouchure de la Rivière site, 49
England: bathrooms in colonial India, 157–58; Caribbean and, 19; Code Noir regulation of slavery, 19, 74, 75; in Guadeloupe history, 20, 21, 99
Entertaining, home. *See* French Creole home entertaining
Entremets, 101, 184n2
D'Esnambuc, Pierre Belain, 18

Faiences (French tin-glazed earthenware), 13, 15, 183n1; brunes, 128, 129; brune tureens, 102–3, *103*, 184n3; chamber pots, 146–48, *147*; flatware, 100–102; pitchers, 52–55, 105, 121–22, *123*; salad bowls, 104, *104*; saucepans, 84, 184n8; sherds from wall fountains, 50–51, *51*; soap dishes, 153, *154*; tableware, 113, 117, *118*, *119*, 119–30, *120*, *121*, *122*, *123*, *126*, *127*, *130*, *131*, 139, 142, 144, 178
Faiences fines, 15; decorative patterns, 124–28, *128*
Feasts: diacretical, 142; meals as feasting rituals, 141–42
Female: feminization of Guadeloupeans, 27. *See also* Guadeloupe female; Women
Female cooks, 177; French, 67–68
Female slave cooks: in French colonies, 68; Guadeloupe, 14, 66, 67, 97–98; overview, 65, 177
Female slaves: Creole medicinal practices and, 162. *See also* Guadeloupe female slaves
Ferguson, Leland, 172
Flatware, 100–102. *See also* Dishes
Floral patterned tableware, 117–22, *118*, *119*, *120*, *121*, 124, *124*, 125, *125*, 126, 129, *130*
Folk medicine: of Americas, 160; cold/hot dualism in, 160–61; magic in, 161, 173; religion in, 161. *See also* Creole folk medicine
Folk therapies: bathing, 166–67, 168–69; ceramics and, 165–73; footbaths, 167; marked ceramics, 171–73, *172*; overview,
165–73; slaves and, 165, 166, 169–70, 173; teas, 166; water and, 165–66, 169. *See also* Folk medicine
Food: colonial, 73–77, 184n4; Creole, 64; Guadeloupe, 74–77, 97, 184n5–6; leftovers, 96–97; slaves and, 75–75, 77, 97
Food storage, 97; garde-manger, 73. *See also* Ceramic food containers; Water storage
Footbaths, 167
Fort Houël site, 24–27, 49, 82, 153, 164
Fountains: overview, 50–52; Paris, 61–62; public, 38–40, 41; wall, 50–51, *51*
France, 1; Guadeloupe and, 6–7; in history of Guadeloupe, 18, 21–22; meals, 136, 141; sets, serialization and, 142–43; tableware, 15; water and bathing in, 158–59; water-storage ceramics from, 56. *See also* Paris
Free mixed-race people: French, 19–20; gens de couleur, 13, 31, 32, 34, 132–33, 140–41
French: administrators, 30; bidets, 150; chamber pots, 148; cooking pots, 88; cuisine, 96; currency, 12; free mixed-race, 19–20; inventories, 11–12, 27; kitchens, 70, 88; low-income women and work, 177; male and female cooks, 67–68; slavery, 19–20; stoneware, 78; West Indies, 19
French Antilles, 130. *See also* Antilles
French Caribbean: colonial society, 30, 34; cuisine, 90; gender and tasks in, 67; history, 19–20
French colonies: Caribbean, 30, 34; female slave cooks in, 68; outdoor cooking in, 69; wall fountains in, 52; water-storage ceramics used in, 56
French Creole home entertaining: behavior and manners, 135–42; caste segregation and, 141–44, 178; dinner parties, 136–37; furniture, 133–35; hospitality, 130–31, 141; overview, 130–35; parties, 135–37; slaves and, 136, 137, 138, 141–44; tableware for, 131–32, 178
French tin-glazed earthenware. *See* Faiences
French water jars, 43, 176. *See also* Biot water jars
Furniture: garde-manger, 73; in salles or galleries, 133–35, 177–78

Galleries, Creole (*galeries*), 14, 132, 133, 134
Garde-manger (food storage furniture), 73

Gargoulette (water vase), 55, 56
Garraway, Doris, 130
Gender, and French Caribbean tasks, 67
Genêt, Nicole, 147
Gens de couleur (freed mixed-race people), 13, 31, 32, 34, 132–33, 140–41
German stoneware jugs, 78
Giraudeau, Jean, 164
Glissant, Édouard, 77
Goglet, 55
Grande-Terre, 17, 20
Granier de Cassagnac, Adolphe, 75, 96–97, 141
Guadeloupe, 11; appraisals, 12; archaeology, 7; cooking essentials, 89; feminization of Guadeloupeans, 27; food, 74–77, 97, 184n5–6; France and, 6–7; kitchens, 70, 72–73, 87–89; overview, 6–7, 17–18. See also Basse-Terre
Guadeloupe ceramic culture: overview, 6, 16, 179–80, 181; slave cooks and, 64; water-storage ceramics in, 36, 176
Guadeloupe ceramics: cadenas, 4–5; Creole life and, 5–6; forms, 2–3; in Guadeloupe inventories, 34–35; overview, 6, 181; therapeutic, 15–16
Guadeloupe ceramic tableware. See Guadeloupe tableware
Guadeloupe ceramic uses, 2, 2–3. See also Guadeloupe ceramic water uses
Guadeloupe ceramic water containers: female slaves and, 60–61; inventory patterns, 55–57; tableware, 105–6. See also Guadeloupe water jars; Guadeloupe water-storage ceramics
Guadeloupe ceramic water uses, 13–14. See also Basse-Terre ceramic water uses; Guadeloupe water-storage ceramics
Guadeloupe chamber pots: overview, 146–51, 147; slaves and, 149, 158; as Thomases, 149, 185n2
Guadeloupe cooks, 67. See also Guadeloupe slave cooks
Guadeloupe domestic water reserves, 14, 36, 37, 38; Basse-Terre, 48; locations of, 56–57; Parisian domestic water reserves compared to, 61–62; water jars as main, 55
Guadeloupe female: cooks, 14, 66, 67, 97–98; servants and water management, 59–61

Guadeloupe female slaves, 33; ceramic water containers and, 60–61; cooks, 14, 66, 67, 97–98; interracial libertinism and concubinage with, 34; water management by, 60–61, 176, 177
Guadeloupe history, 13; England in, 20, 21, 99; France in, 18, 21–22; overview, 17–22, 30. See also Basse-Terre study sites
Guadeloupe homes: organization of, 135. See also Creole homes
Guadeloupe hygiene. See Creole hygiene
Guadeloupe inventories: ceramics in, 34–35; demographic information, 27–35, 28, 183n3; material context, 13; occupations in, 27–29, 28; overview, 8, 10, 11–13, 34–35; patterns in ceramic water containers, 55–57. See also Basse-Terre inventories
Guadeloupe male cooks, 65, 67
Guadeloupe servants: slave cooks versus, 64–68; water management and female, 59–61
Guadeloupe slave cooks: African slaves as, 65; Antillean cuisine and, 64; female, 14, 66, 67, 97–98; Guadeloupe ceramic culture and, 64; kitchen accessories of, 89–90; male, 65, 67; overview, 64–65, 180–81; poisoning of masters by, 68; servants versus, 64–68
Guadeloupe slaves, 4, 5, 12, 19, 22; domestic, 33–34; food and, 75–76, 77, 97; in Guadeloupe inventories, 31–35; kitchen, 73; overview, 18, 35; water supply of, 60. See also Guadeloupe female slaves
Guadeloupe study: data sources, 6–13; overview, 4–6, 13–16. See also Basse-Terre study sites
Guadeloupe tableware: beverage services, 107–11, 115–17, 143; bols and écuelles, 106–7, 112; colors, 122–23; comparisons, 111–17; for condiments, 104–5; Creole cuisine and, 114; faiences, 113, 117, 118, 119, 119–30, 120, 121, 122, 123, 126, 127, 130, 131, 139, 142, 144, 178; flatware, plates and dishes, 100–102, 111; overview, 15, 99–100, 142–44, 177–78; pewter, 99–100; pitchers, 121–22, 123; porcelain, 112–13, 122, 124; salad bowls, 103–4, 112; style and decoration, 117–30; tureens, 102–3, 103, 112, 184n3; utensils, 99, 184n1; for water, wine, and cold drinks, 105–6

Guadeloupe water, 37; bathing and, 159; female servants and, 59–61; management, 59–61, 63, 176, 177; quality, 57–59, 61–62; supply, 59–60. *See also* Basse-Terre water; Guadeloupe domestic water reserves

Guadeloupe water jars, 46, 175, 176; as domestic water reserve, 55; drip jars, 49–50, 55; Paris fountains compared to, 61–62; size, 59. *See also* Basse-Terre water jars

Guadeloupe water-storage ceramics: in Guadeloupe ceramic culture, 36, 176; pitchers, 52–55; wall fountains, 50–52, 51, 55. *See also* Basse-Terre water-storage ceramics; Guadeloupe ceramic water containers

Guéridons (high round table), 133, 184n4

Health: Basse-Terre water and, 40, 42. *See also* Creole health
Hearn, Lafcadio, 145, 181
Hellman, Mimi, 142–43
History: ceramic use throughout, 2. *See also* Caribbean history
Holy water, 165
Homes. *See* Creole homes
Hot/cold dualism, in folk medicine, 160–61
Hot drinks, and socializing, 138–40, 139
Houël, Charles, 18, 24–26
Hugues, Victor, 21
Hydrotherapies, 159–60
Hygiene: Dessalles and, 151, 156, 157, 158, 167, 170. *See also* Creole hygiene

Ile Bourbon, 6, 52, 56, 60, 65
Inca, 4
Interracial libertinism and concubinage, 34
Inventories: French, 11–12, 27; probate, 27, 183n3. *See also* Guadeloupe inventories

Jarres à l'eau (water jars), 43
Jars: olive, 175. *See also* Water jars
Joseph, J. W., 172
Joséphine, 155–56
Jugs: German stoneware, 78; Rhenish Bartmann, 78; water, 55–56

Kakukera (Guadeloupe), 17
Karaf, 55
Kitchens: accessories, 87–90, 184n9;

American planter, 70–71; Antilles, 70; Basse-Terre, 70; ceramic kitchen equipment, 77–78, 79, 80–82, 81; Creole, 69–73, 88, 97; detached, 70–71; French, 70, 88; Guadeloupe, 70, 72–73, 87–89; slaves and detached, 71
Kneading troughs, 89
Krish (water jug), 55

Labat, Jean-Baptiste, 49, 50, 68, 69, 74, 76, 159, 165, 184n4
Leg baths, 167
Lélé (Creole kitchen tool), 88
Livre coloniale (currency), 12
Livre tournois (currency), 12
Longin, 38, 39, 42
Louis XIII, 18
Louis XIV, 19

Magic, in folk medicine, 161, 173
Male cooks: French, 67–68; Guadeloupe slave, 65, 67
Mallet, 39, 40, 41
Manioc flour, 71–72, 89
Manners. *See* Behavior and manners
Marked ceramics, 171–73, 172
Martinique, 157; in Caribbean history, 17–22, 30; ceramic water containers, 55; water jars, 45–46, 175
Le Masurier, 138–39
Meals: as feasting rituals, 141–42; in France, 136, 141. *See also* Dinner; French Creole home entertaining
Medicinal practices. *See* Creole medicinal practices; Folk medicine
Mehta, Brinda J., 77
Metallic cookware, 87
Montlezun, Baron de, 40, 132, 135
Moreau de Saint-Méry, Médéric-Louis-Élie, 131, 140, 157
Mosquitoes, 57
Muid (130 liters), 47, 184n3

Oleoresin, 163, 185n7
Olive jars, 175
Oplas, Mathieu, 26, 83

Palais de Justice site, 22–23, 27, 50, 82
Paragot, Veuve, 26
Pardailhé-Galabrun, Annick, 53, 61, 112, 155

Paris: barber's bowls, 150–51; Creole hygiene ceramics compared to, 148–51; Creole hygiene practices compared to, 155, 157; decorations, 134; fountains, 61–62; Guadeloupe ceramics compared to, 179; Guadeloupe domestic water reserves compared to, 61–62; metal objects, 179. *See also* France

Paris water management, 37; compared to Guadeloupe, 61–62

Parlors, Creole. *See* Salles

Parties, French Creole home, 135–37

Pearlware bowls and saucers, 124, *125*

Peeters, Alice, 158, 168, 169

Pérotin-Dumon, Anne, 28–33, 38, 57, 60, 75, 168, 178

Petrucci, Jean Ferdinand, 82, 83

Pewter tableware, 99–100

Pillulier (drugpot), 164

Pitchers: coarse earthenware, 52–55, *54*; faience, 52–55, 105, 121–22, *123*; overview, 52–55; 28 Rue Amédée Fengarol site, 54, *54*, 173; for washing, 53

Planters: American kitchens of, 70–71; in Basse-Terre inventories, 28–31

Plates and dishes, 100–102, 111. *See also* Flatware

Pointe-à-Pitre, 20, 21, 32–33

Poison, and slaves, 68, 170–71

Population, transient, 30

Porcelain Guadeloupe tableware, 112–13, 122, *124*

Pots: coffeepots, 108, 109, 110, 115–16; drug, 164; teapots, 108, 109, 110, 115. *See also* Chamber pots; Cooking pots

Pots à eau, 52

Pott l'eau (pitcher), 55

Power: cooking and, 180–81; social, 4–5

Probate inventories, 27, 183n3. *See also* Inventories

Professional cooks: kitchen accessories of, 89–90; slave cooks and, 65–66, 89–90

Provence, 80–81

Public fountains, 38–40, 41

Reciprocity, 140

Régent, Frédéric, 64, 65, 75

Religion, in folk medicine, 161

Rhenish Bartmann jugs, 78

Rim decorations, 121, *122*

Roche, Daniel, 27

Rouen patterns, 118, *118*, 119, 120, 121, 128–29

Rum, 169

Saint-Domingue, 20, 21, 30, 131–32, 157, 162

Saint-François, 24, 38–39

Salad bowls, 103–4, 112

Salles (spaces in Creole homes), 14, 132–34, 177–78

Saucepans: coarse earthenware, 83–84, *85*; faience, 84, 184n8

Saucers: cups and, 108, 109, 110, 115; pearlware, 124, *125*

Scalloped vessels, 117

Schiffer, Michael, 4–5

Schoelcher, Victor, 137

Segregation, caste, 141–44, 178

Serialization, 142–43

Servants. *See* Guadeloupe servants

Service régional de l'archéologie (SRA), 7

Services tableware: faience, 130, *131*; overview, 107–11, 115–17, 143

Sets: France, serialization and, 142–43. *See also* Services tableware

Shaving: barber's bowls, 150–53, *152*; bar soap and, 153–54; overview, 153

Sites, study. *See* Basse-Terre study sites

Slave cooks: Antillean cuisine and, 64, 97–98, 177; male, 65, 67–68; overview, 64–66; professional cooks and, 65–66, 89–90. *See also* Female slave cooks; Guadeloupe slave cooks

Slavery: Caribbean history of, 19, 21, 22; English Code Noir regulation of, 19, 74, 75; French, 19–20

Slaves: African, 65; chamber pots and, 149, 158; Creole, 65, 157, 158; Creole medicinal practices and, 161–62; detached kitchens and, 71; domestic, 33–34, 180; drugs and, 165; folk therapies and, 165, 166, 169–70, 173; French Creole home entertaining and, 136, 137, 138, 141–44; poison and, 68, 170–71. *See also* Guadeloupe slaves

Soap: bar, 153–55; dishes, 153, *154*, 155; washerwomen and, 168

Socializing: around hot drinks, 138–40, *139*; reciprocity in, 140–41

Social power, 4–5

Spanish dripstones, 59

Spyglasses, 133, 134

SRA. *See* Service régional de l'archéologie

St. Lucia, 46, 55, 175

Stoneware: French, 78; German stoneware jugs, 78

Stoneware ceramics: cannes, 77–79, 184n7; food containers, 78, 79

Stone water filters, 57–59, 58

Style and decoration. See Tableware, style and decoration

Sugar: molds, 49–50; production and trade, 21–22; wares, 48

Table, Creole art of, 99, 138, 144. See also Guadeloupe tableware

Table manners, 136, 141

Tableware: French, 15; for French Creole home entertaining, 131–32, 178; in salles or galleries, 134, 177. See also Guadeloupe tableware

Tableware, style and decoration, 127, 128, 131; floral patterns, 117–22, 118, 119, 120, 121, 124, 124, 125, 125, 126, 129, 130; overview, 117–30; rim decorations, 121, 122; Rouen patterned, 118, 118, 119, 120, 121, 128–29; scalloped vessels, 117

Tea: coffee and tea ware, 110, 115, 116; in folk therapies, 166

Teapots, 108, 109, 110, 115

Tea sets or services. See Services tableware

Terrines (coarse earthenware bowls), 84, 167–68

Du Tertre, Jean-Baptiste, 25, 74, 88, 130–31, 141, 159, 160, 183n2

Thistlewood, Thomas, 131

Thomases (Guadeloupe chamber pots), 149, 185n2

Thunderbox (commode), 158, 185n6

Trade: Caribbean, 20, 21; Dutch merchants and traders, 18–19; sugar, 21–22

Trivets, 88

Tubers, in Caribbean, 77

Tureens (serving bowls), 102–3, 103, 112, 184n3

28 Rue Amédée Fengarol site: overview, 26–27; pitchers, 54, 54, 173; Vallauris cooking pots from, 82, 83, 84; water jars, 48

Utensils, 99, 184n1

Vallauris cookware, 79, 82–85, 85, 86, 87–90

Vanony-Frisch, Nicole, 12–13, 32, 64, 65, 162, 168

Vessels: condiment ceramic, 104–5; scalloped, 117. See also Ceramic food containers; Ceramic water containers

Walker, William, 4–5

Wall fountains, 50–51, 51

Walthall, John, 121

Waselkov, Gregory, 121

Washerwomen, 168

Water: archaeology of, 7; folk therapies and, 165–66, 169; France, bathing and, 158–59; holy, 165; hydrotherapies, 159–60; jugs, 55–56. See also Antilles water; Bathing

Water filter: Peruvian, 58; stone, 57–59, 58

Water jars: Biot, 43–45, 44, 47, 176; French, 43, 176; Martinique, 45–46, 175. See also Guadeloupe water jars

Water management: Basse-Terre, 56, 62–63; female servants and, 59–61; female slaves and, 60–61, 176, 177; Guadeloupe, 59–61, 63, 176, 177; Neolithic, 176; Paris, 37

Water quality, 36–37; Guadeloupe, 57–59, 61–62; water storage and, 59

Water reserves. See Guadeloupe domestic water reserves

Water storage, 175; sheds, 56–57; storeroom, 57; water quality and, 59

Water-storage ceramics: from France, 56. See also Ceramic water containers; Guadeloupe water-storage ceramics

Water supply, 36–37; Basse-Terre, 39–43, 59, 62, 63, 183n1; Guadeloupe, 59–60; of slaves, 60

Weaver, Karol, 162, 170

West Indies, French, 19

Whites, as caste, 31

Wilkie, Laurie, 173

Wine glasses, 105–6

Women: chamber pots and, 149–50, 185n3; hot drinks and socializing by Creole, 138–40, 139; washerwomen, 168; work and French low-income, 177. See also Female

Wooden bathtubs, 156

MYRIAM ARCANGELI's research on colonial-era ceramics within the historical context of Creole culture in Guadeloupe informs the original approach used for analyzing and interpreting ceramics in this book. Showing her long interest in ceramics, Arcangeli's first research projects examined the history of local potteries near Toulouse in southwestern France. Intrigued by the colonial period, she traveled to the United States where she discovered American archaeology while excavating at Mount Vernon, the plantation home of George Washington. Currently, she is publishing her research in both French and English journals and recently contributed a chapter to Karen B. Metheny and Mary C. Beaudry's edited volume, *The Archaeology of Food: An Encyclopedia.*